AF594546

DRAWING
FARM & ZOO ANIMALS

Raymond Sheppard § C. F. Tunnicliffe

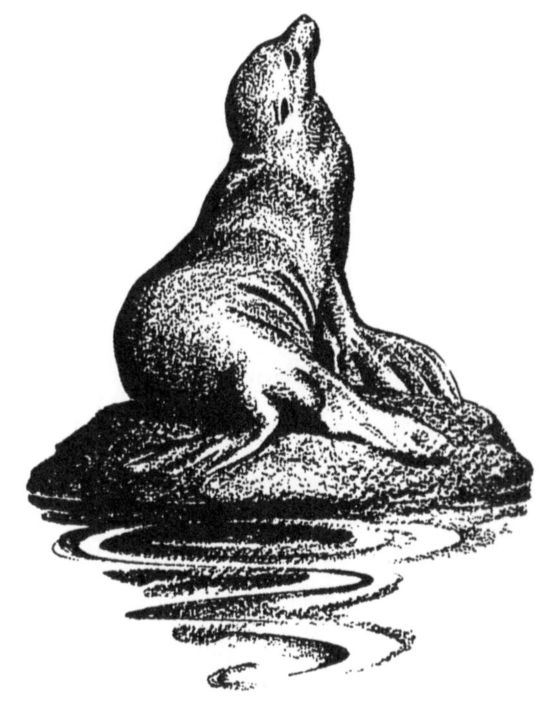

DOVER PUBLICATIONS, INC.
Mineola, New York

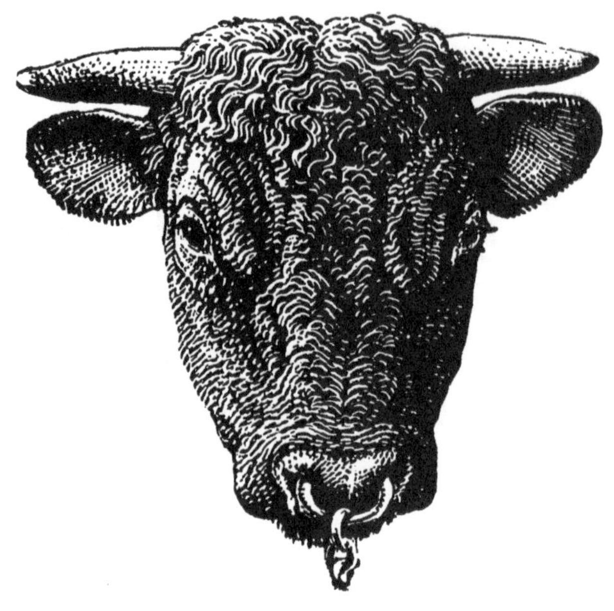

Copyright

Bibliographical Note

This Dover edition, first published in 2018, is a republication in one volume of the following works: *How to Draw Farm Animals* by C. F. Tunnicliffe (The Studio: London and New York, 1952) and *Drawing at the Zoo* by Raymond Sheppard (The Studio Publications: London and New York, 1949). The text has been newly reset.

Library of Congress Cataloging-in-Publication Data

Names: Container of (work): Sheppard, Raymond. Drawing at the zoo. | Container of (work): Tunnicliffe, C. F. (Charles Frederick), 1901–1979 How to draw farm animals.
Title: Drawing farm and zoo animals / Raymond Sheppard, Charles Frederick Tunnicliffe.
Description: Mineola, New York : Dover Publications, 2018. | Series: Dover art instruction | "This Dover edition, first published in 2018, is a republication in one volume of the following works: How to Draw Farm Animals by C. F. Tunnicliffe (The Studio: London and New York, 1952) and Drawing at the Zoo by Raymond Sheppard (The Studio Publications: London and New York, 1949)."
Identifiers: LCCN 2017046138| ISBN 9780486819150 (paperback) | ISBN 0486819159
Subjects: LCSH: Animals in art. | Drawing—Technique. | BISAC: ART / Techniques / Drawing.
Classification: LCC NC780 .D724 2018 | DDC 743.6—dc23
LC record available at https://lccn.loc.gov/2017046138

Manufactured in the United States by LSC Communications
81915901 2017
www.doverpublications.com

CONTENTS

PAGE

How to Draw Farm Animals 1

Introduction 2

Model and Mode. 4

Horses. 6

Cattle 18

Pigs. 32

Sheep 40

The Farmer's Dog 50

The Farmyard Cat 57

Drawing at the Zoo. **61**

Introduction 62

Materials. 66

The Method of Approach 68

Construction 76

We Make a Start 78

studies of iguana, crocodiles and alligators, hippopotamus and rhinoceros, polar bears, brown bears, drawing the tiger and lioness

Animal Movement 90

the lion walks, rapid outline studies, the panda, the tiger dines, gibbons, the chimpanzee, rhesus monkeys, a page of baby monkeys, drawing zoo babies, the antelope

Pattern 104

Camels and Elephants 106

Sea-Lions. 108

Zoo Birds 109

flamingoes, the ostrich, the peacock, pelicans

The Aquarium. 114

Turtles 115

Using your drawings for painting a picture or illustrating a story. . . . 117

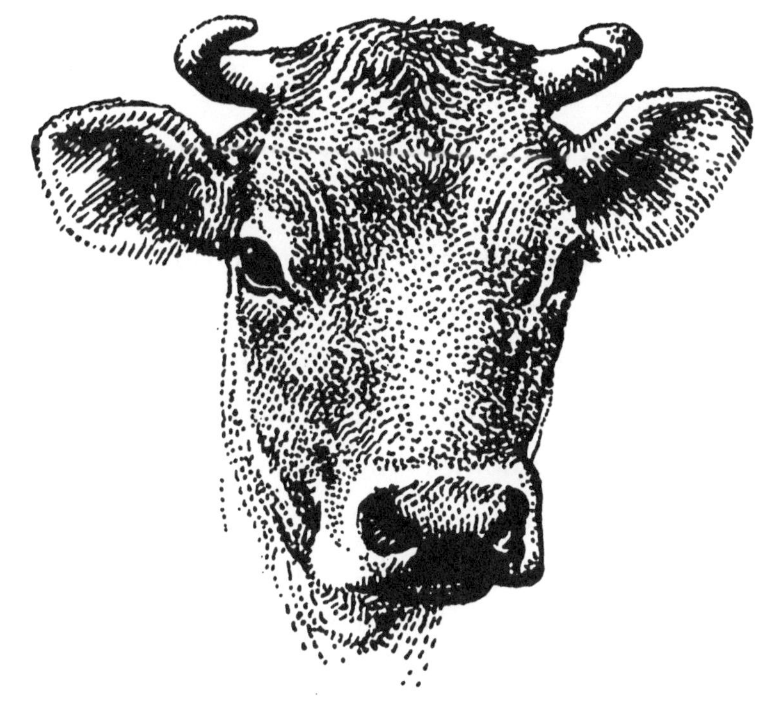

HOW TO DRAW
FARM ANIMALS

Charles F. Tunnicliffe

INTRODUCTION

"The Common Boar is, of all other domestic quadrupeds, the most filthy and impure. Its form is clumsy and disgusting and its appetite gluttonous and excessive." Thus wrote Thomas Bewick in his "History of Quadrupeds," below his excellent wood-cut of the despised beast. But that was nearly one hundred and fifty years ago and since Bewick's time many changes have occurred in the breeding and in the appearance of our domestic animals. Gone is his "Black Horse," his "Long Horned or Lancashire breed of cattle" (except for a few remnants) and his old "Tees-water" breed of sheep. To-day, if you were to ask a farmer where you could find a Common Boar he would probably look perplexed and might reply "I dunno about 'Common' but I *can* tell you where there is a Large White or a Wessex Saddleback or a Tamworth boar." And there you have it: the great majority of our modern domestic animals are of definite breeds which are the result of many years of trial and type selection in the endeavour to evolve an animal which will fulfil a particular purpose, with the result that there are fewer and fewer nondescript beasts to be seen on our farms to-day, their place being taken by animals of specialised breeds.

To-day the farms in Britain are being cultivated more intensively than ever before, and the animals of the farm are inseparable from this great activity.

The Horse is still a useful and valued helper in spite of the great increase in mechanical cultivation, while cattle, sheep, and pigs are all very important members of the farming economy, and their importance will probably increase as farming becomes more balanced and passes from this emergency period of strenuous ploughing and crop-raising to one of stock raising.

It seems then that the grandeur of the Shire Horse, the impressive shape of the Shorthorn Bull and the delicate beauty of the Jersey Cow will, for many years to come, be part of the farming scene, not only for the profit of the Farmer but for the delight of the Artist also.

As you persevere with your drawing of the animals you will inevitably gain some knowledge of farming ways and procedure, and this will be a good thing, for it will increase your understanding of your models. You will soon realise that, in spite of Thomas Bewick's devastating remarks, the Boar is no longer a despised animal. His form is neither clumsy nor disgusting but has a strong virile beauty of its own, and, given the chance, he is a cleanly beast, both in his habits and his feeding. There is no doubt that, if he could return to us, Bewick would see many and great changes in our domestic animals.

MODEL & MODE

The only practical and sure foundation on which to build your representation of farm animals will be the close study of the living creature.

You may at first find it a little difficult to obtain suitable models but if you make a friend of the farmer and his assistants, and do not make a nuisance of yourself by interrupting farm work, your difficulties will disappear. You may indeed find the farmer a willing helper, for he takes a pride in his animals as a rule and may be a little flattered by your desire to draw them. Also he is an expert judge of an animal, and if you can satisfy him with your drawings of them you may, I think, mildly congratulate yourself.

Afterwards, that which remains to be done is to develop your technique and mode of expression, but in this no farmer can help you, for you will be ploughing a lone furrow, slowly evolving an individual method, stimulated perhaps by the study of the achievements of the masters of animal and figure draughtsmanship of all ages. Remember that animal drawing is almost as old as mankind itself and there is a great and varied field to be explored.

I would suggest that in all cases you begin your studies by drawing animals which are at rest. This will give you an opportunity to make complete studies of form and of more detailed drawings than would be possible from the moving animal.

Later on you can attempt studies of movement. These will of necessity be more generalised statements, but your first drawings of form and details will help enormously in your understanding of movement. Whenever possible handle your animal model. There is no better way of understanding shapes and contours than by having a knowledge of that which is just under the skin. It may be bone, muscle, tendon, or fat, but to know just where these occur is absolutely essential; so run your fingers over shoulders, ribs, hips, and joints, until knowledge gained by touching is linked to that acquired by seeing. In time the correct drawing of the contours of your animals will become instinctive.

When drawing from life, a sketch book with a good stiff binding is desirable. Often you will be standing whilst drawing and in the majority of cases you will be in the open air, so a stiff, board-like backing to the pages is essential. Do not forget to include two elastic bands in your equipment. These will prevent the sketch book pages from blowing about while you work. There will often be a breeze.

For drawing I use a H.B. or a hard carbon pencil and sometimes work over this with ink—in my case, brown or black, carried in a fountain pen. But the matter of medium is a very personal one and I suggest you try as many methods as possible from the great variety available until you find the one which suits you best.

And now "to Horse!"

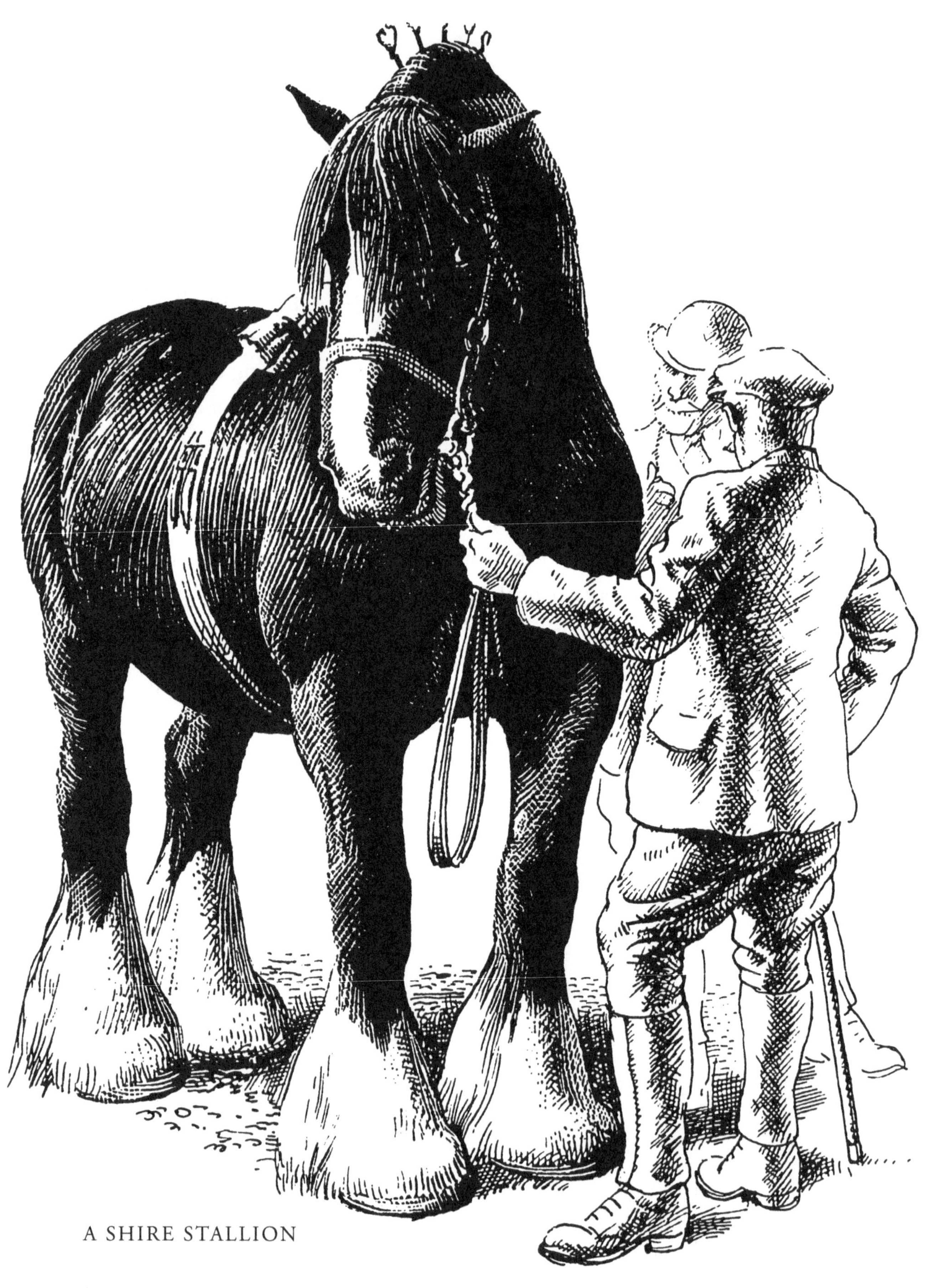

A SHIRE STALLION

HORSES

Among the animals, probably none has stimulated the artist more, or been responsible for so many masterpieces, as the Horse. As you search among the works of the ancients you will find him in wonderful Chinese paintings and colour wood-cuts. You will take pleasure in the horses of the Parthenon frieze and in those little horses of the lion hunt in the Assyrian low relief sculpture. Nearer our own time you will discover Dürer and his engraving of The Great Horse, and later still our own George Morland and George Stubbs. But the horse we shall be dealing with in this little book will be no fiery war horse or swift race horse, but the strong serviceable draught horse of the farm.

In England the Shire horse is the breed most favoured for heavy work, except in certain of the Eastern counties where a horse called the Suffolk Punch is used. In Scotland a breed known as the Clydesdale is the favourite draught horse.

At one time most farmers kept a more lightly built horse either for riding or for harness work, and on market days they could be seen in their smart gigs and traps, polished wheel spokes glittering, and harness buckles flashing, driving briskly along the country lanes. But alas, nowadays the motor car is more esteemed, and a horse-riding farmer is the exception in most parts of this country, unless he be a follower of the Hunt.

How are we to begin our study of the Horse, bearing in mind that it will not pose to order, but will move often and just when it feels inclined? If you are observant you will soon notice that there are certain times when the horses are quiet or at rest and when quite detailed drawings can be made; for instance, on a hot summer day you will often see a group of horses in the shade of a tree, sleepy and unmoving except for a swish of the tail or a toss of the head. They will sometimes drowse away a whole afternoon in this fashion. At other times

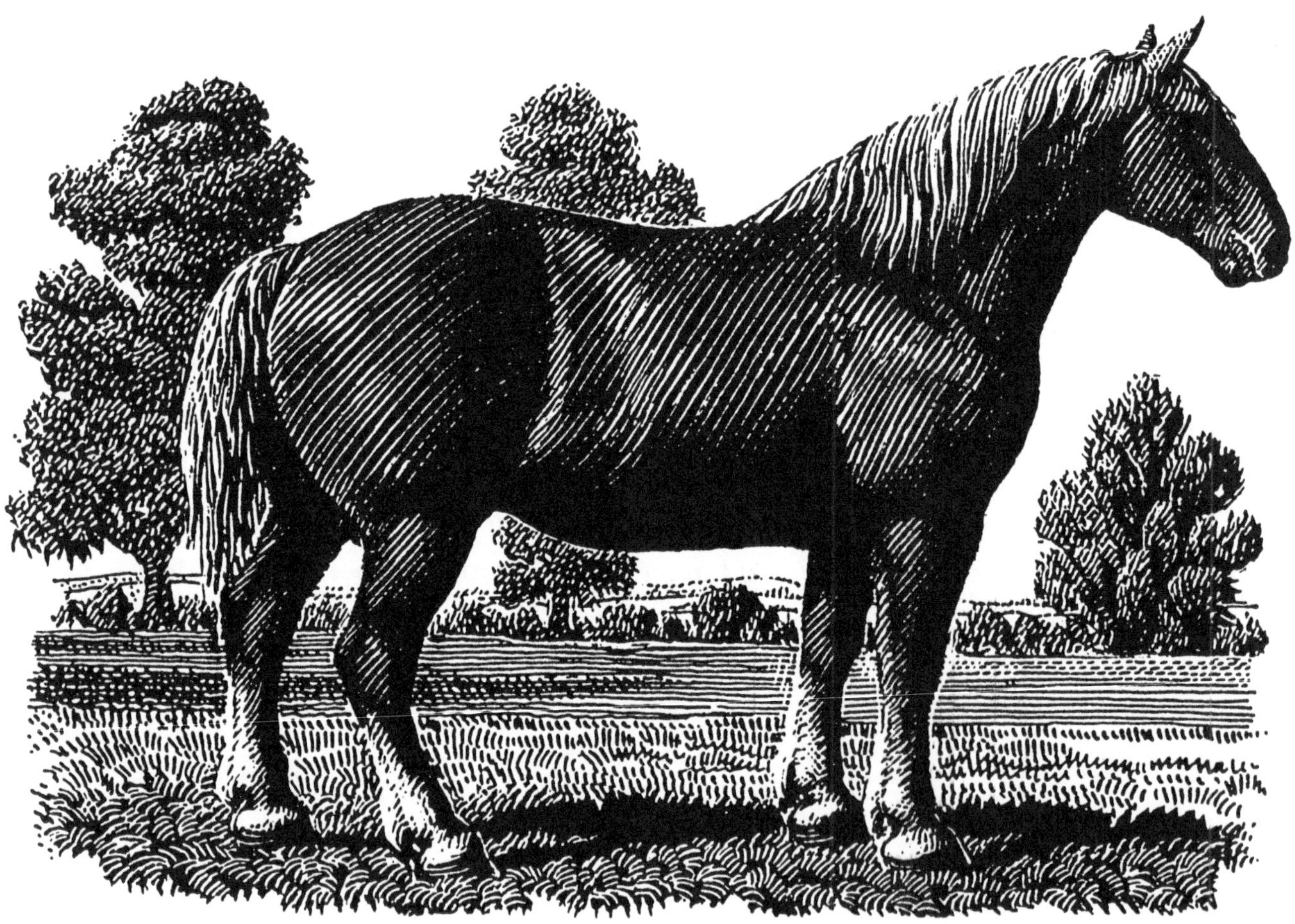

A SUFFOLK PUNCH

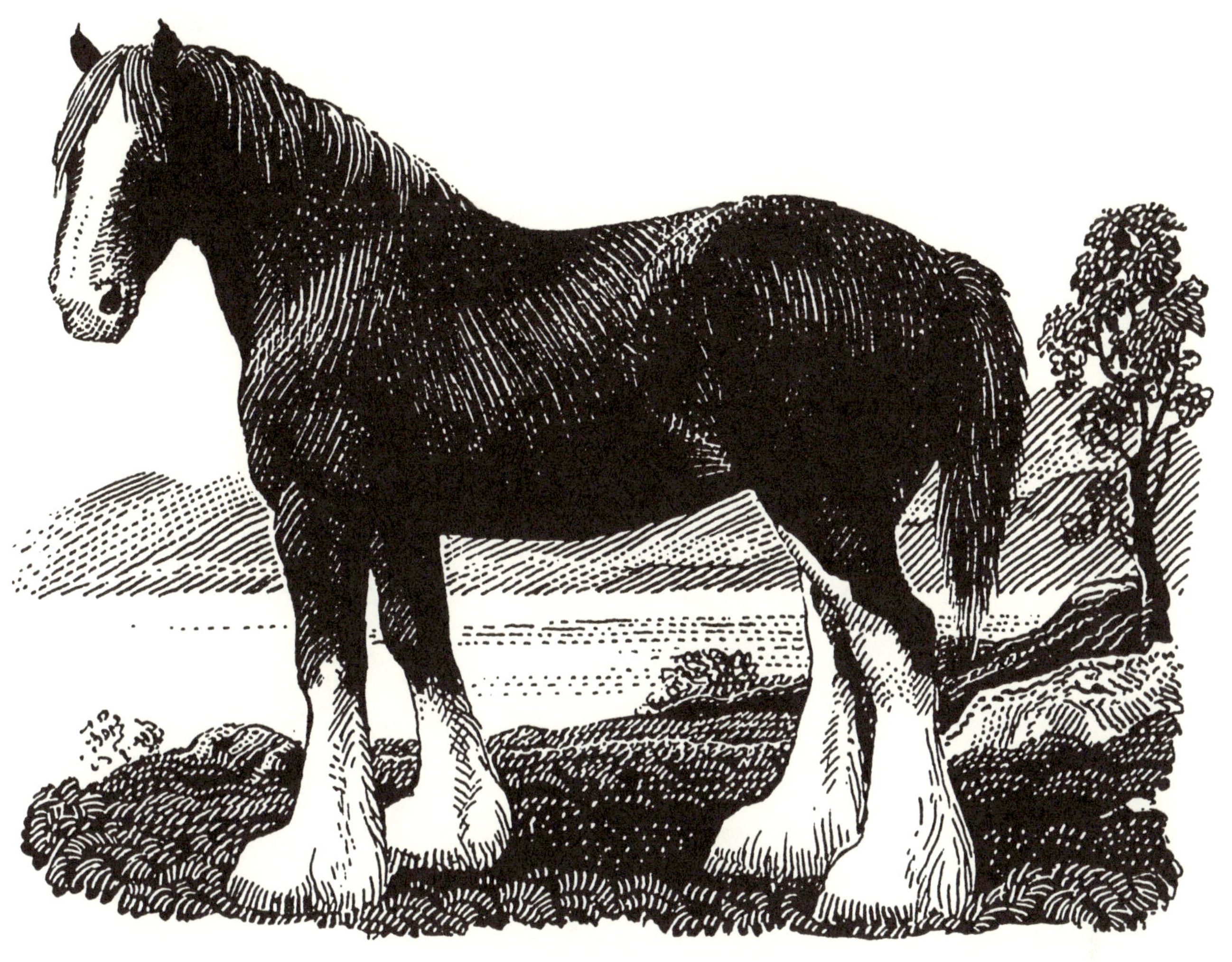

A CLYDESDALE

you will see the horse in harness probably standing quite still while the cart is being loaded or unloaded—a good opportunity for in spite of the harness there is still plenty of horse to be seen. (It would be no bad thing to make studies of harness also; you are bound to need them later). Try to get the very essence of the animal's shape, remembering that there is nothing so much resembles a horse as a horse.

When you have become familiar with its form you will doubtless want to make some studies of movement, and for these I suggest that at first you follow the horse about the field as it grazes. It would be as well to fix the position of the legs in your drawing and work only when the animal, in its striding, returns to that position. Or again, concentrate on the drawing of one limb, noting the various positions of the stride and the effect they have on the muscles and

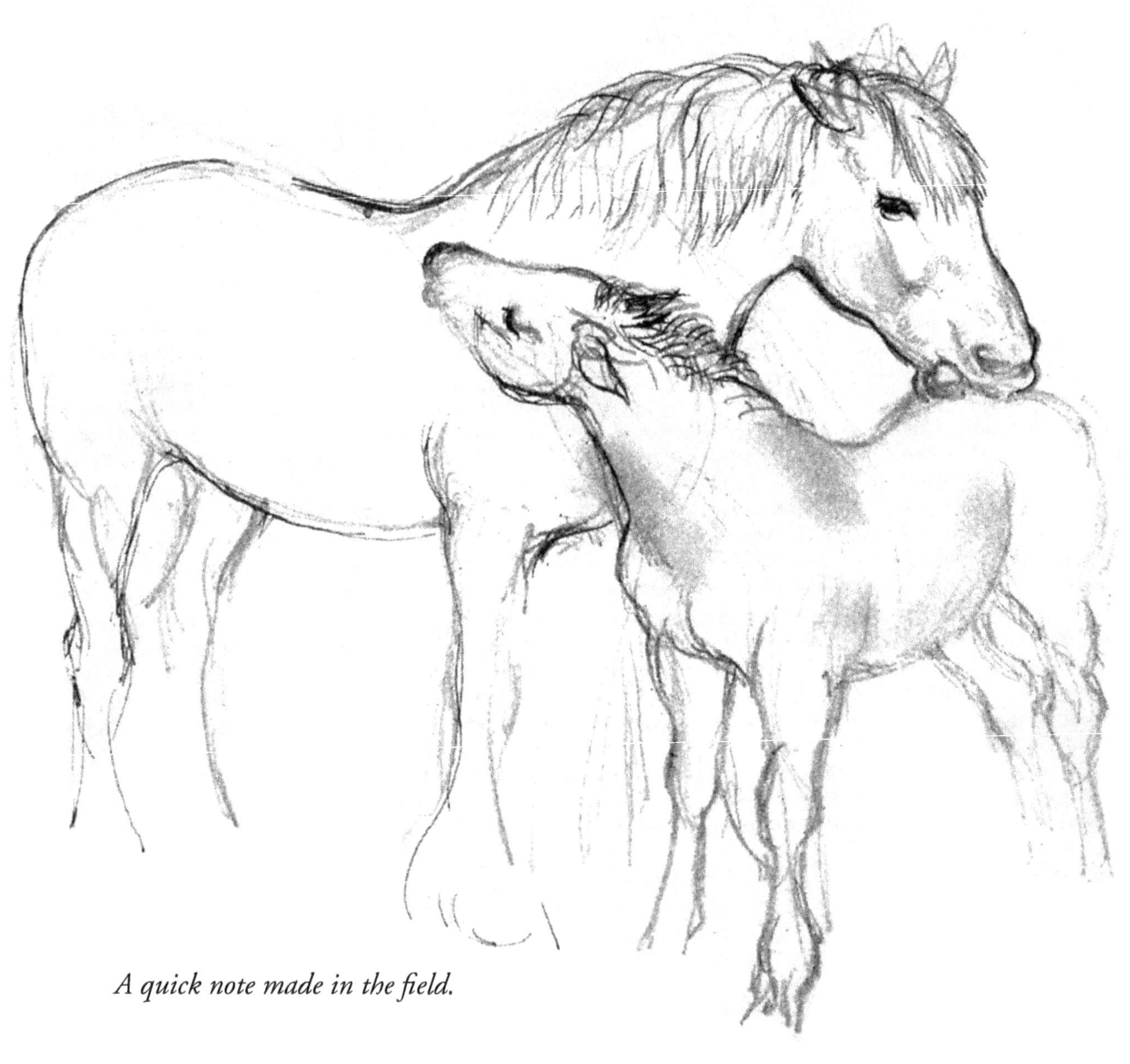

A quick note made in the field.

tendons when the limb is tensed and relaxed. Move round your model and draw front and back views as well as side views.

For your studies of more violent movement you must watch your model carefully, long and often, recording your impressions as soon as possible afterwards. Try to set down the movement of the whole horse so that you synchronise front and back legs. This will be difficult at first but "practice makes perfect."

This type is known as "half-legged," that is, neither light nor heavy in build and is used for the less heavy work on the farm.

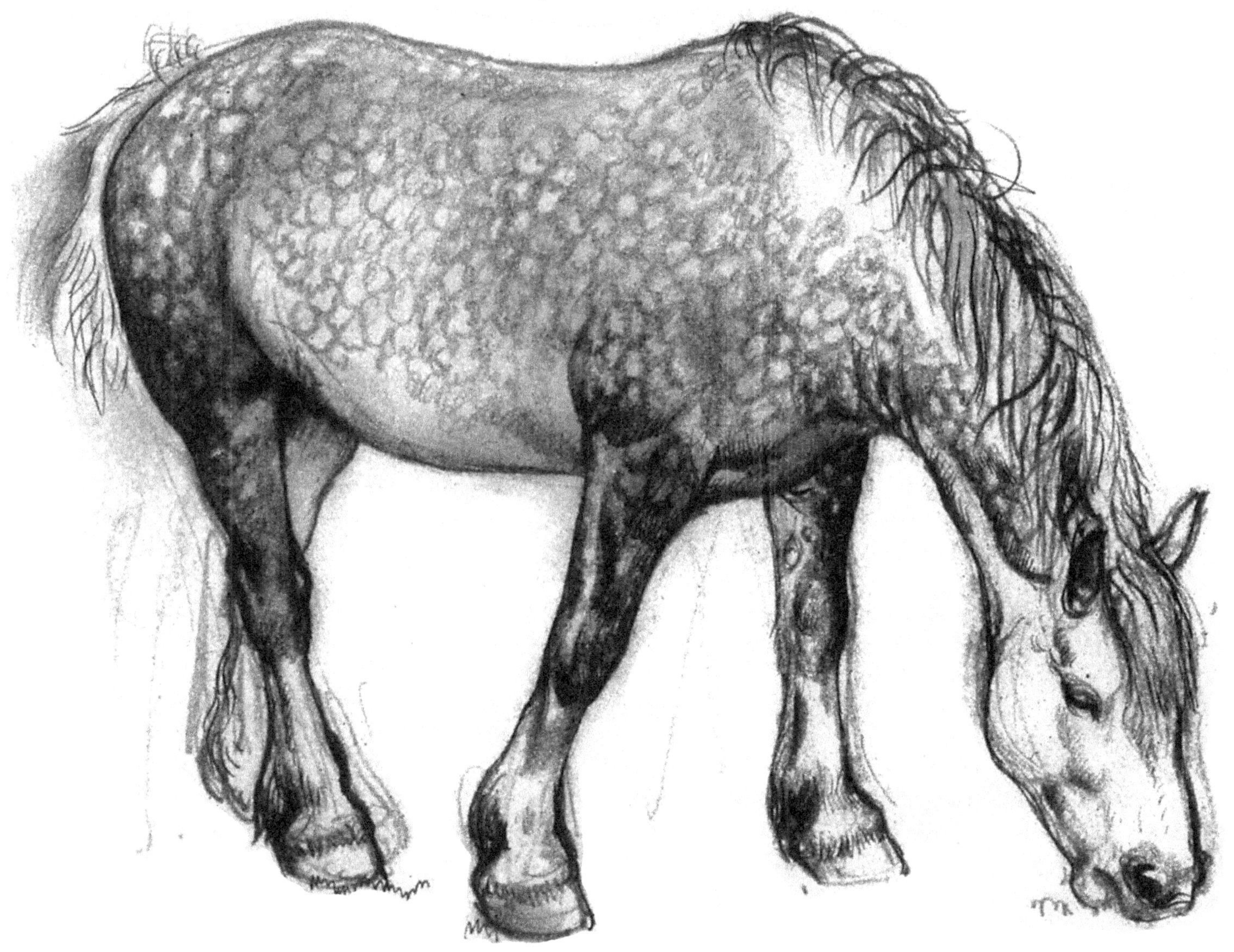

A DAPPLED GREY COB

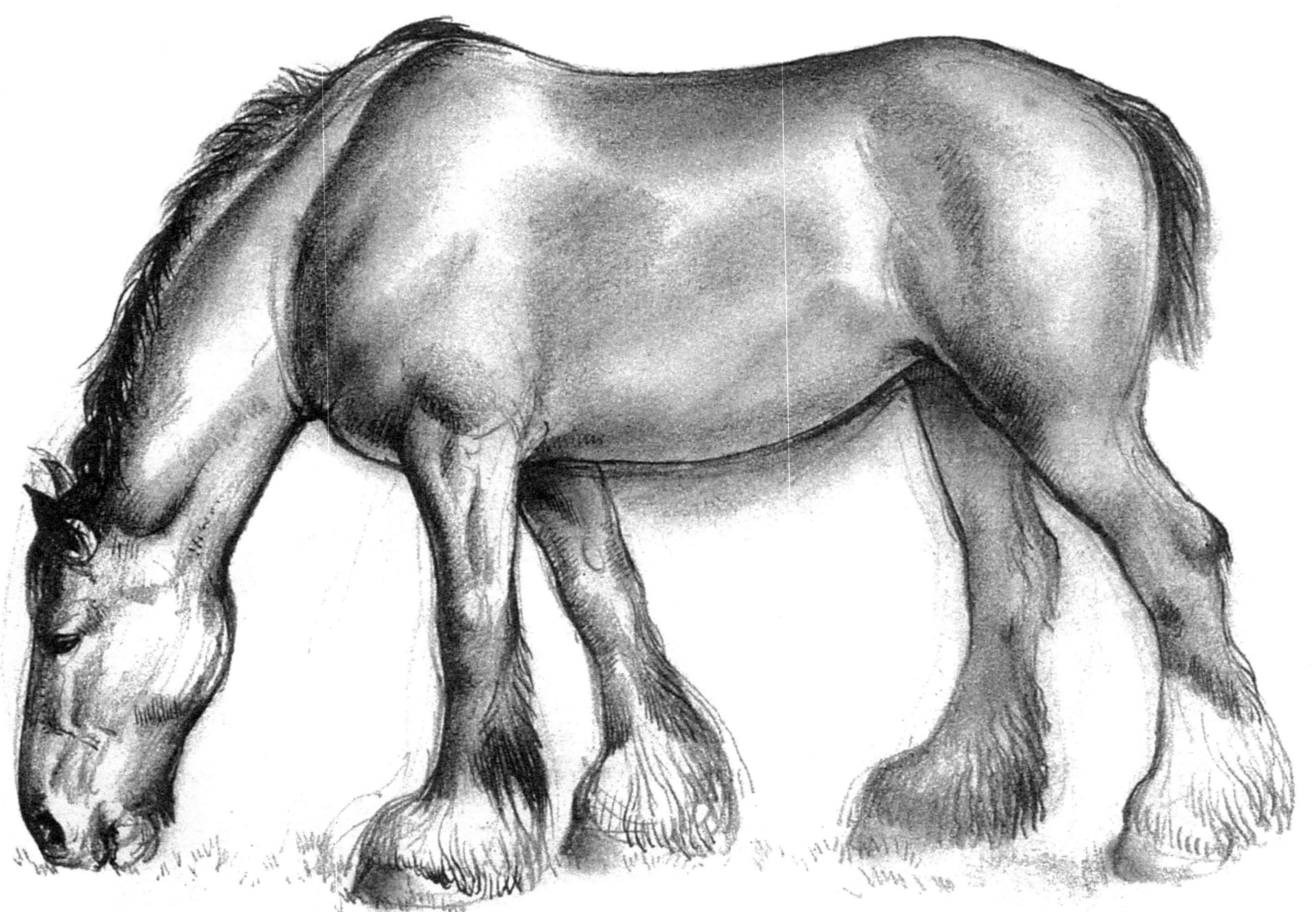

The drawings on these two pages were made from a big Shire mare as she grazed. She is immensely powerful and a typical draught horse.

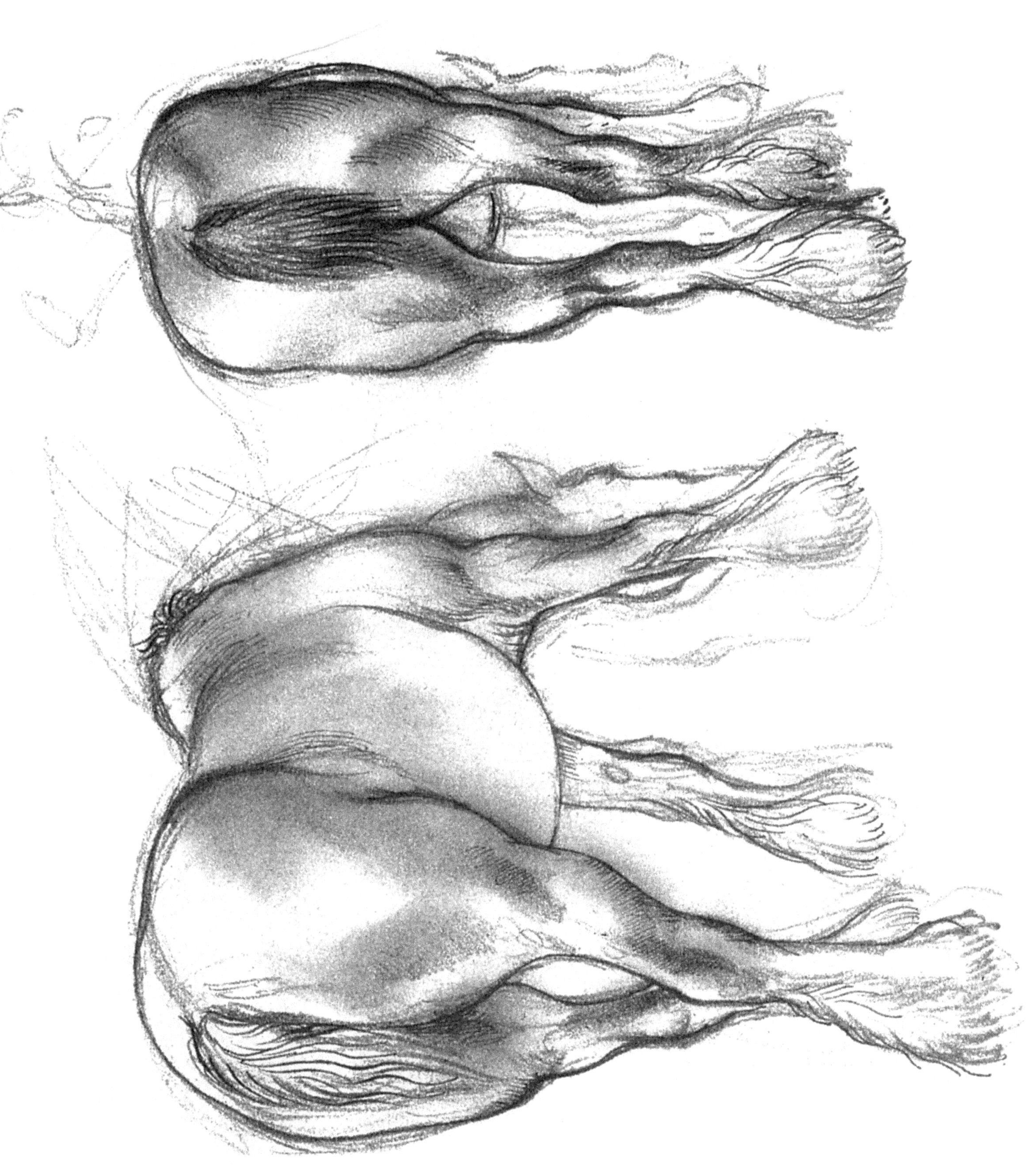

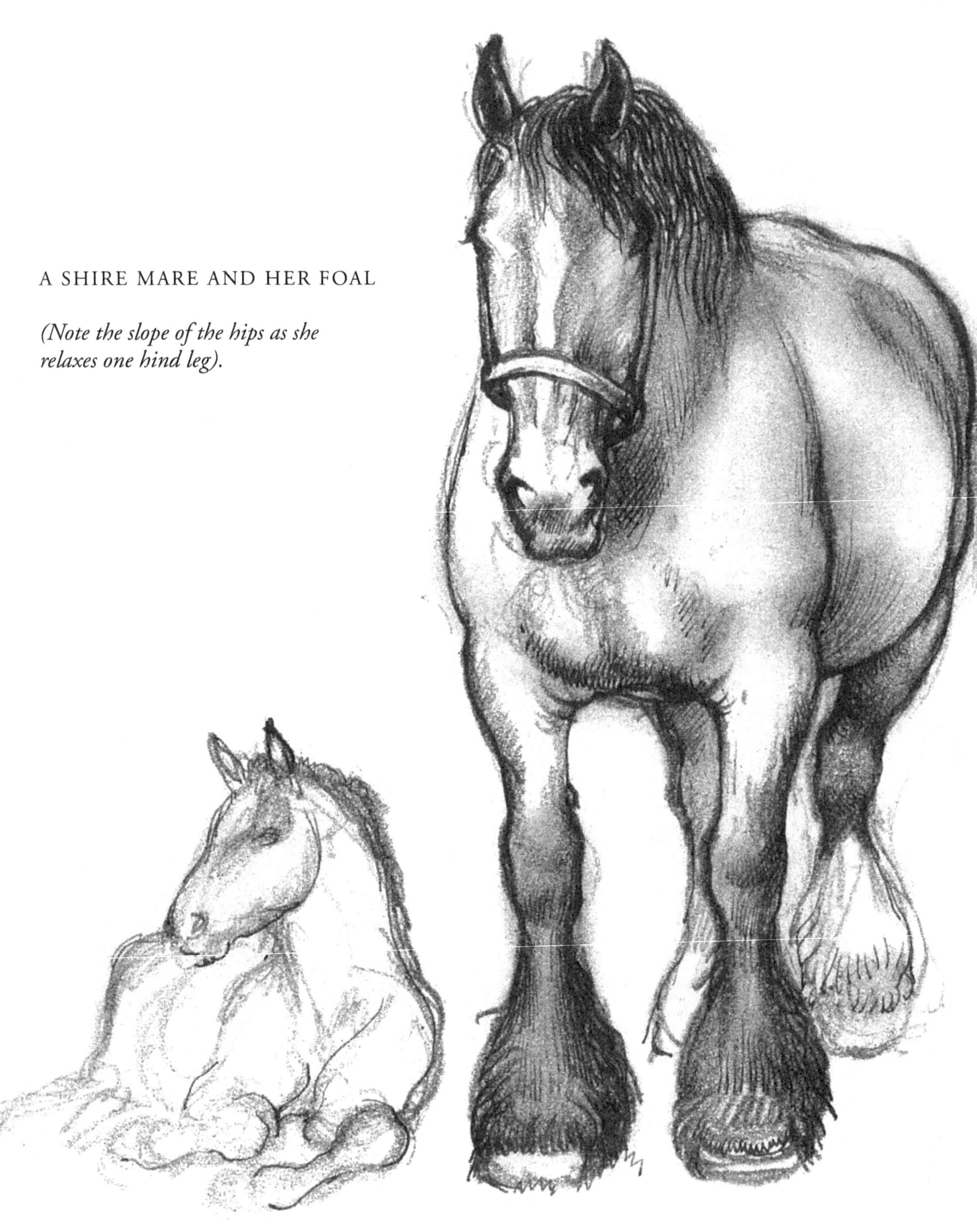

A SHIRE MARE AND HER FOAL

(Note the slope of the hips as she relaxes one hind leg).

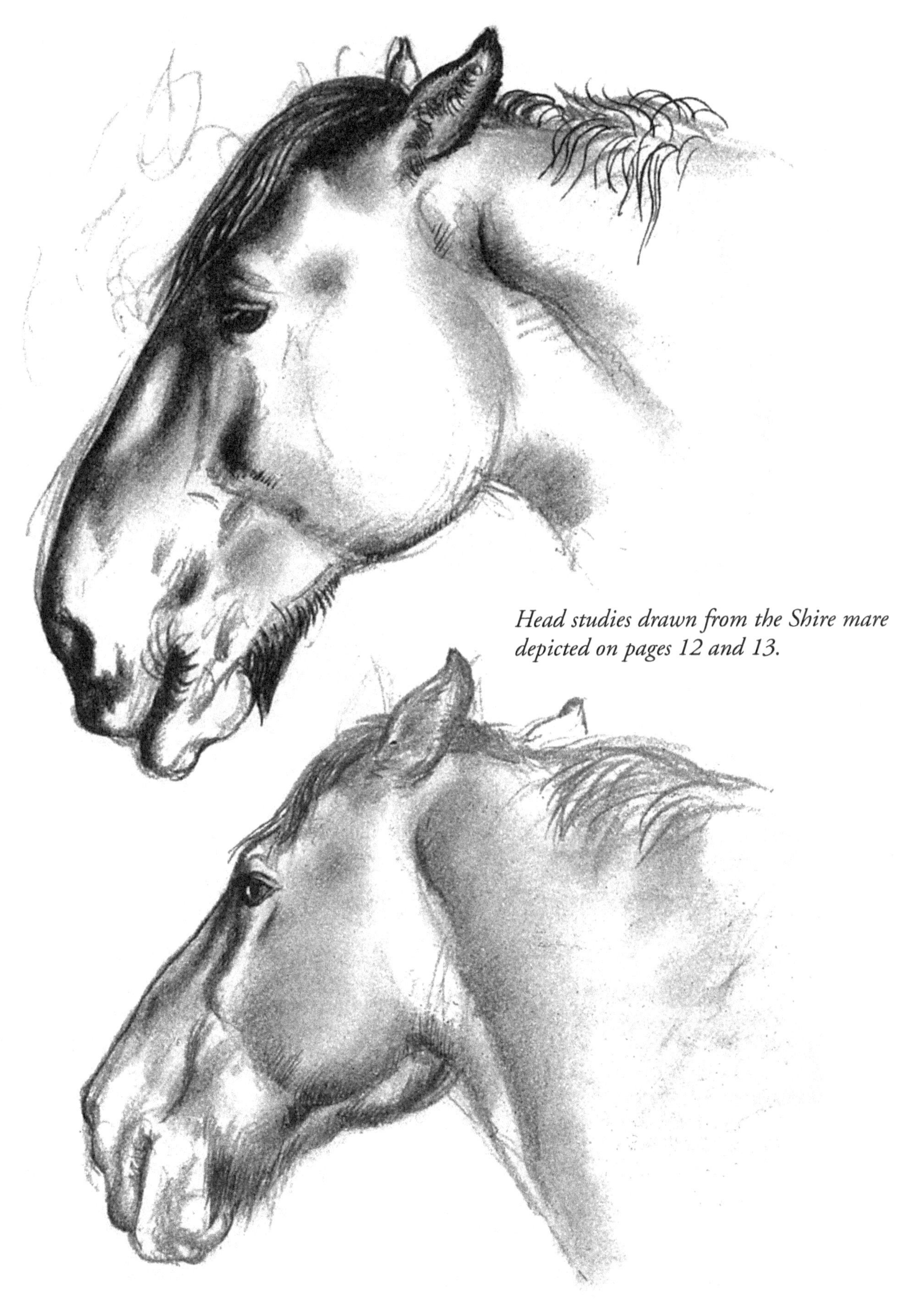

Head studies drawn from the Shire mare depicted on pages 12 and 13.

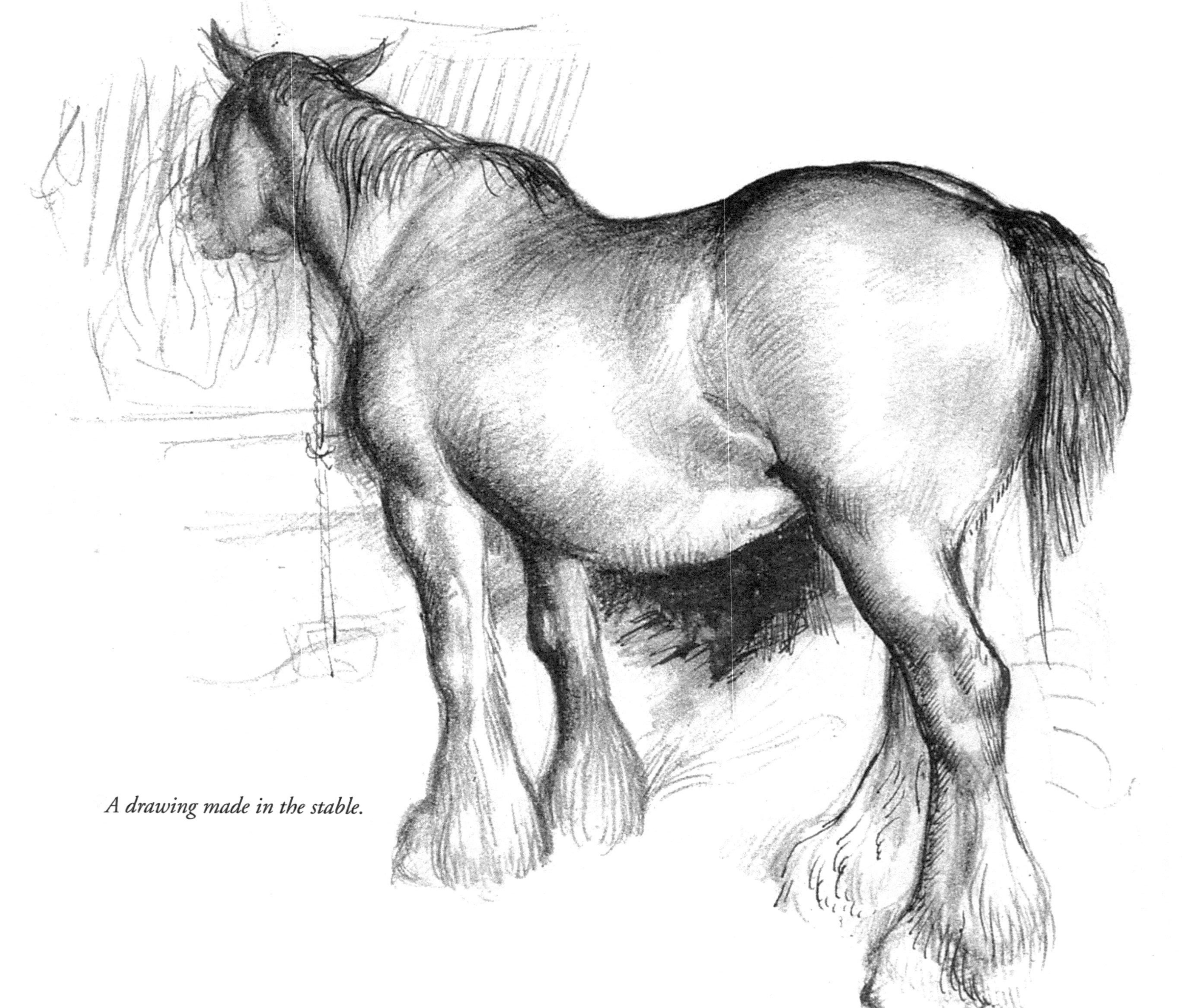

A drawing made in the stable.

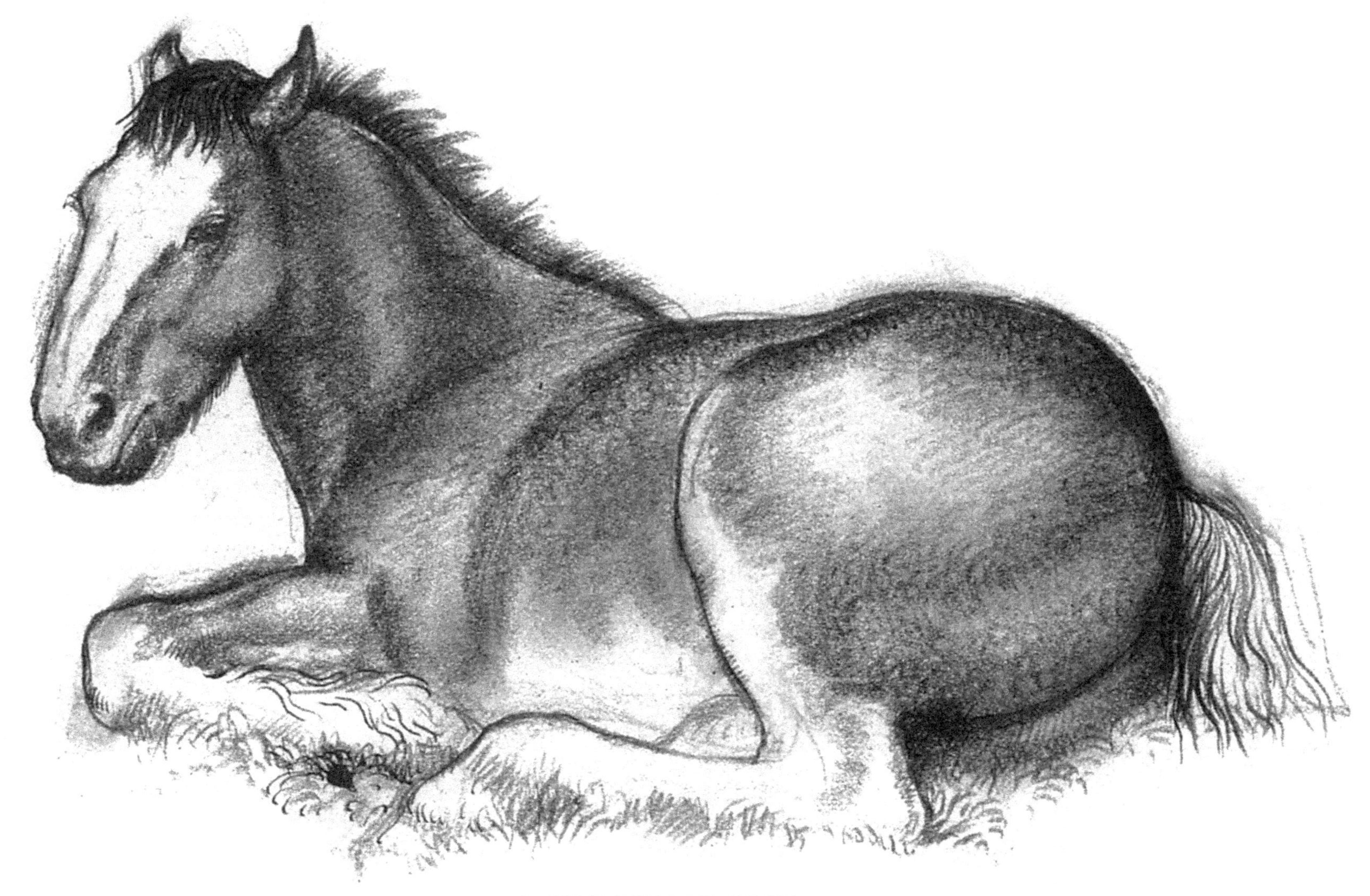

A CLYDESDALE COLT

CATTLE

Cattle as a rule are most obliging models: indeed, all you have to do is to sit quietly in the middle of a pasture, where they are feeding, and wait. Soon you will be surrounded by a ring of beasts all filled with a great curiosity towards you. You will be able to draw as many front views as you desire but for other views of cows this method is not entirely satisfactory. However, cattle, like horses, have their quiet periods when they can easily be studied and drawn. When they have finished grazing they will stand, or lie, quite still chewing their cud for a

Shorthorns resting and chewing their cud after a morning's grazing.

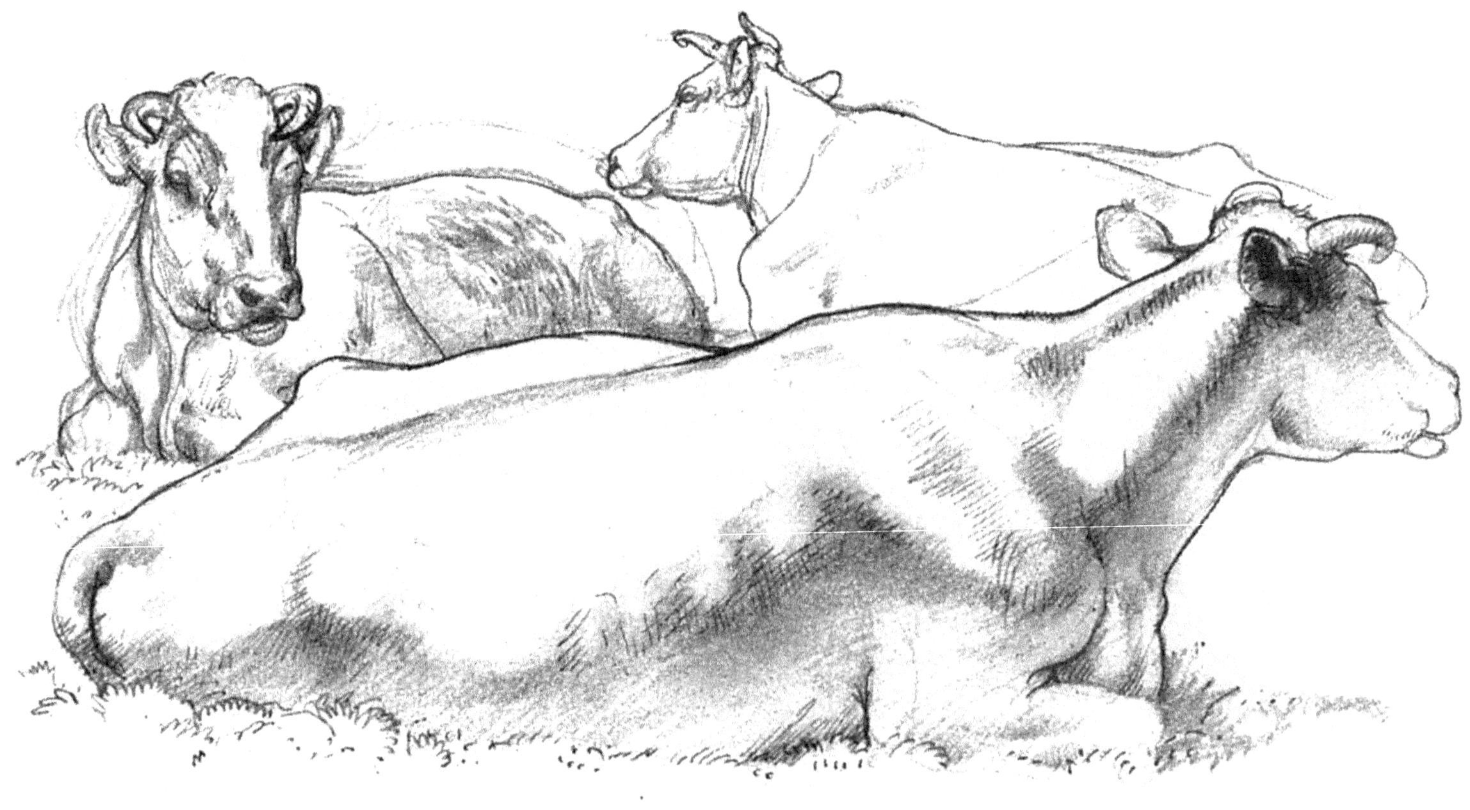

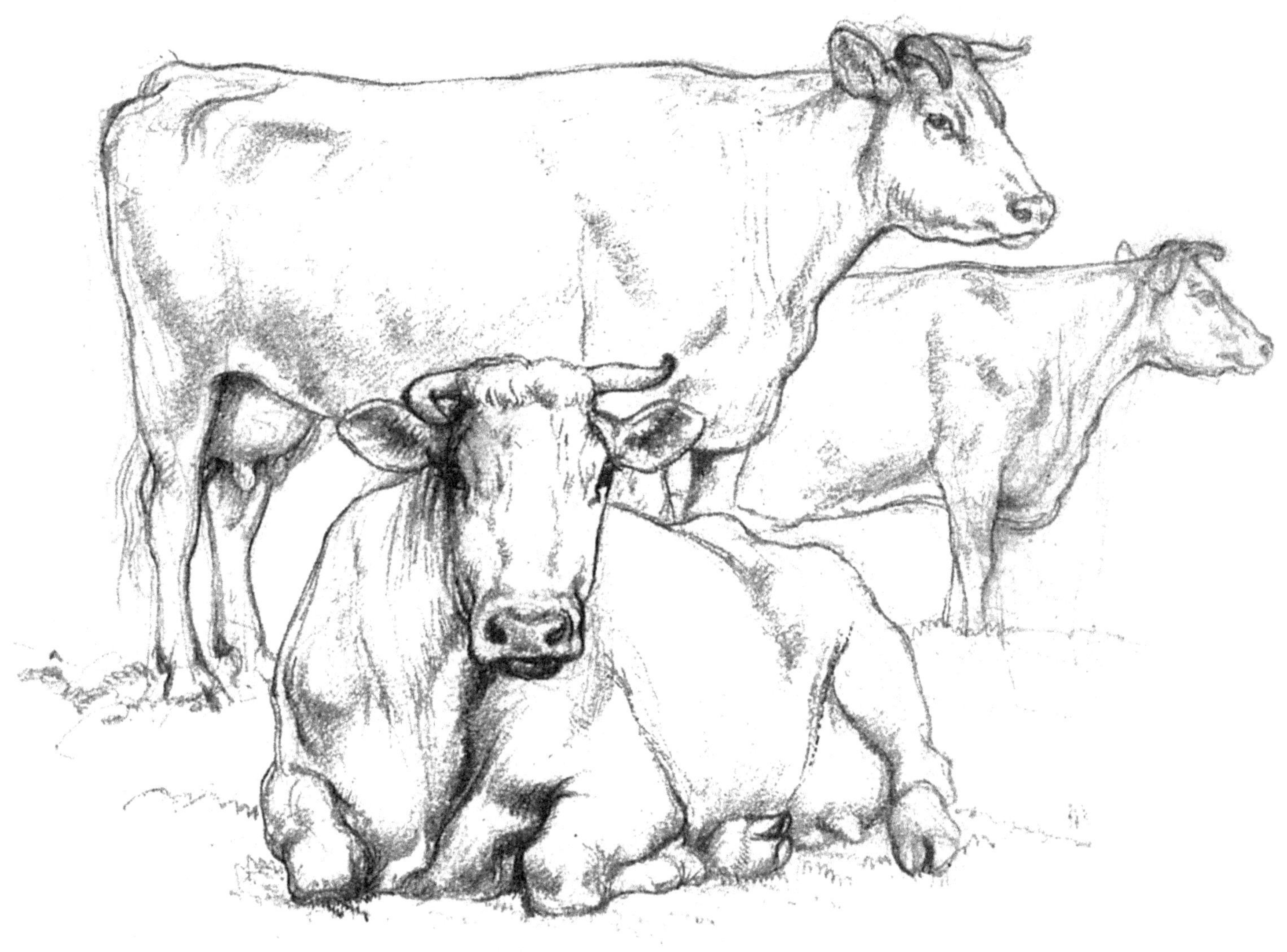

A group of Shorthorns waiting near the yard gate for milking time.

length of time which is amply sufficient to allow detailed studies to be made. Well before milking time they may often be seen by the pasture gate, awaiting the feed of corn which they associate with milking. Often they will stand in interesting groups which I suggest you try to draw. Your studies of groups will be most useful when you begin to compose more finished works.

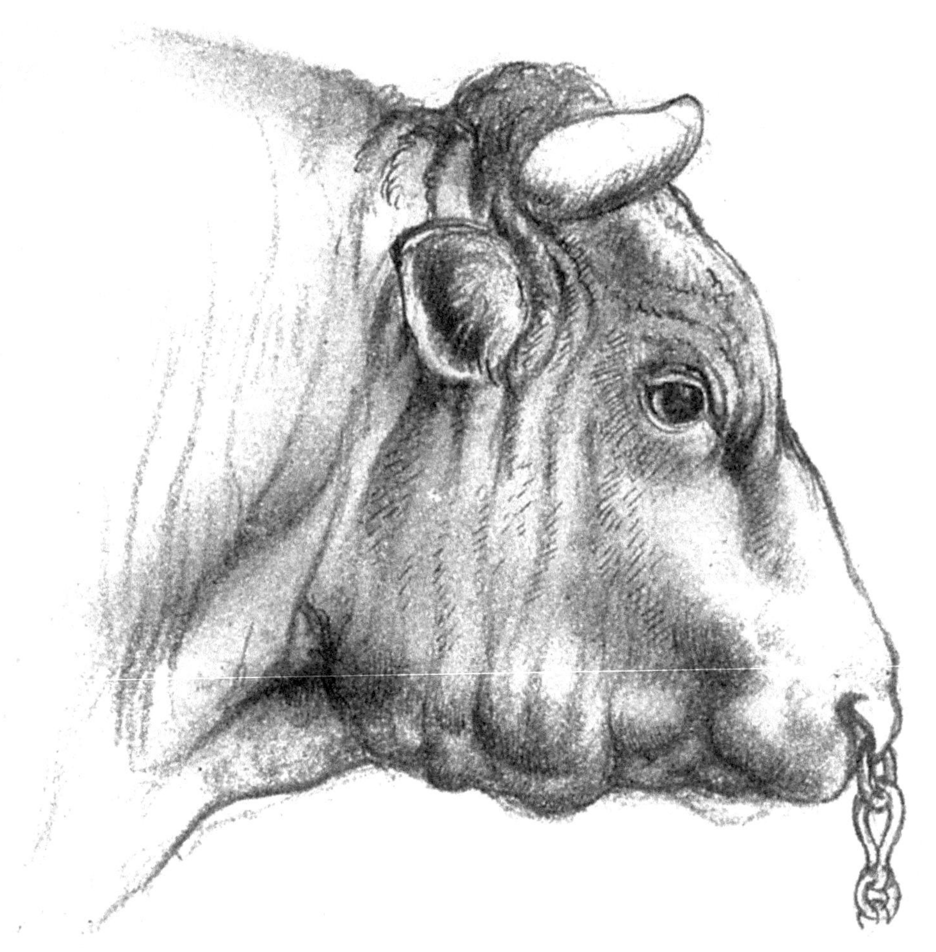

A SHORTHORN BULL

This bull, which was tethered by a chain to a fifty-six pound iron weight, was a very bad model; it resented the presence of a stranger and gave me an awe-inspiring display of bovine fury. Above is a study of the head made in the intervals between its snorting, pawing, and goring of the ground.

The foregoing suggestions apply to cow models only. As for William the bull, take no risks with him. Do not go into the middle of a field where he is unless you know that he is quiet and good tempered. Even then I doubt if the middle of a field is a fit place to test this. A cattle auction or a market often presents far better opportunities to make studies of bulls. There you will see them tethered in a line and these conditions, besides eliminating any qualms concerning the temper of your models, have the added attraction of variety, for you will rarely find two bulls which are identical. Note how their shape and build differs from that of the cows.

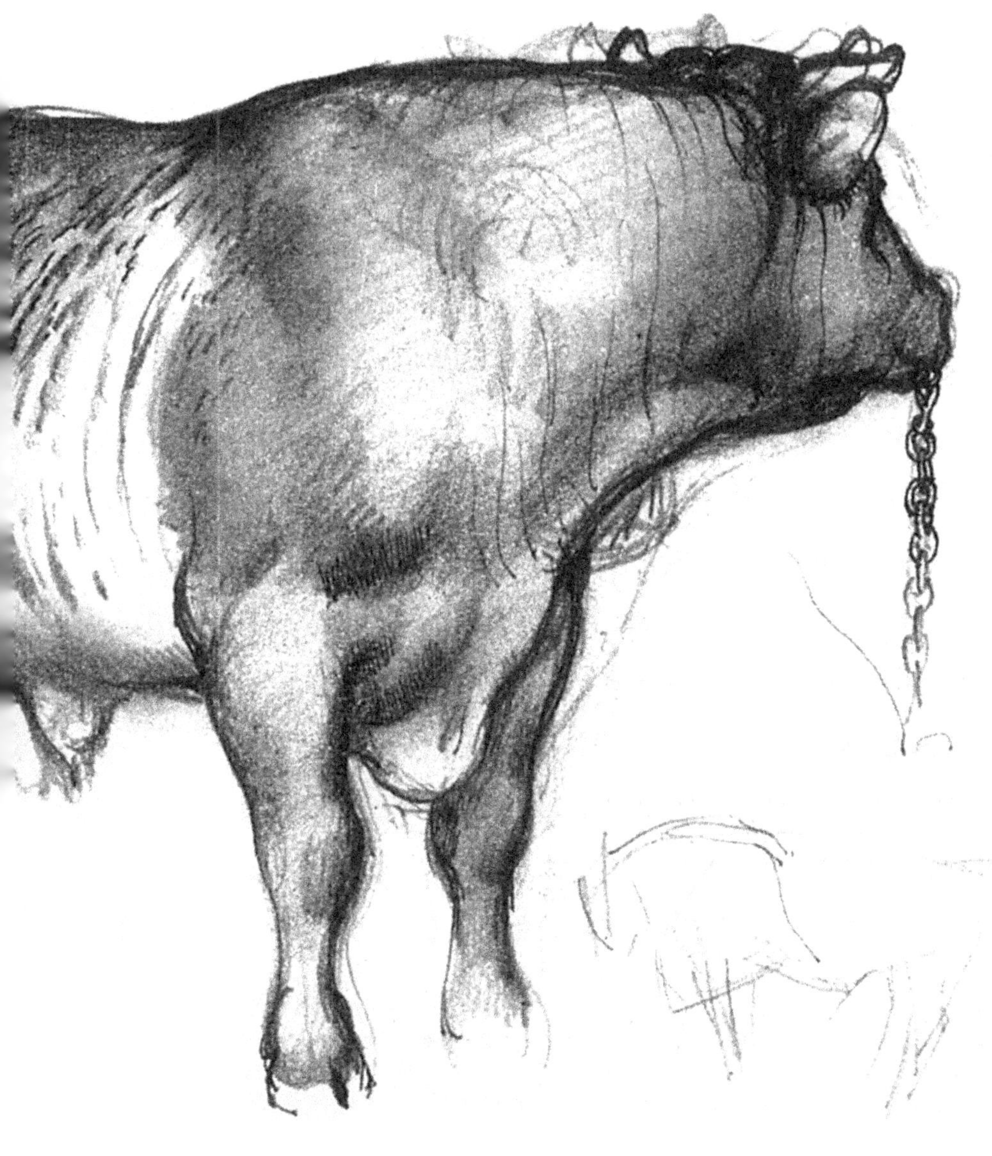

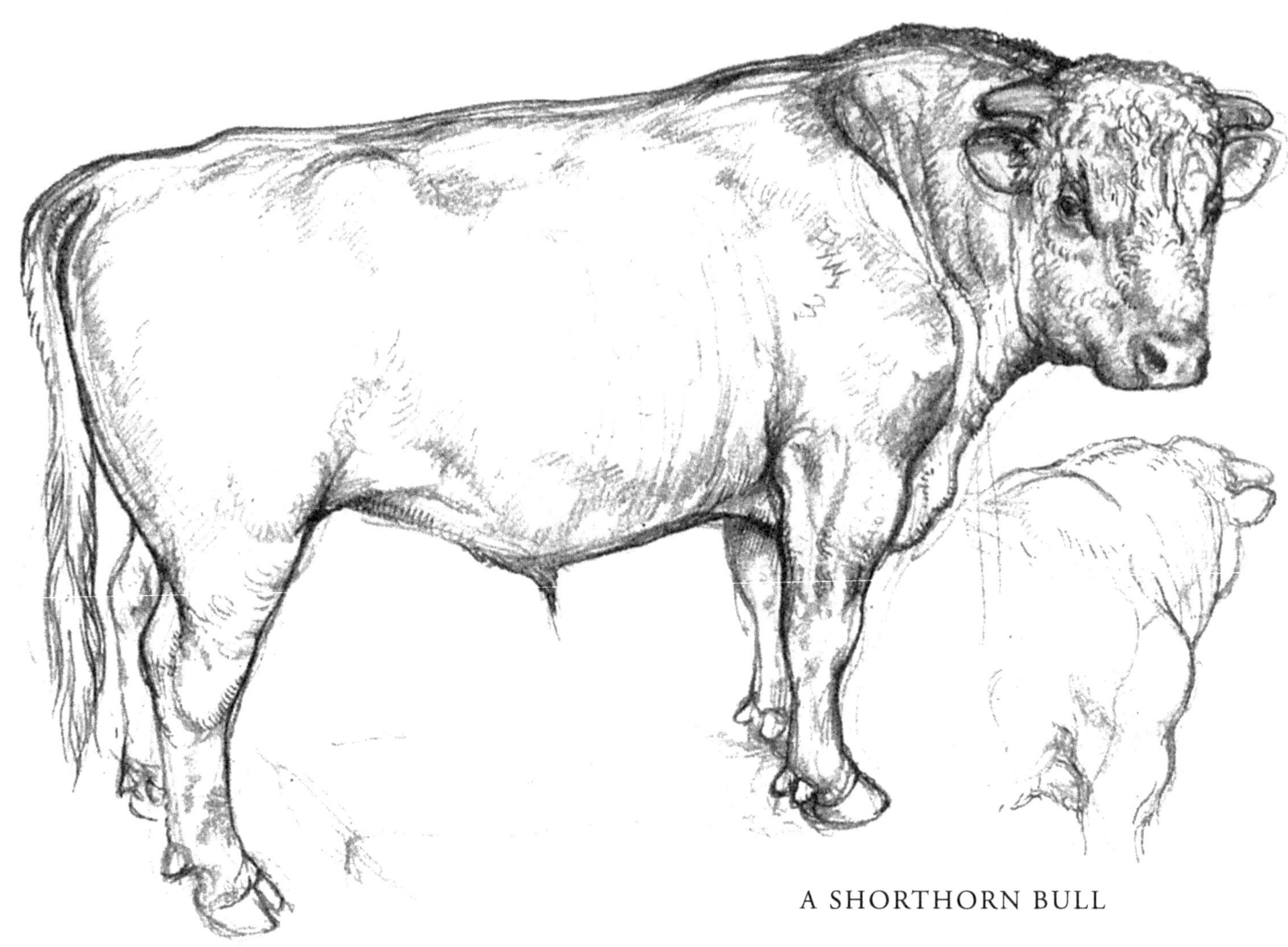

A SHORTHORN BULL

Note the powerful neck and shoulders and the lean loins.

We have, in this country, many breeds of cattle and the one you will be most familiar with will depend on the district in which you live. If your home is in Devon you will know the big red cattle with the long horns. If you hail from Herefordshire you will be familiar with the red cattle with the white faces, or if from southwestern Scotland the spotted Ayrshire cattle will be first in your mind's eye. But wherever you go in Britain there is one breed which is well known and that breed is the Shorthorn. Because of its general usefulness it is a favourite with farmers, for it gives good quantities of milk, and when its milking days are over it fattens well for beef. For our purpose it is a good "average" sort of beast to draw: neither too big nor too small and with a shapely head. If you wish to see many of our breeds together, try to attend a big Agricultural Show where you will find our Shorthorn cheek by jowl with perhaps the Welsh Black or the Aberdeen Angus. There you will be able to compare the smooth delicacy of the Jersey with the hairy bulk of the Highlanders, and the red and white of the Lincoln Red with the black and white of the Belted Galloway. All will display differences of shape and colour which should keep your pencil busy for many hours.

Compare the oblong shape of her body with the tapering one of the bull's.

A SHORTHORN COW

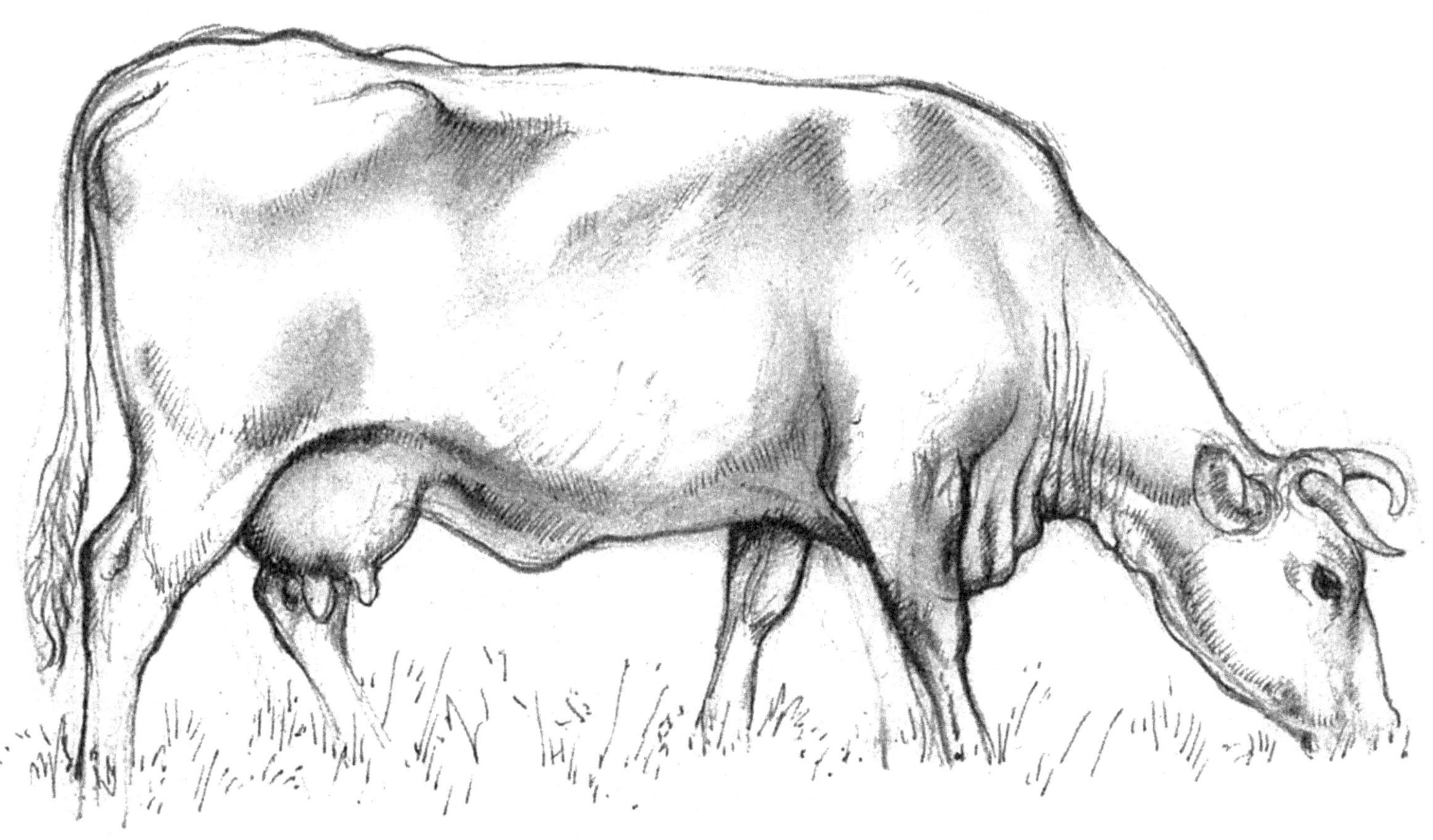

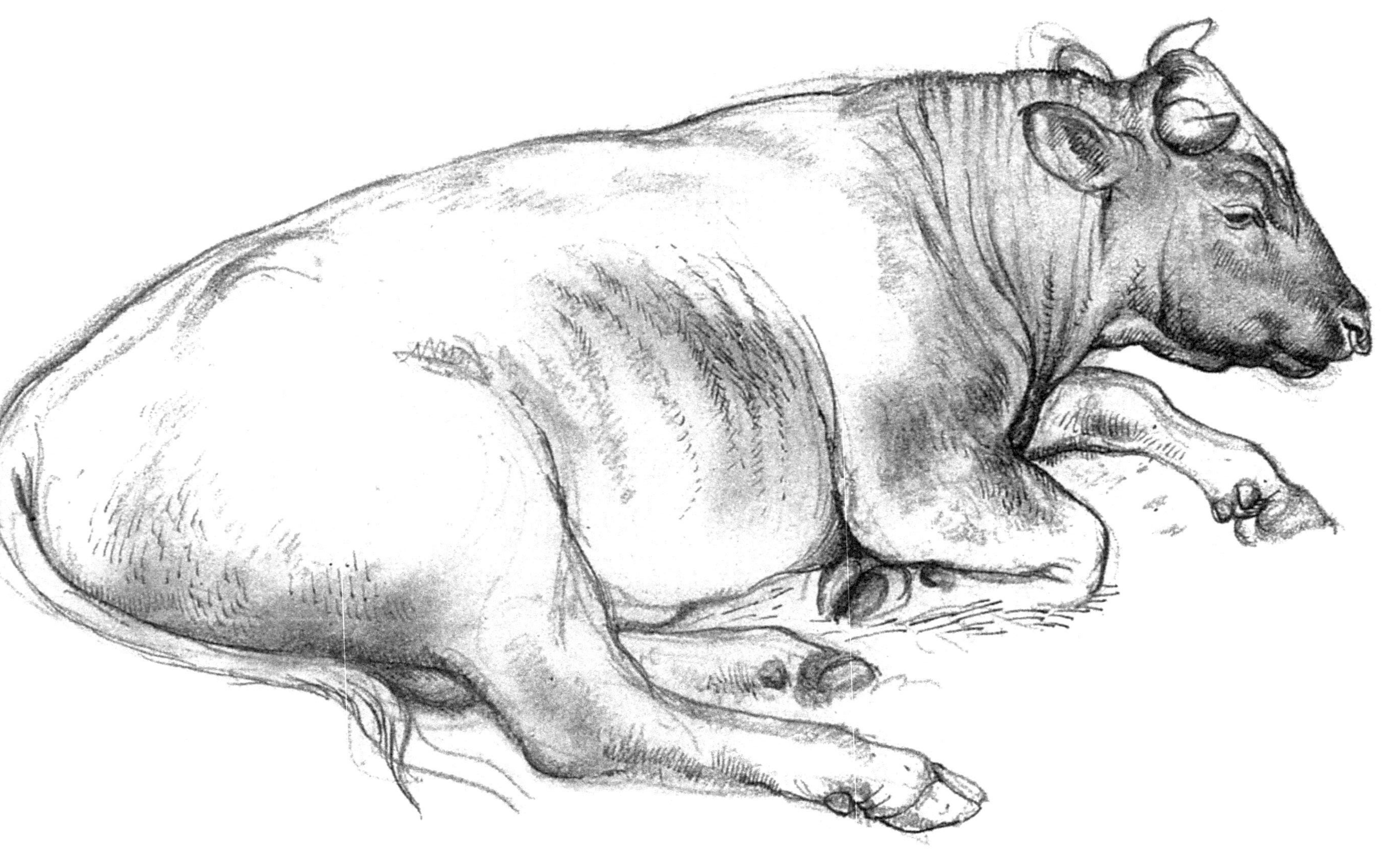

This drawing and the one on the next page were made from a very sleepy young Shorthorn Bull as it rested in a loose box. Note the shape of the head, especially the width of the skull between the horns.

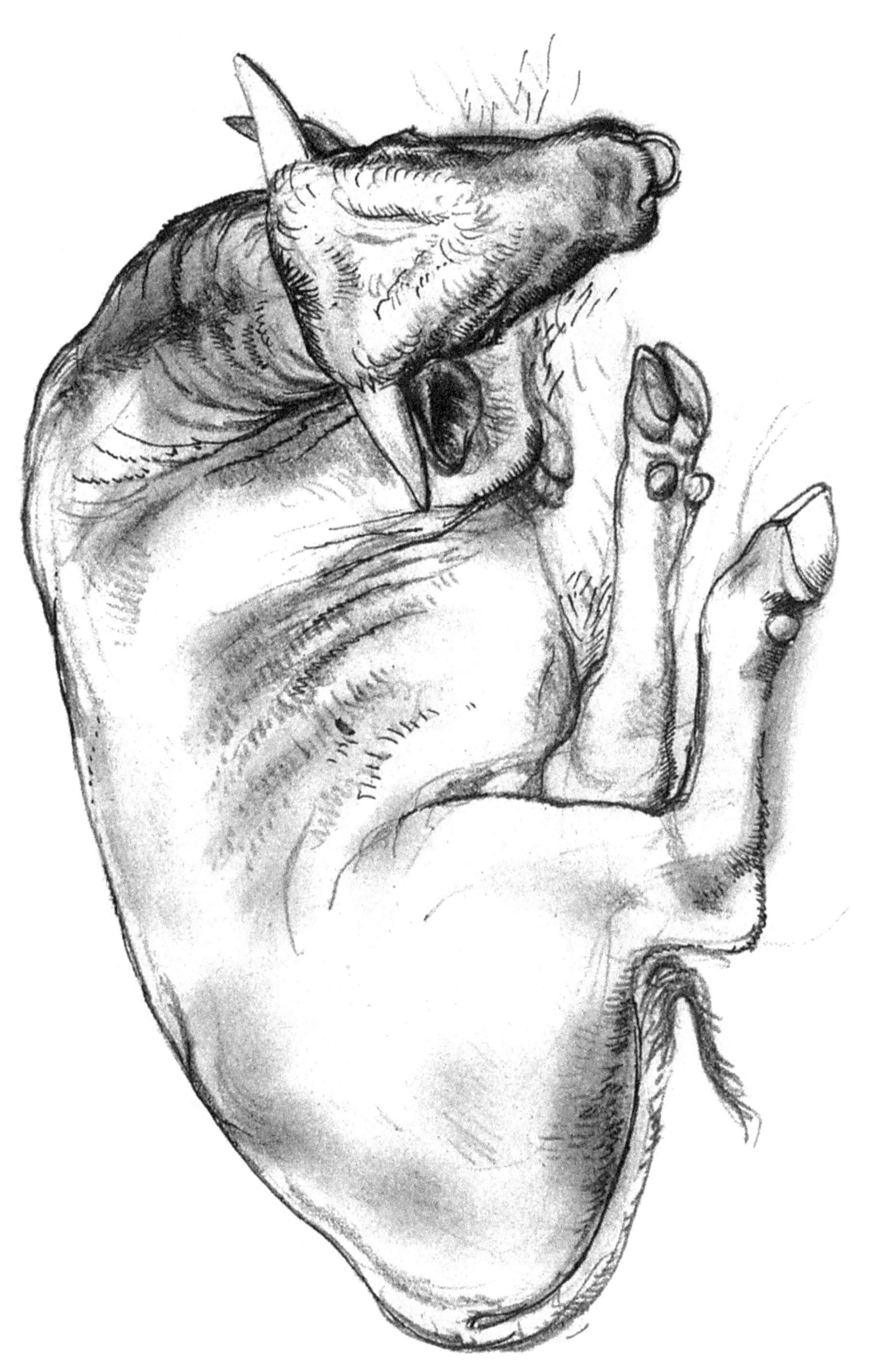

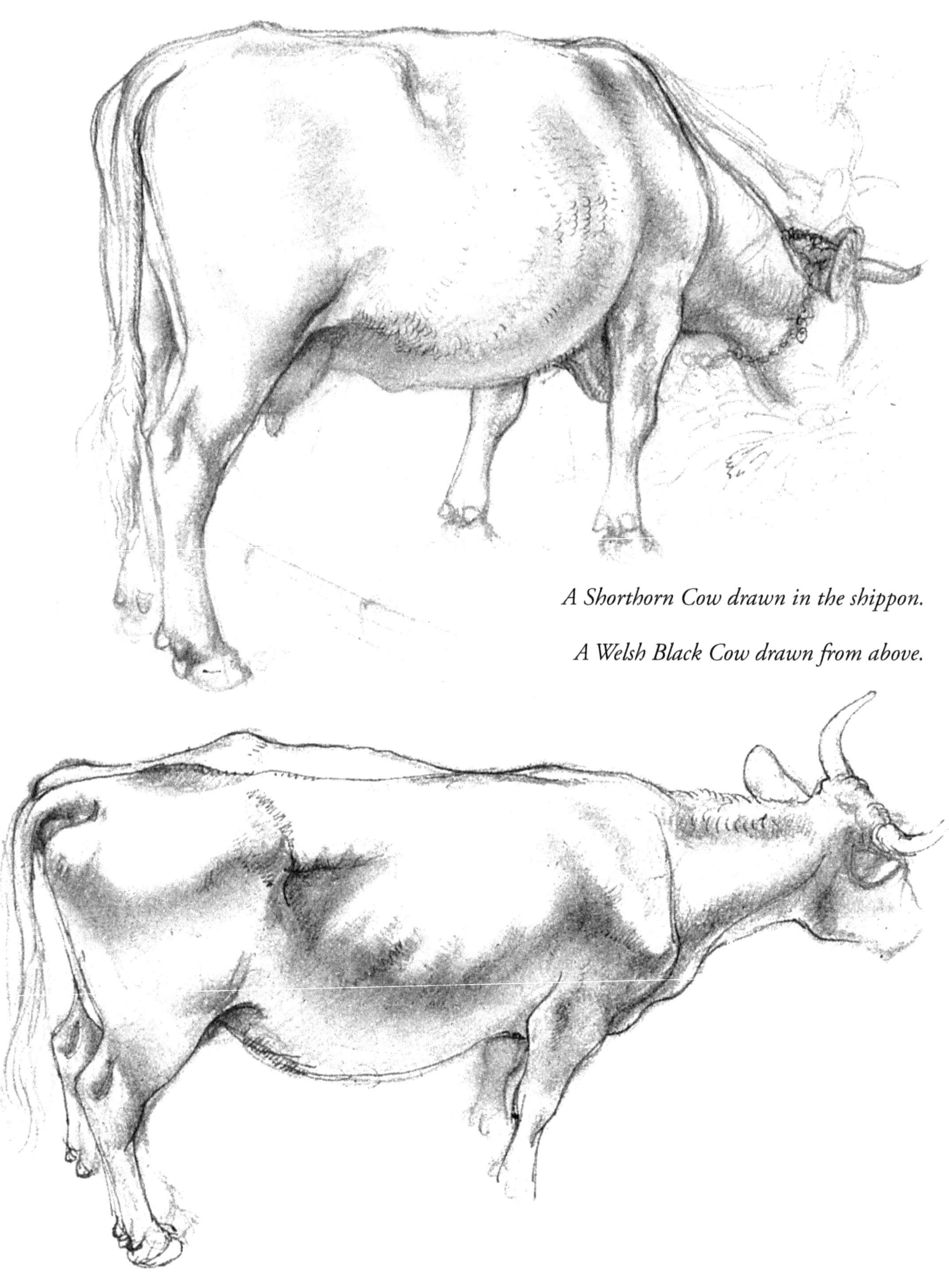

A Shorthorn Cow drawn in the shippon.

A Welsh Black Cow drawn from above.

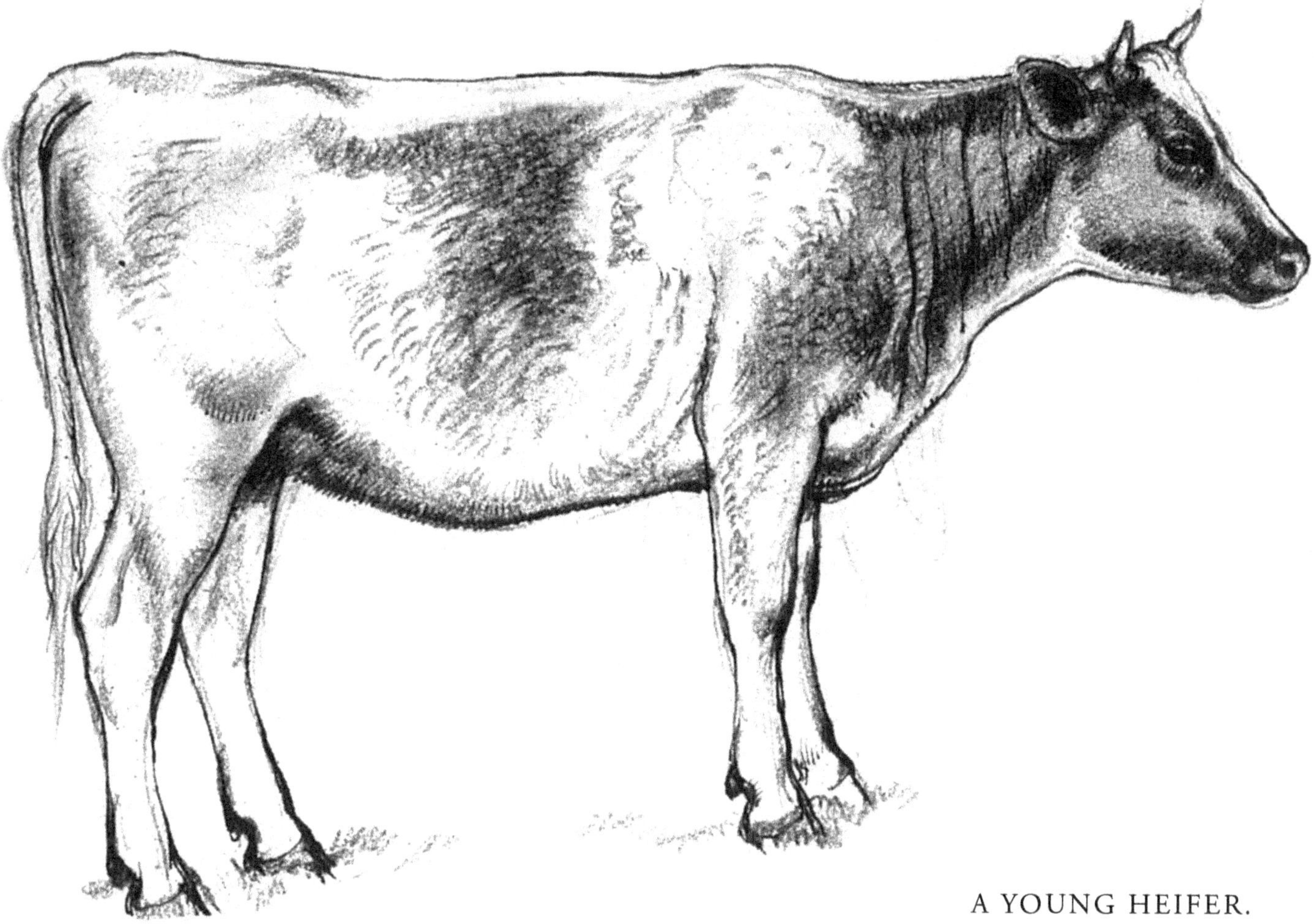

A YOUNG HEIFER.
A SHORTHORN-AYRSHIRE CROSS

AN AYRSHIRE CALF

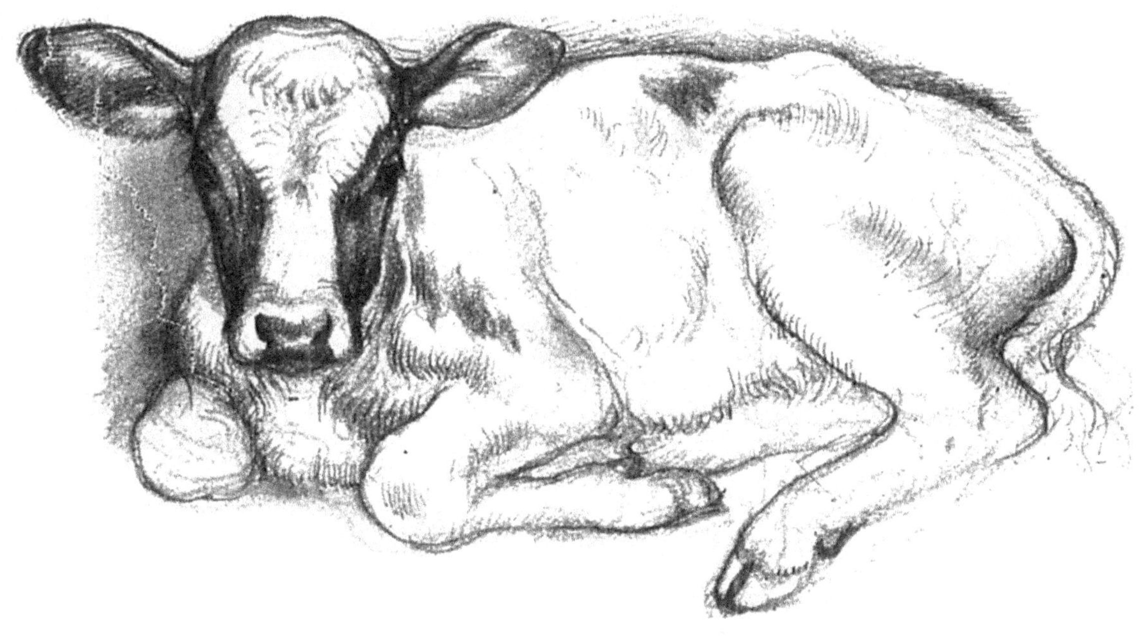

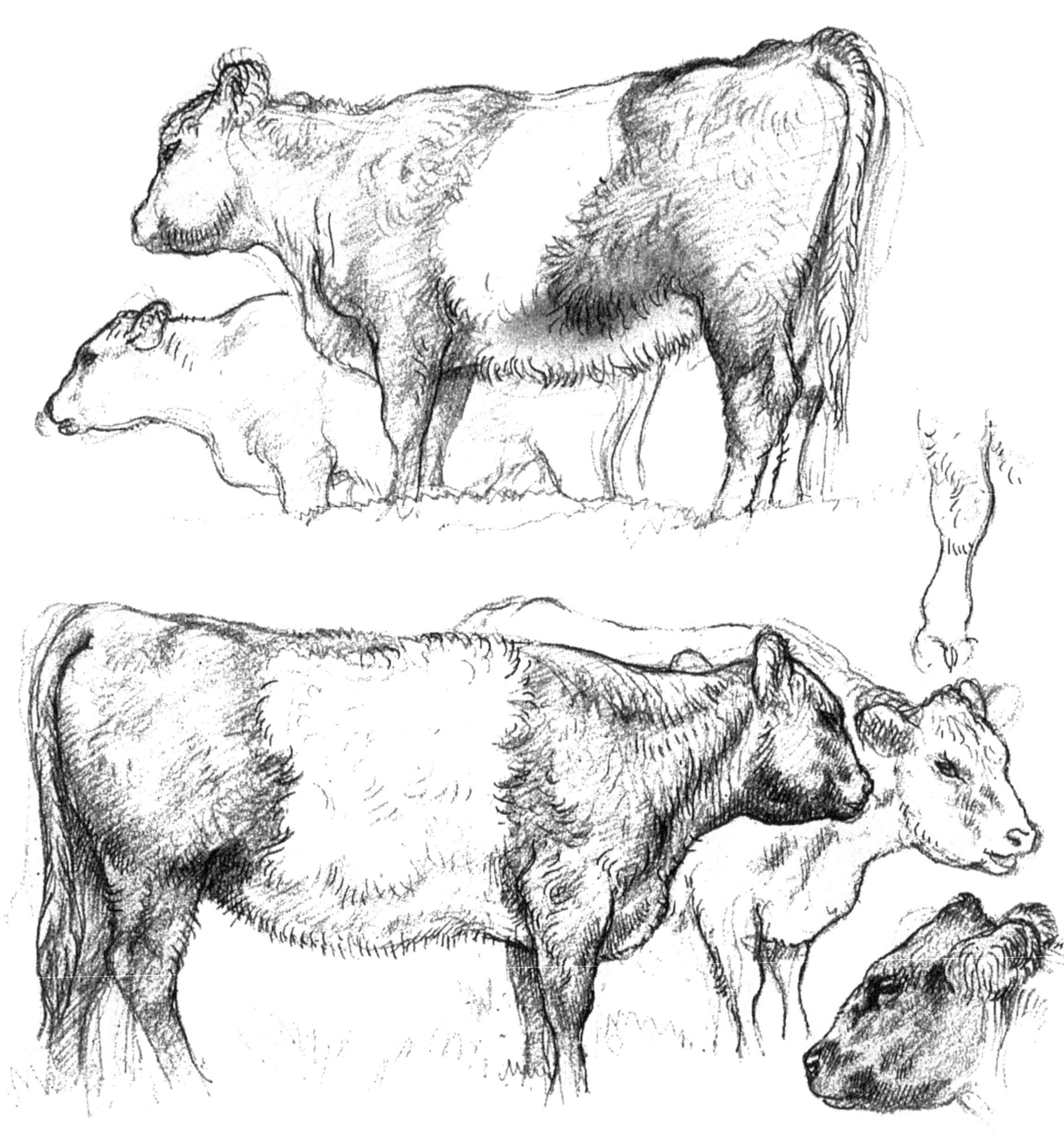

Sketches of Belted Galloways drawn on a wild hillside in North Staffordshire. They are black and white in colour and hornless.

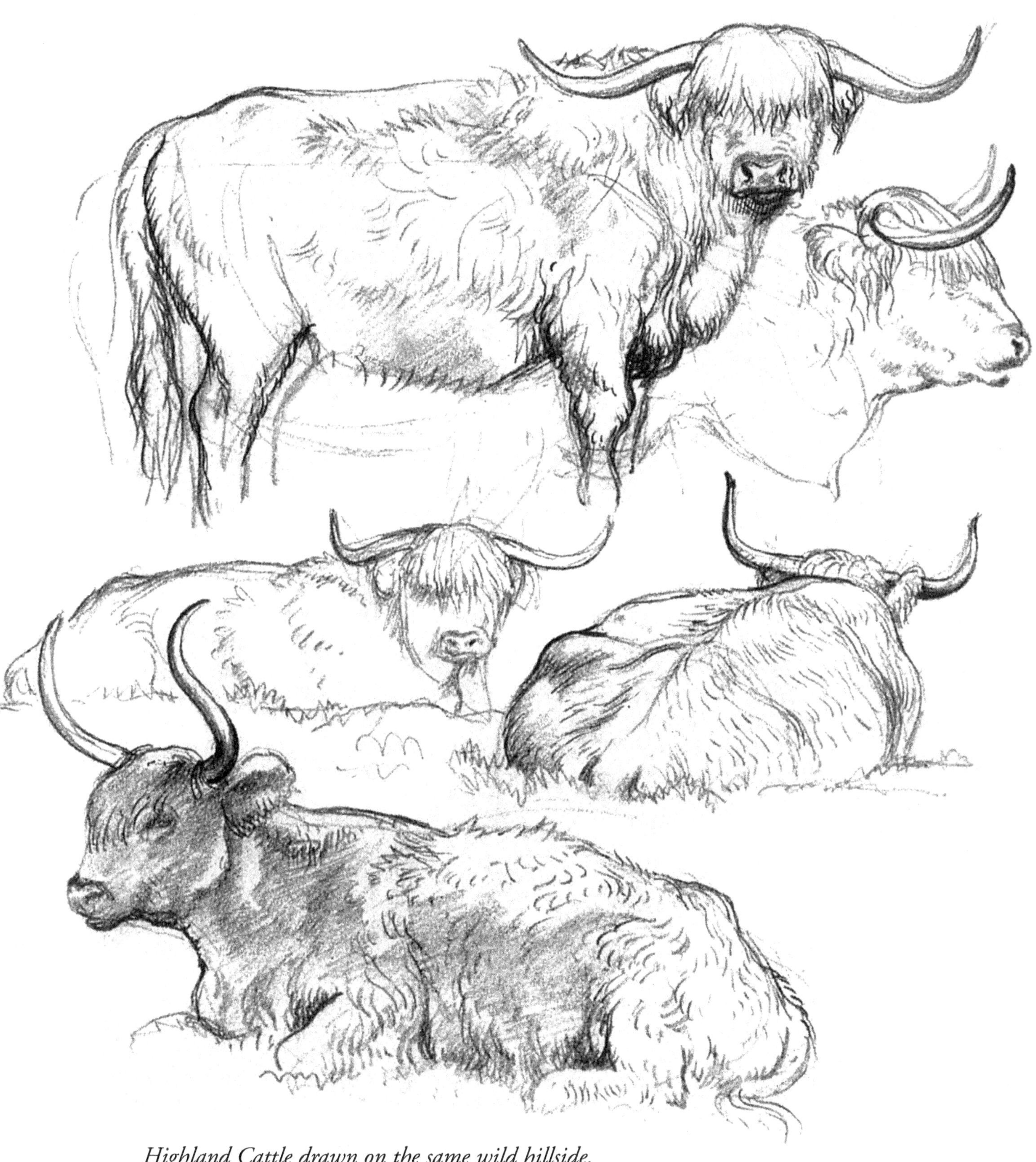

Highland Cattle drawn on the same wild hillside.

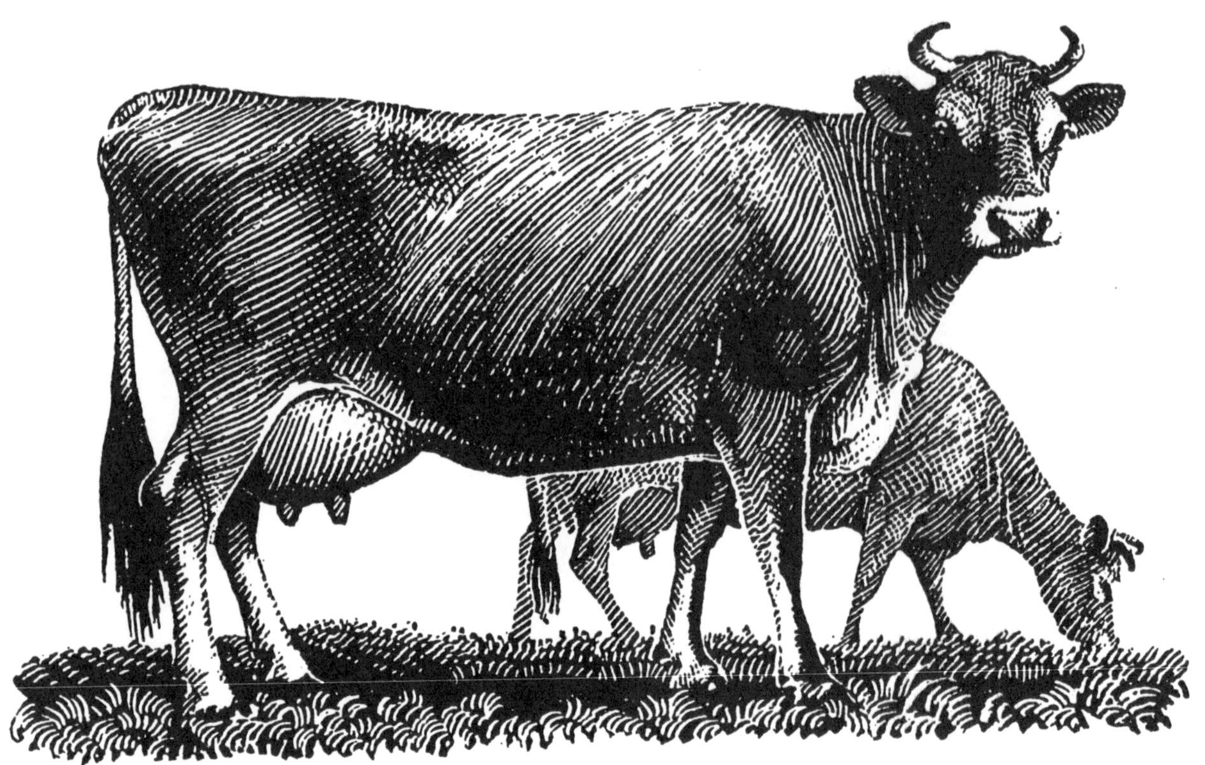

A JERSEY COW

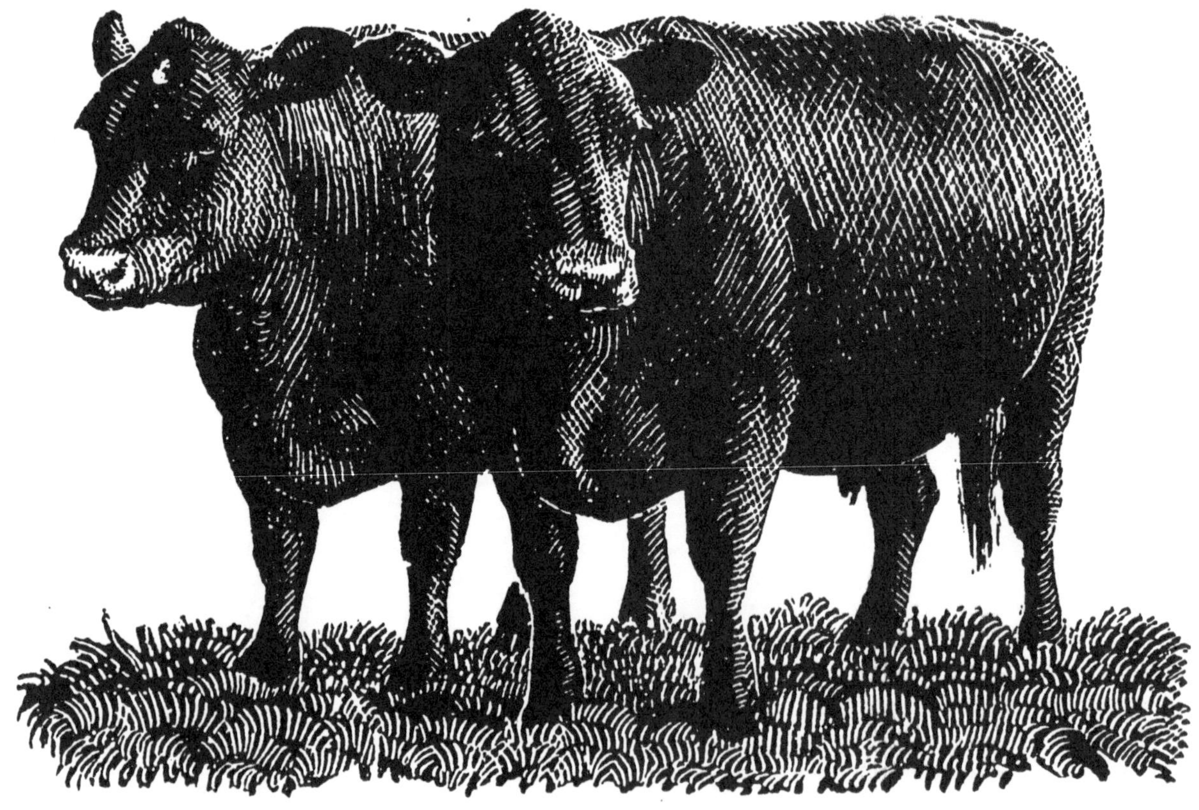

ABERDEEN ANGUS BULLOCKS

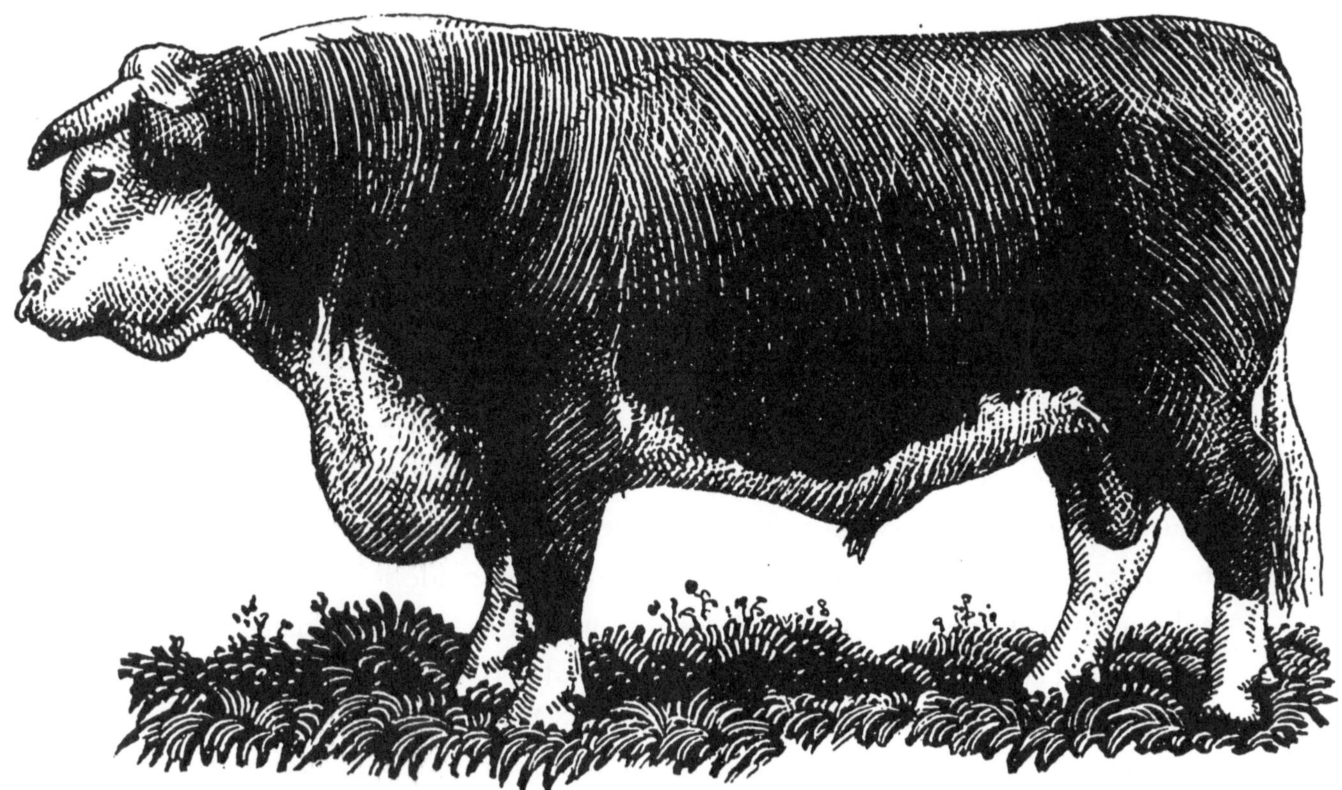

A HEREFORD BULL

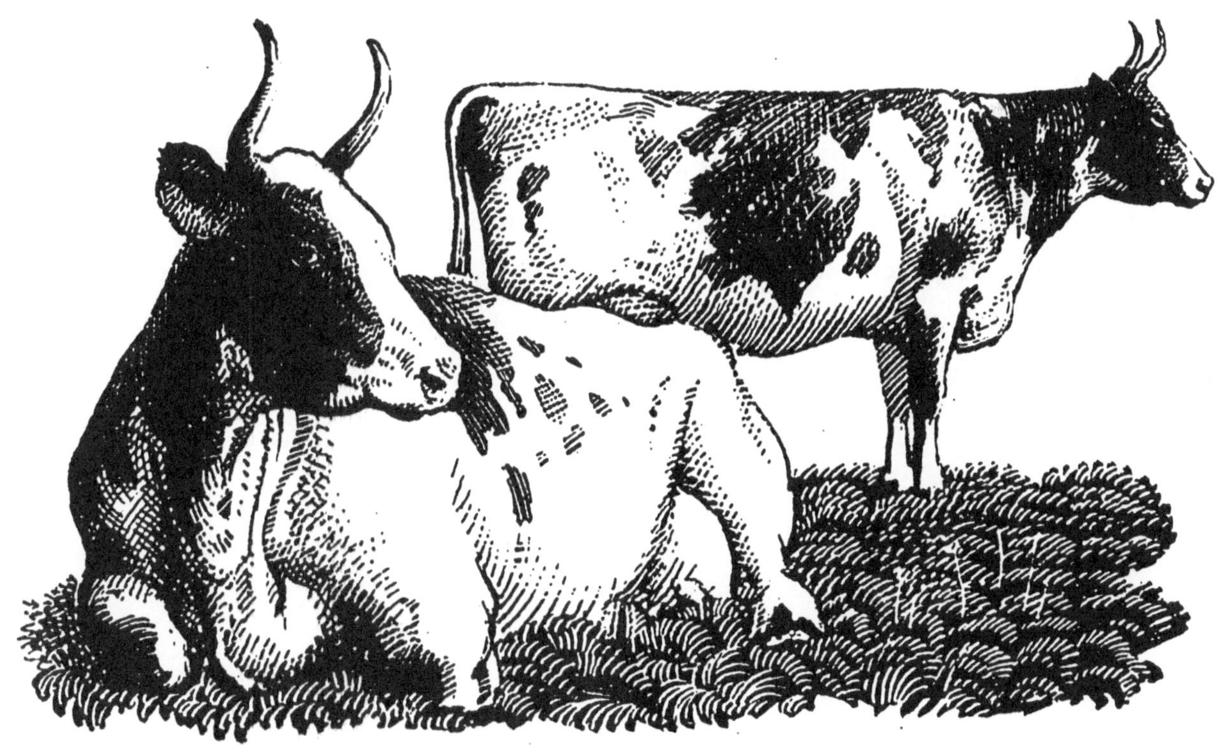

AYRSHIRE COWS

PIGS

Pig, Swine, Hog; how often one hears these words used to describe some objectionable person or thing! A pity: for the pig has not deserved these insults. Most of the objectionable habits which are supposed to be part of the pig's nature have been imposed on it by its connection with man. In the wild state the pig is a clean animal. A dirty pig has usually been made so by neglect and bad housing conditions. True the pig loves to wallow in mud, especially in hot weather, but mud is not necessarily unclean, and certain human beings have been known to do likewise! Therefore, when you begin to draw pigs it would be well to rid yourself of the usual conventional ideas concerning them. Your pig models will be, above all else, very individual, with minds of their own and impulses which do not coincide with the desires of humans. They are rarely completely domesticated and tame, so you will realise that your approach to them should be rather more cautious than was necessary in the case of horses or cattle. Pigs are, by nature, restless creatures, and the only time you may be sure of drawing them line by line is when they are sleeping. Even so you should approach them with care for they are easily startled. When pigs sleep they tend to lie close together—sometimes one on top of the other—and, under these circumstances, you will find it easy to make detail studies but rather difficult to make drawings of the complete animal.

Opposite: Large White gilts (young females).

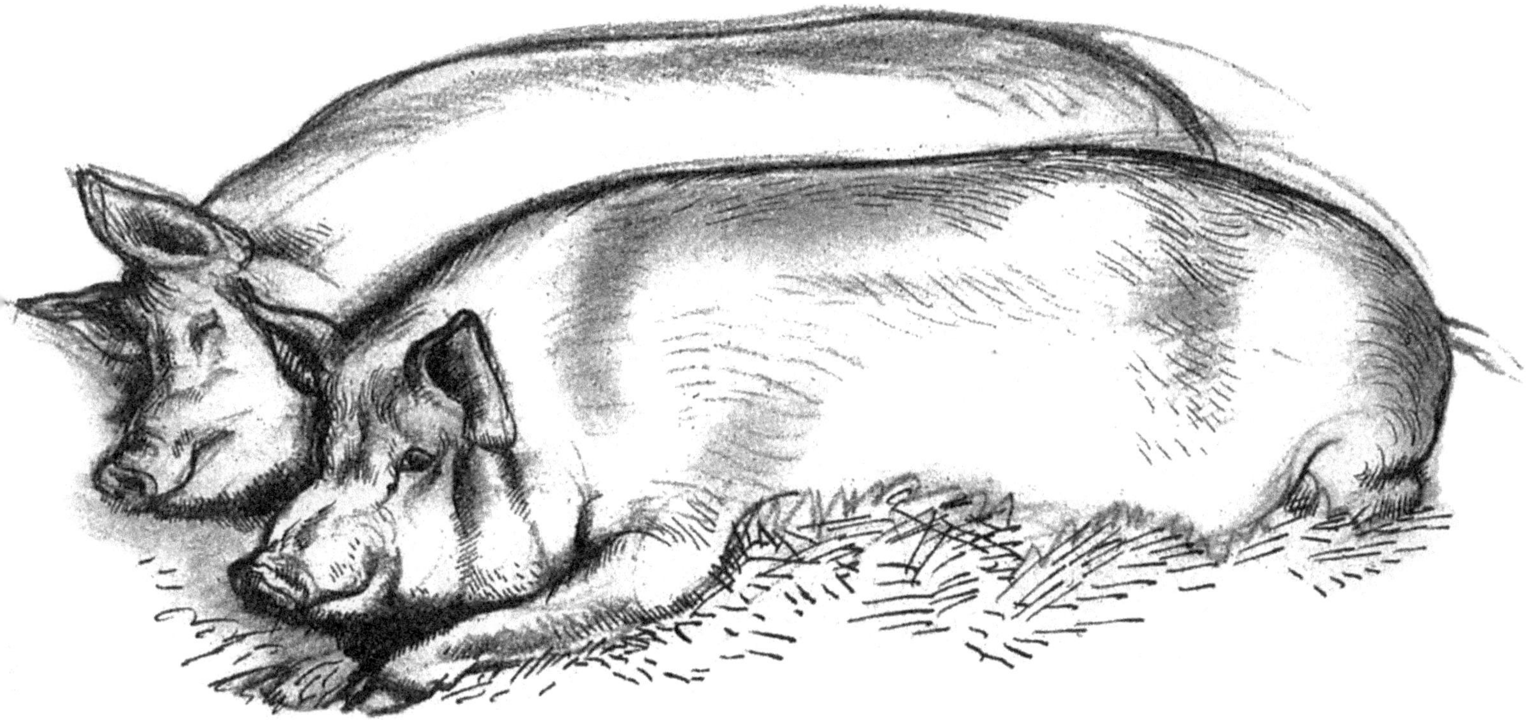

You may find that feeding time is more favourable for this, though for the most part our model will have its head lowered in the feeding trough. Again I suggest that you attend the auction, the show, and the market for some of your pig studies, and for the rest there will be many occasions when you can make quick sketches. Be alert, and take advantage of the fortunate moment; and though your sketches will be, in many instances, the merest fragments, you will be gaining valuable knowledge of your models.

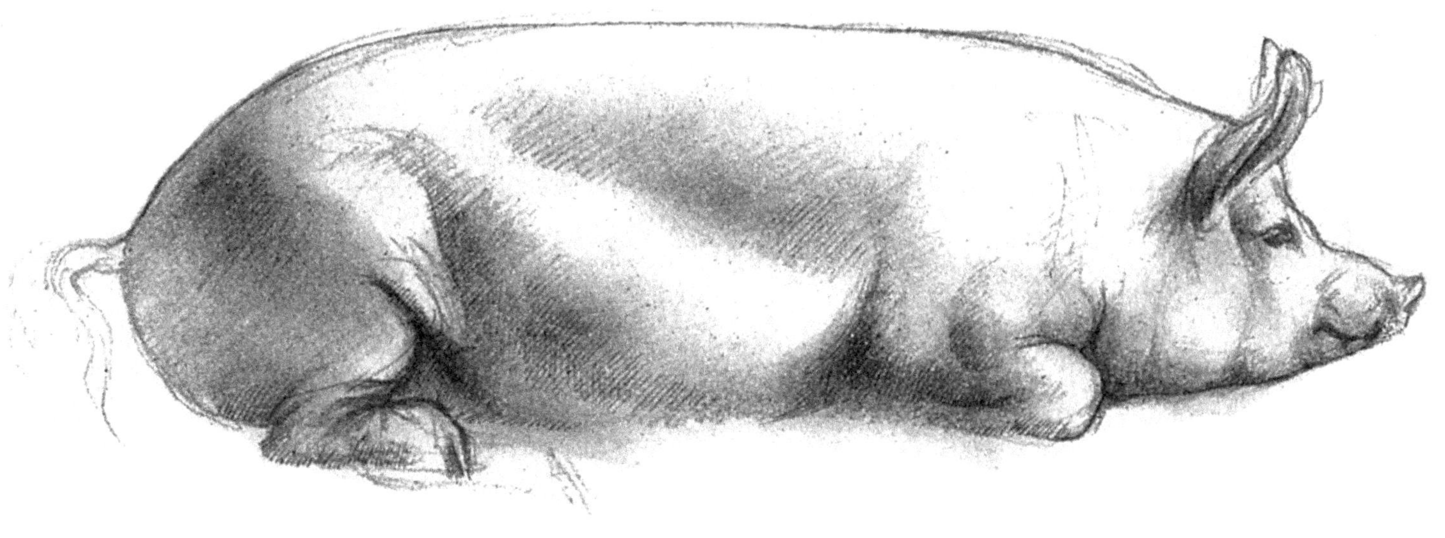

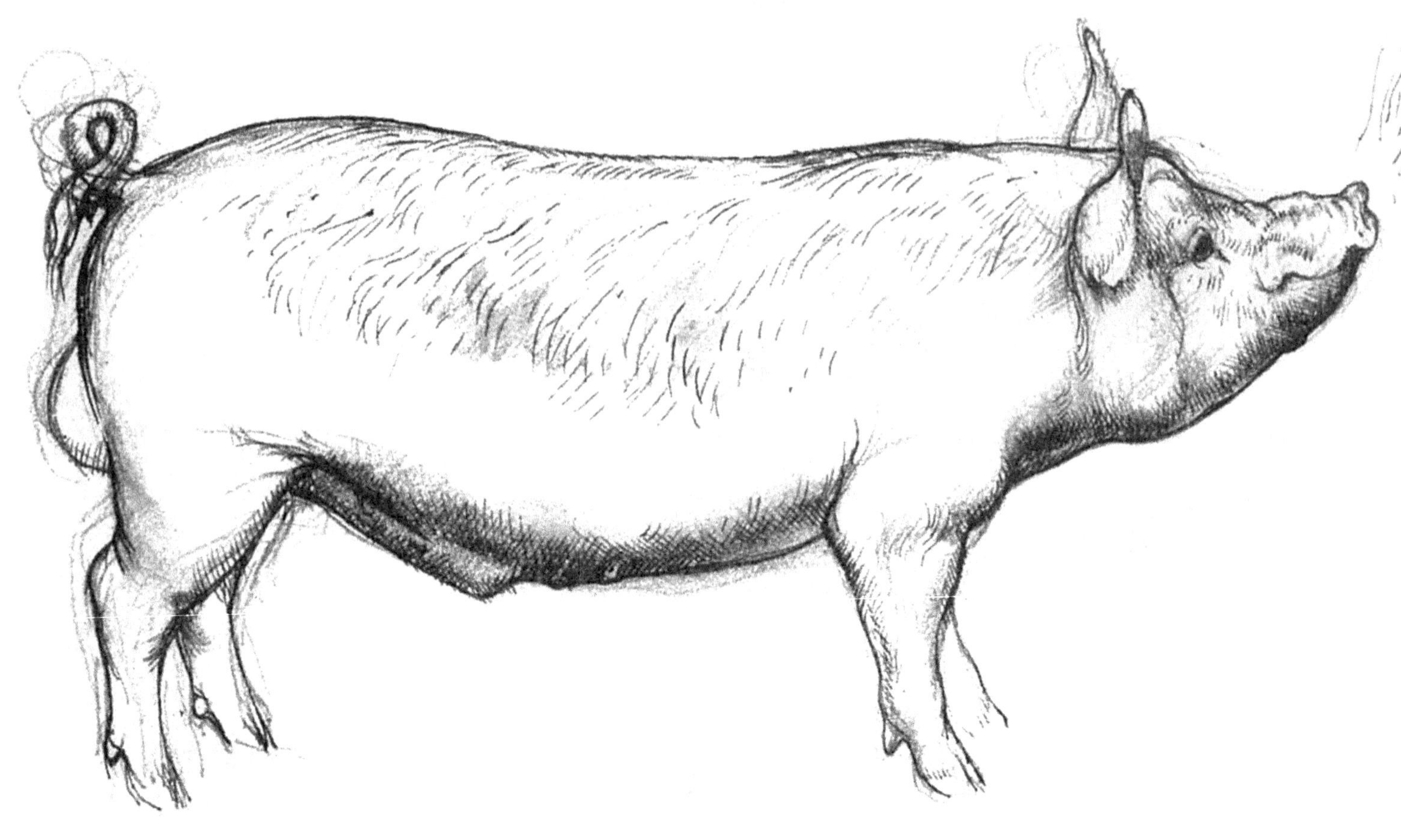

A LARGE WHITE BOAR

Probably the oldest of our many breeds of pigs is the Tamworth, a neat, alert looking animal of a most beautiful reddish orange colour. It has an almost straight profile from forehead to snout, rather reminiscent of the profile of the wild boar, the ancestor of our domestic pigs.

In marked contrast with the Tamworth, both in colour and shape, is the Wessex Saddleback. This pig is chiefly black, except for a broad area of white which encircles the body in the region of the shoulders, upper ribs, and forelegs.

Its build is heavier and not so racey as that of the Tamworth, this heaviness being further emphasised by the drooping ears which fall forward and hide the eyes. Its facial contour is concave, or "dished," as the farmer terms it. Somewhere between these two extremes in pig shapes we have the breed which is probably the big favourite with pig farmers—the Large White Yorkshire. It is a long, shapely animal with upright ears, and will be the breed you see most often. But you will also meet the pug-faced Middle White (which always looks as if it had charged a too solid obstacle and never quite recovered) and perhaps the piebald or spotted Gloucester Spot and the all-black Large Black. All are interesting and good to draw and I have no doubt that you will become quite fond of pig models.

A LARGE WHITE GILT

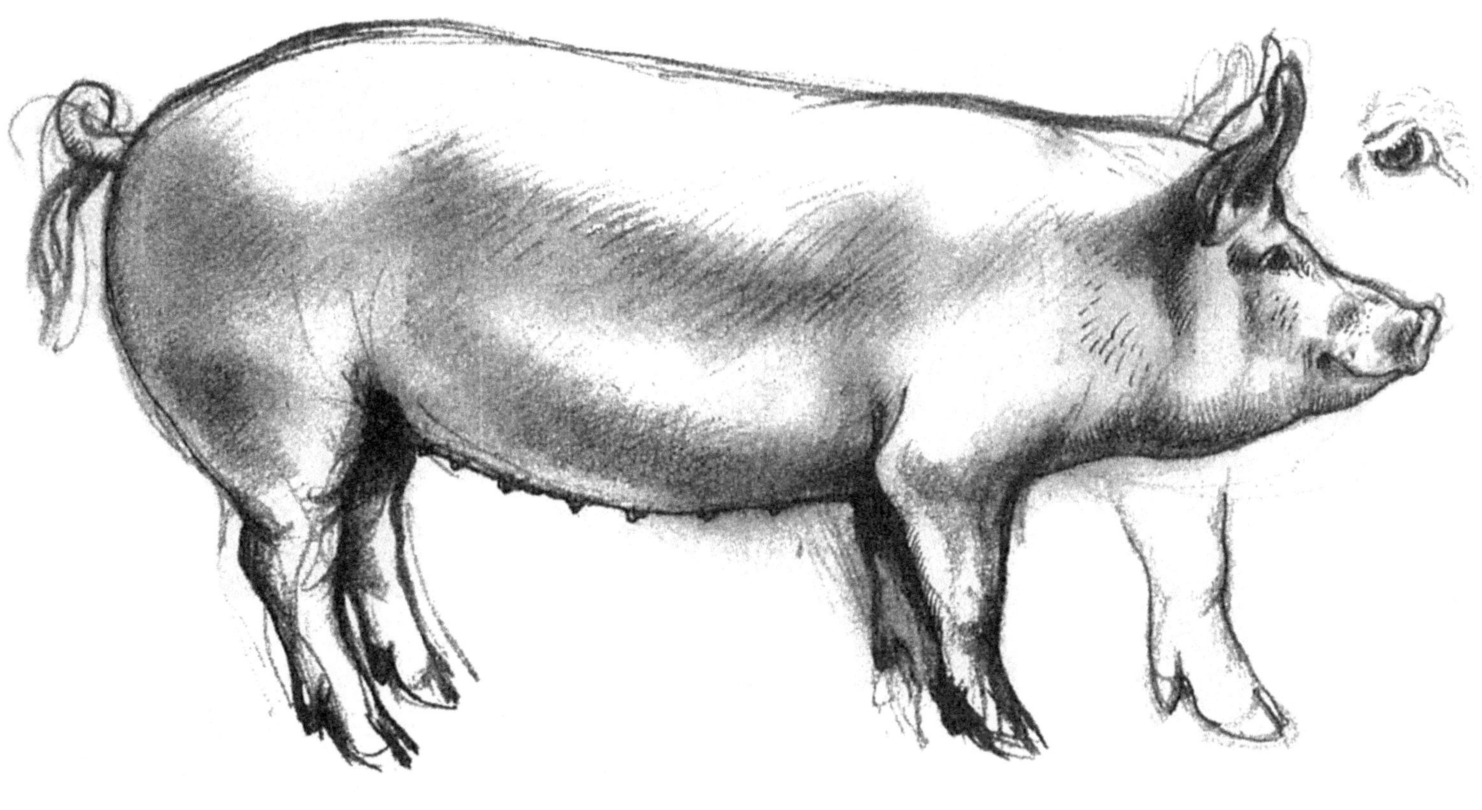

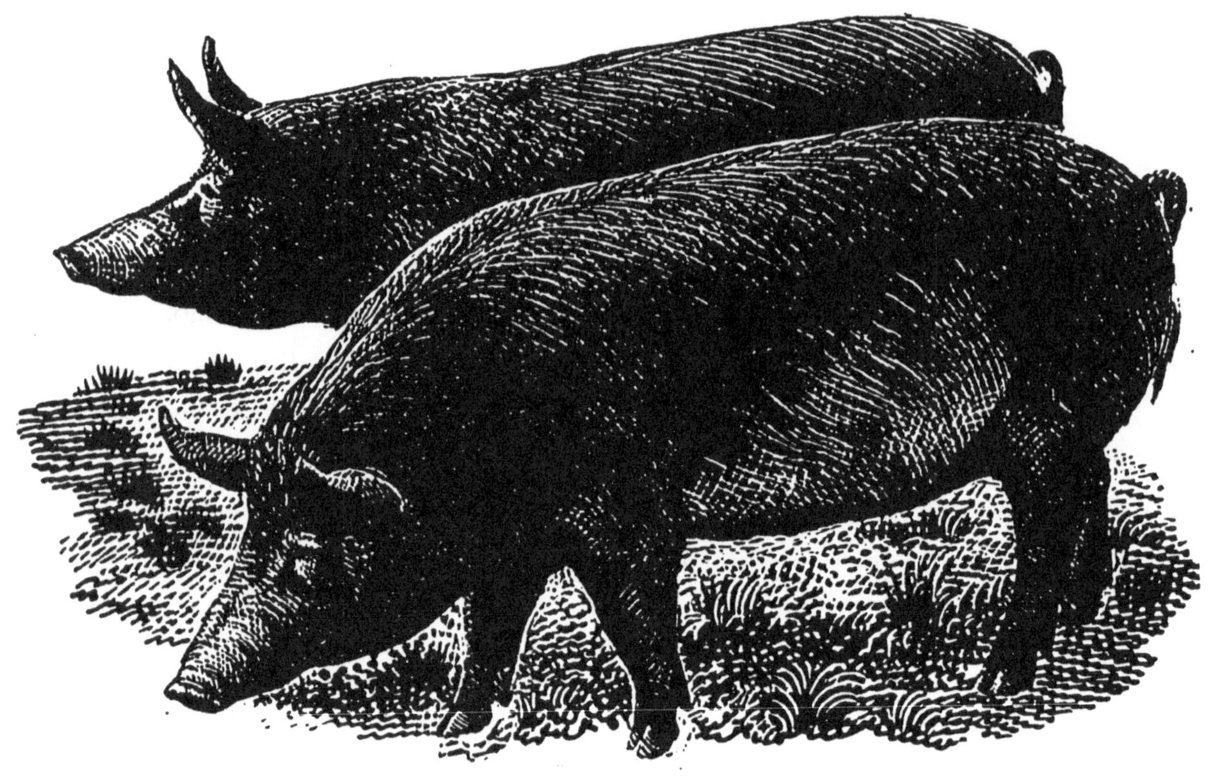

TAMWORTH GILTS

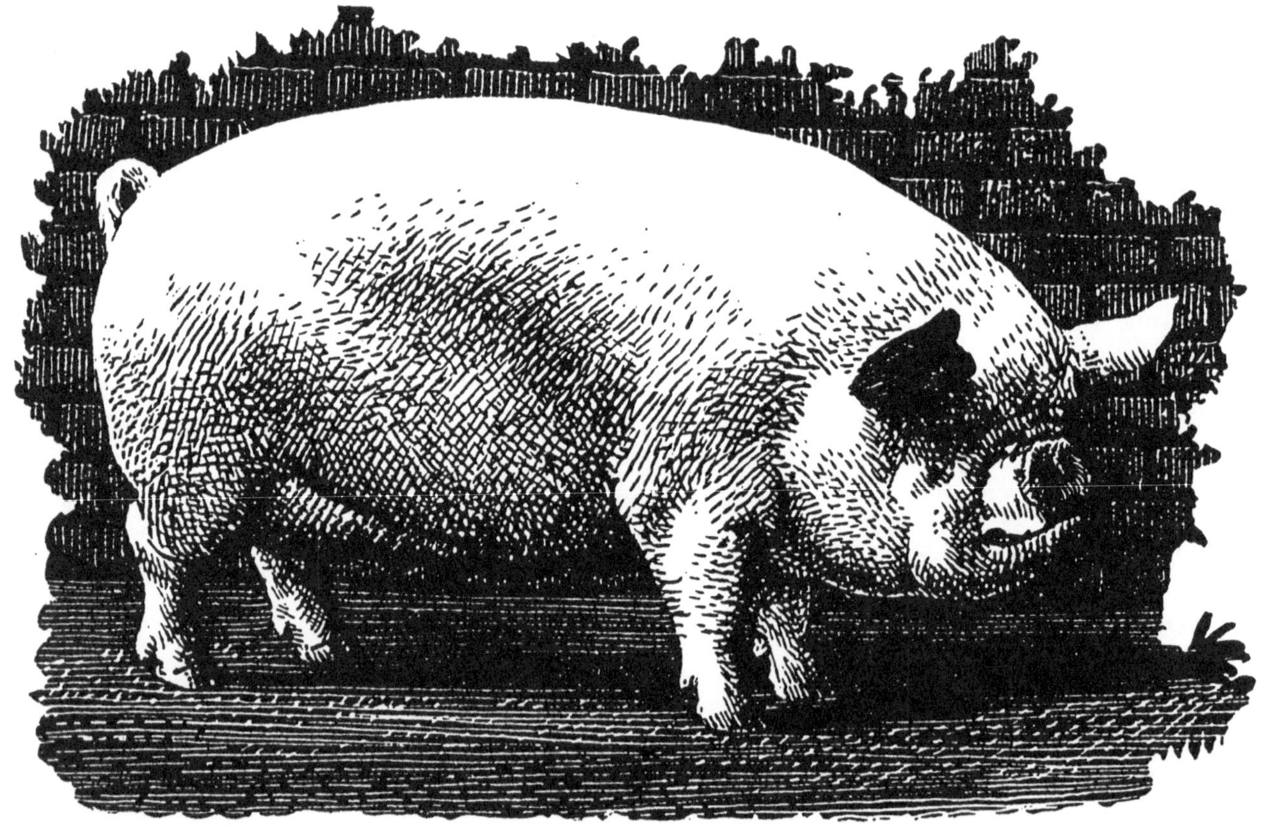

MIDDLE WHITE SOW

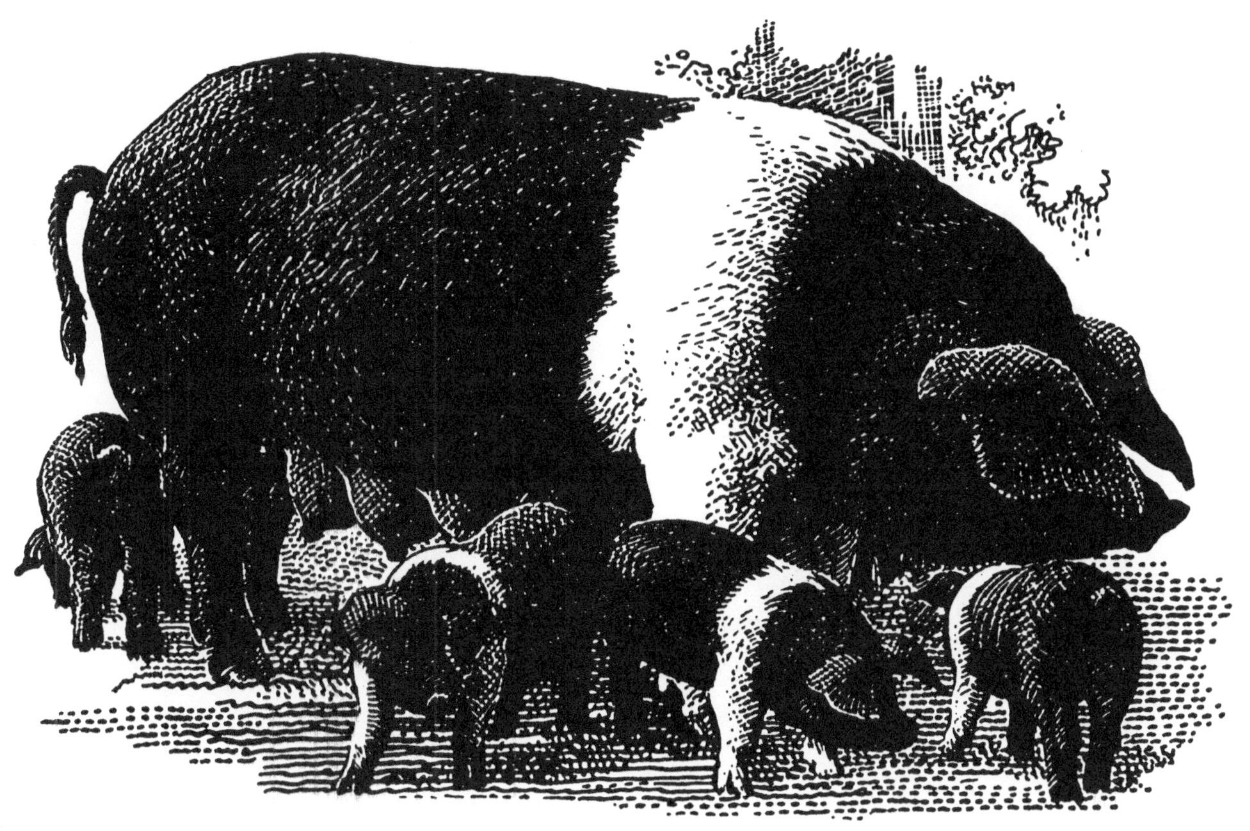

WESSEX SADDLEBACK SOW AND LITTER

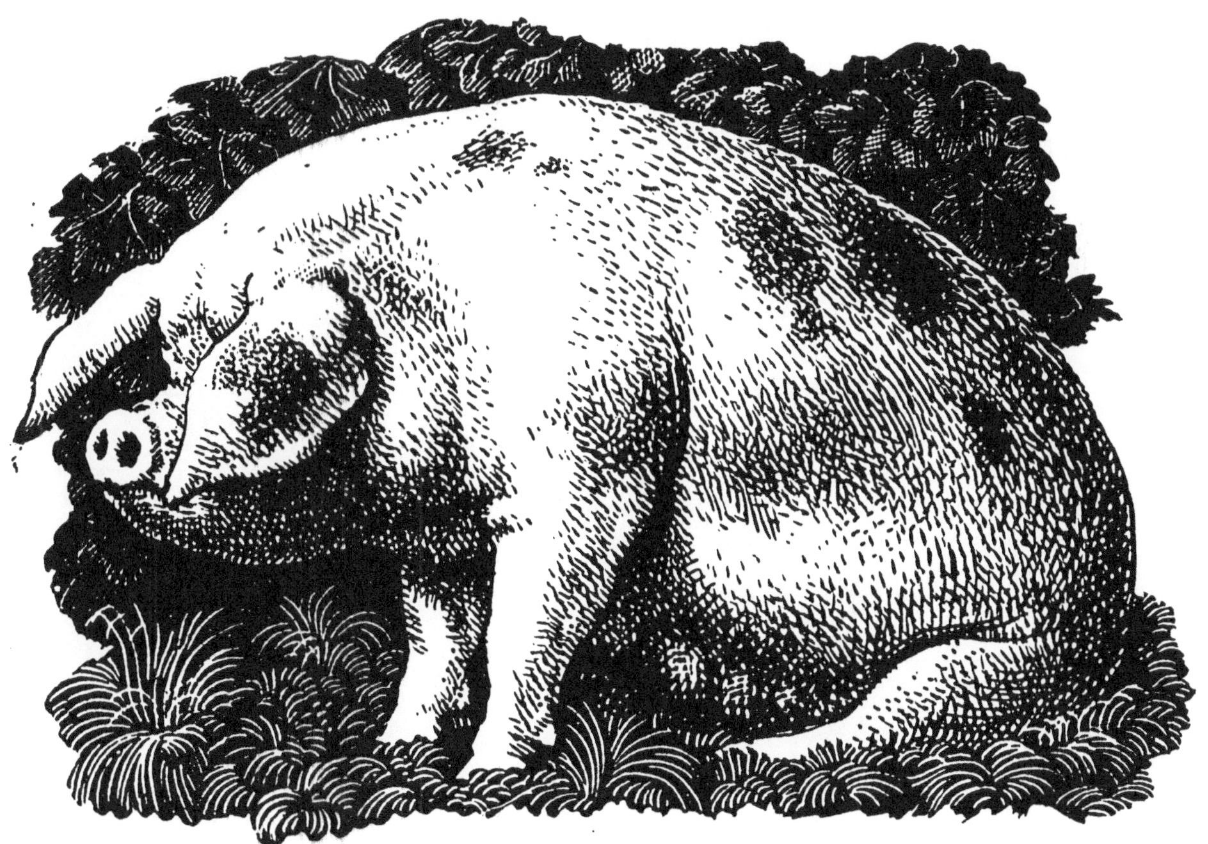

A SOW OF THE OLD GLOUCESTER SPOT BREED

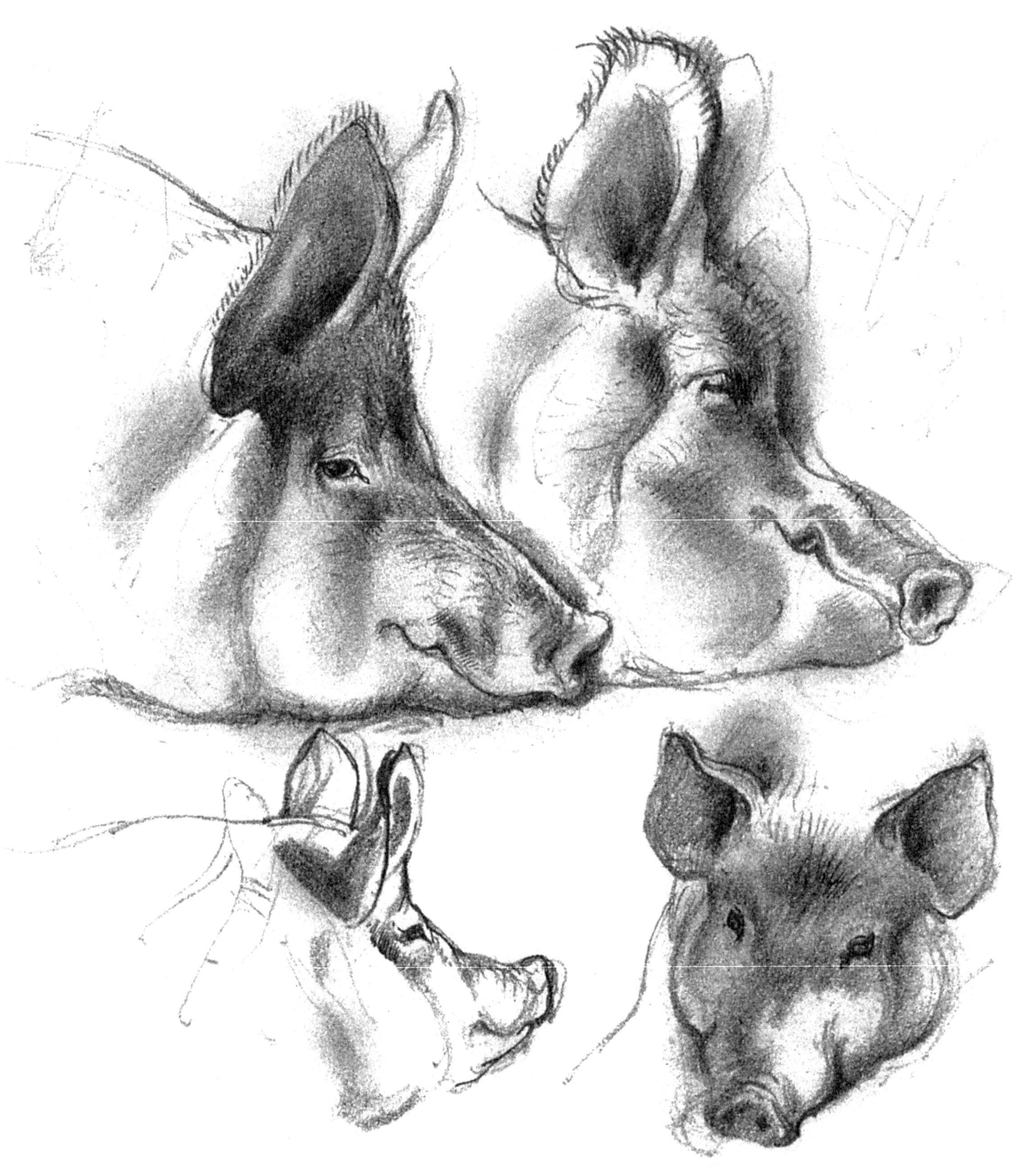

Head studies. Upper, heads of a sow; lower, of young pigs.

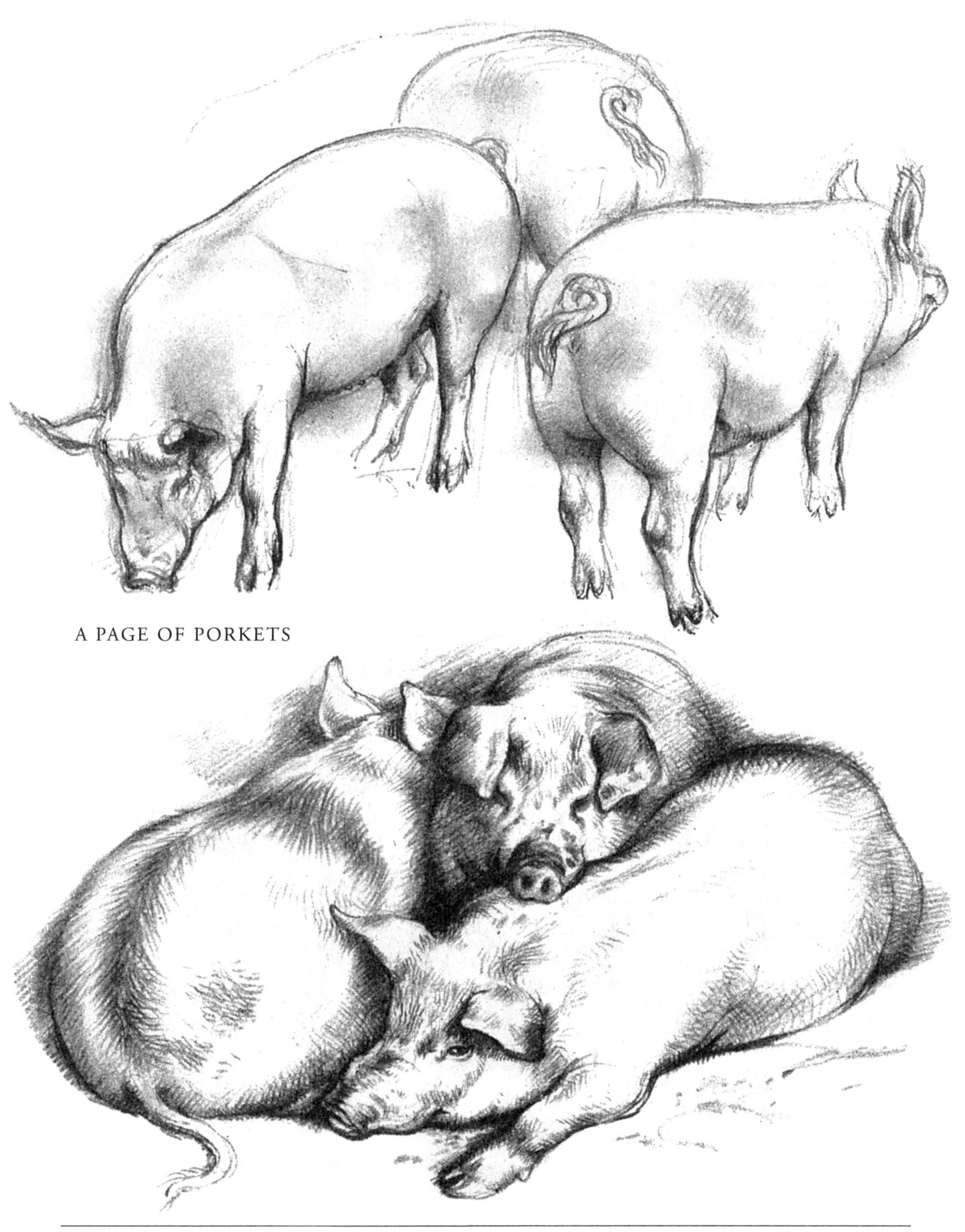

A PAGE OF PORKETS

SHEEP

When you begin your study of Sheep you will encounter a problem which did not occur in your drawing of Horses, Cattle and Pigs. In these latter the presence of muscle and bone below the skin was apparent and directly affected the contours. With Sheep, except in the case of newly-shorn animals, this will not be the case. The fleece, even in the short-wooled sheep, hides the anatomy, and when you draw sheep, instead of expressing bony or muscular contours you will be much preoccupied in drawing the masses and folds of wool. From breed to breed the amount, length and texture of the fleece varies considerably, but

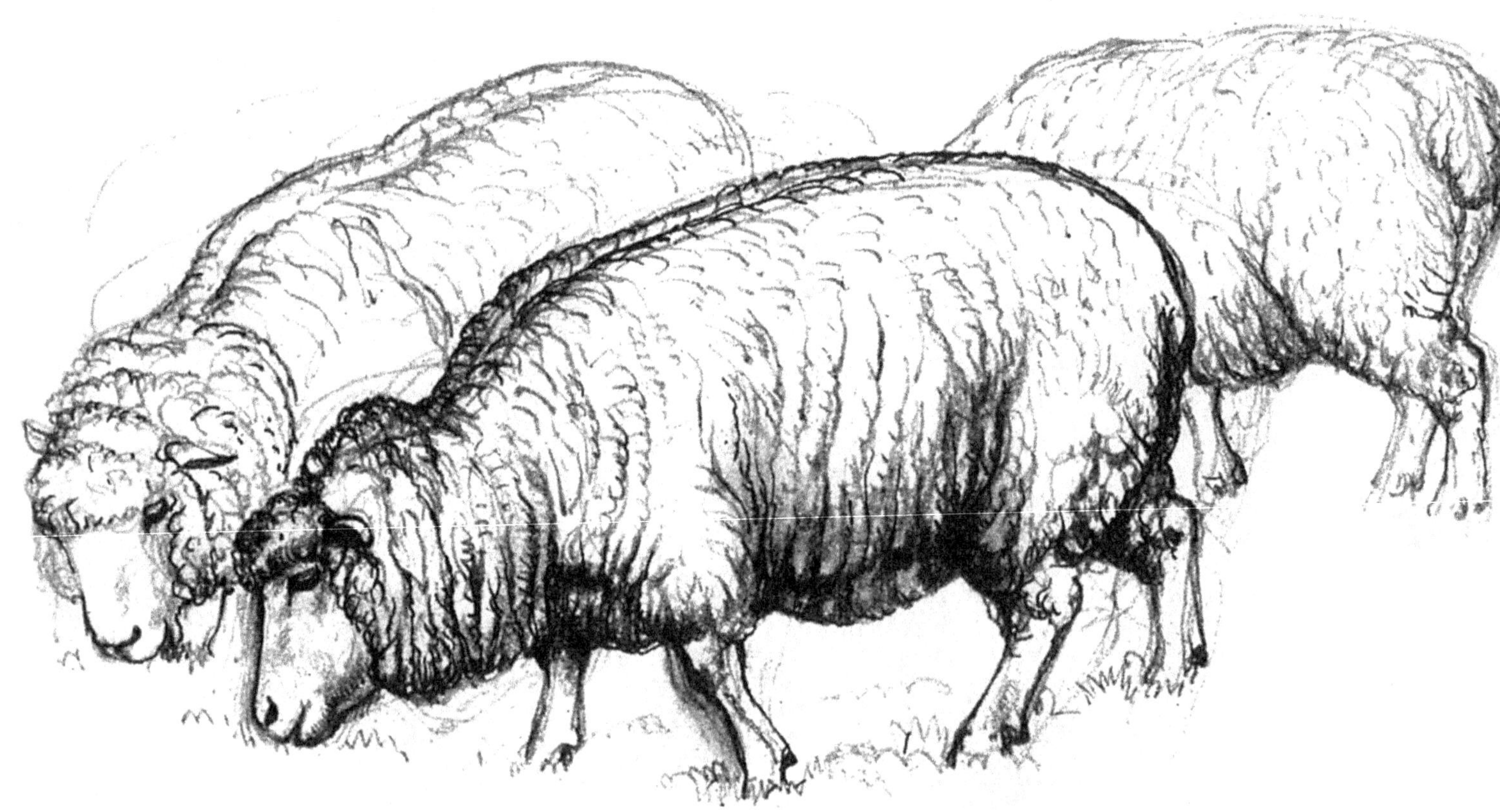

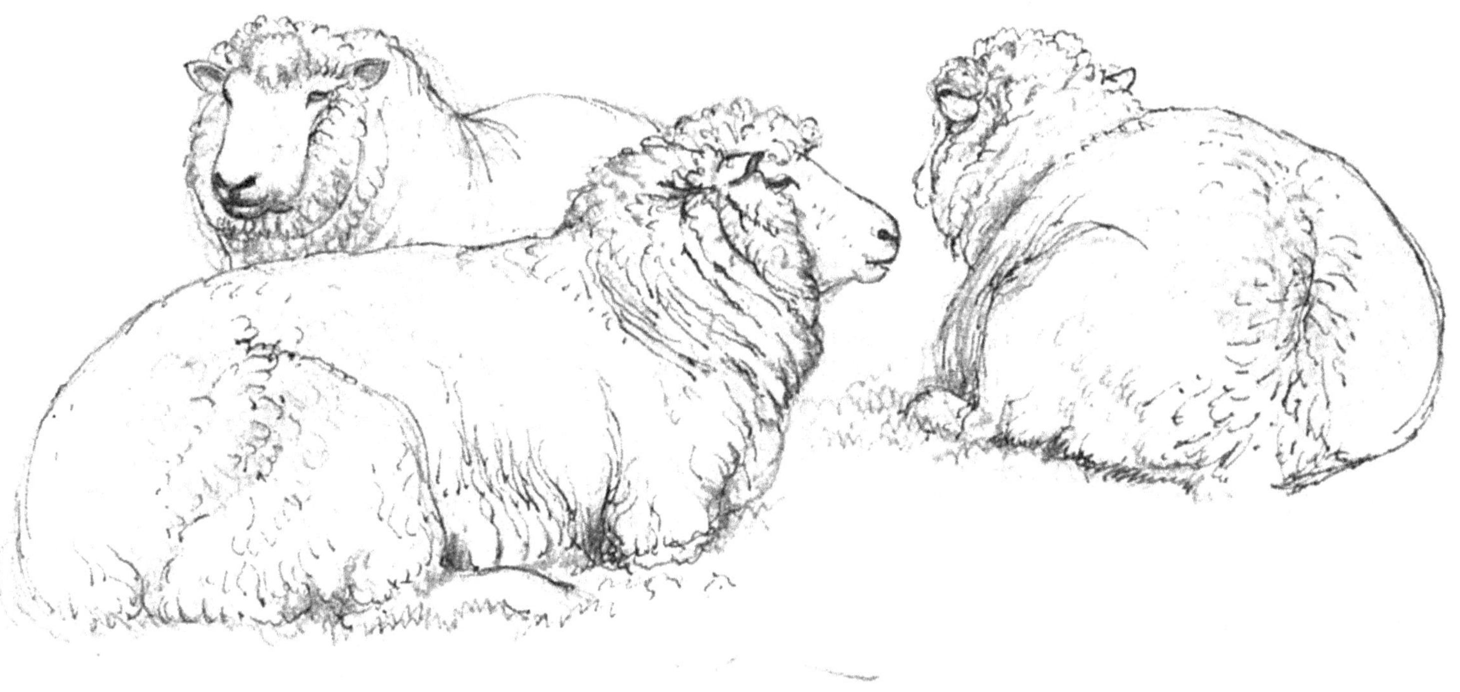

in all it will be seen that the wool is arranged in well-defined areas. These areas, especially in the short-wooled sheep, have a close connection with the anatomy (in spite of the fact that they hide so much of it) and are greatly influenced by the flesh contours. The greatest care should be given to the study of the fleece, for your drawings of sheep will not be convincing if you neglect it. It is just as important as the study of the head and limbs.

Take every opportunity to draw the new-shorn sheep. Shearing time comes but once a year, and soon after a sheep is shorn a growth of new wool

Left: This drawing and the one above are of Kent sheep, drawn from life as they grazed between the trees of a Kentish cherry orchard.

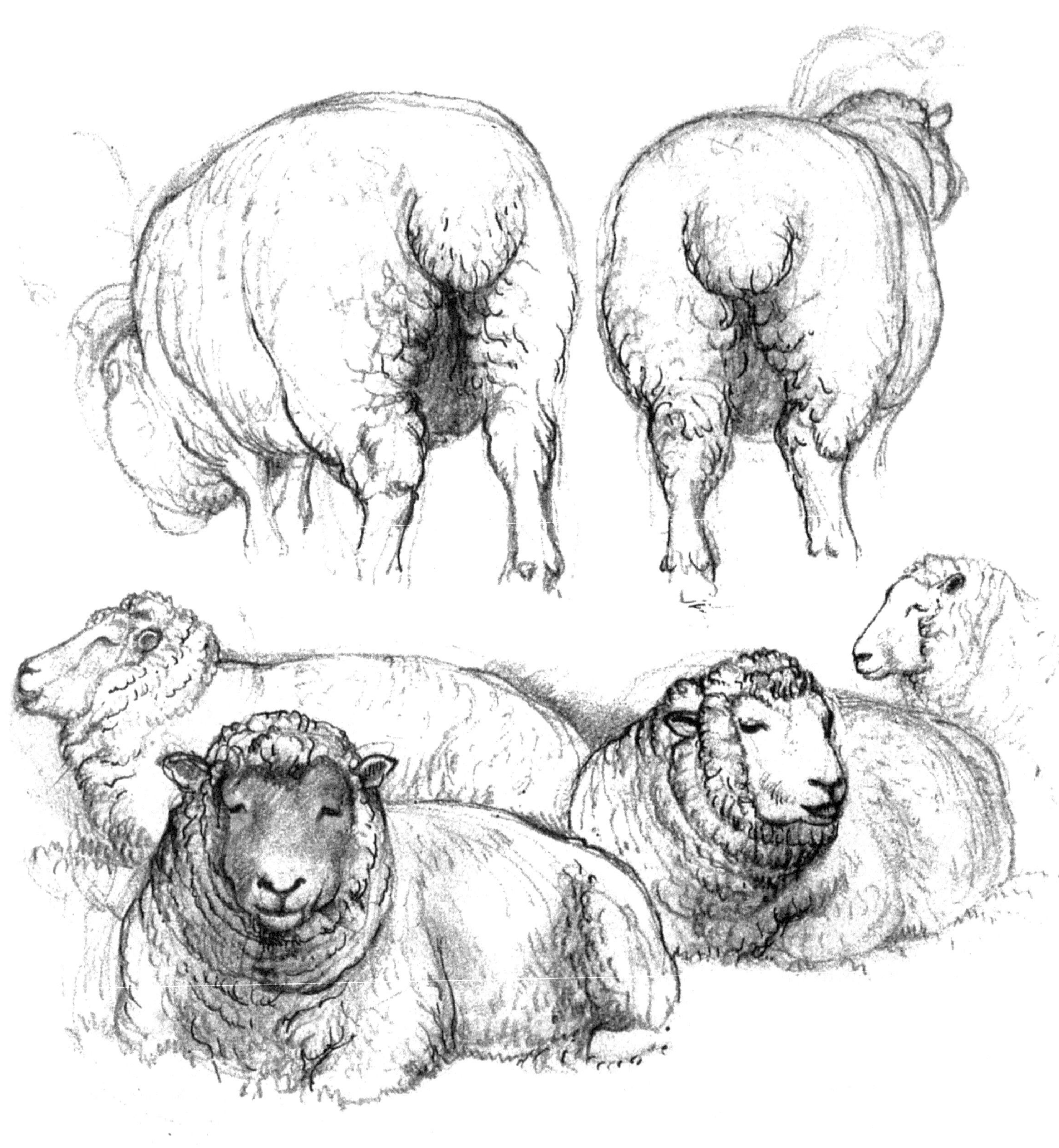

KENT SHEEP

(the lower sheep is a Kent-Southdown cross breed).

Studies of shorn sheep. Note the definite arrangement of the wool.

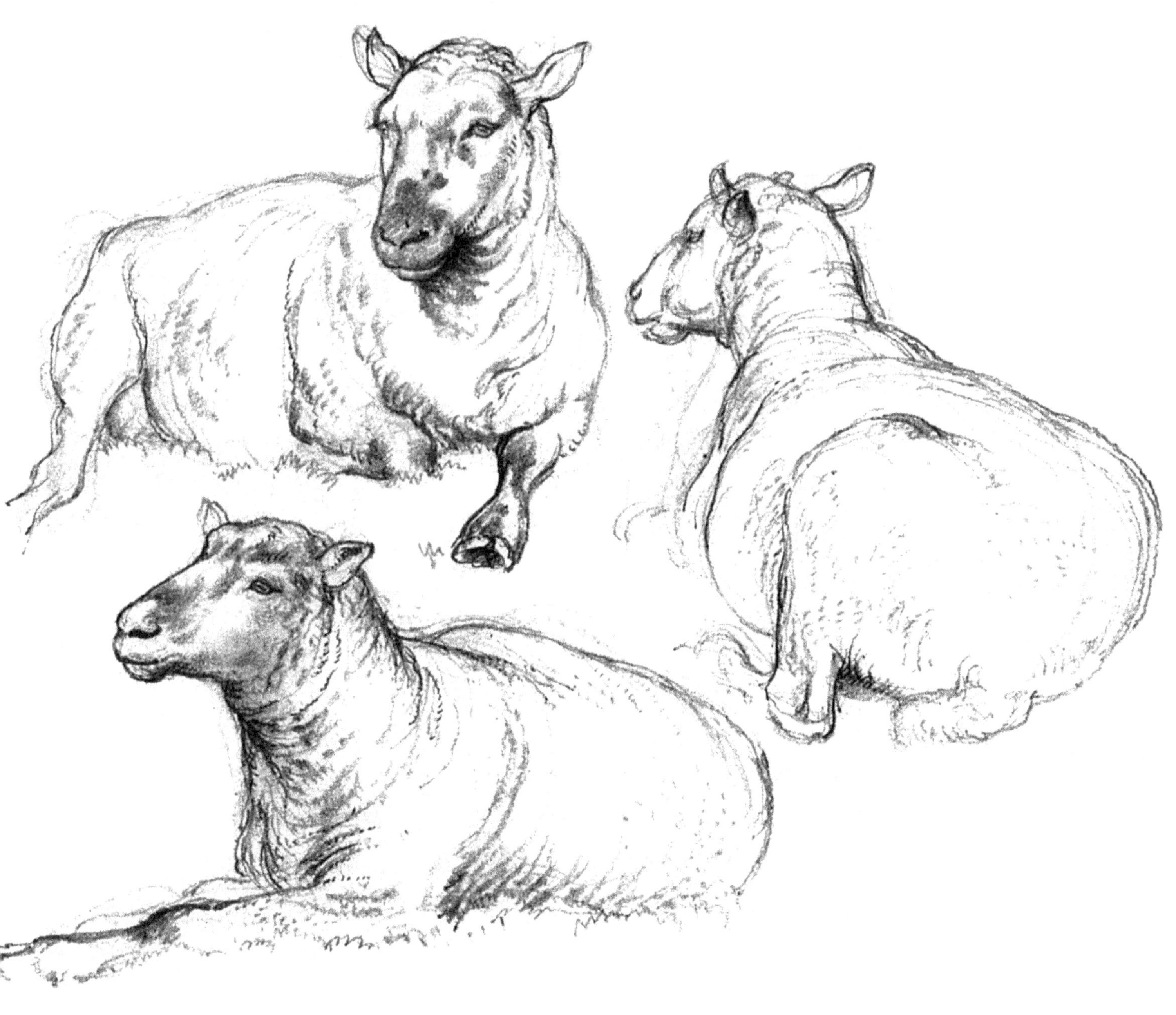

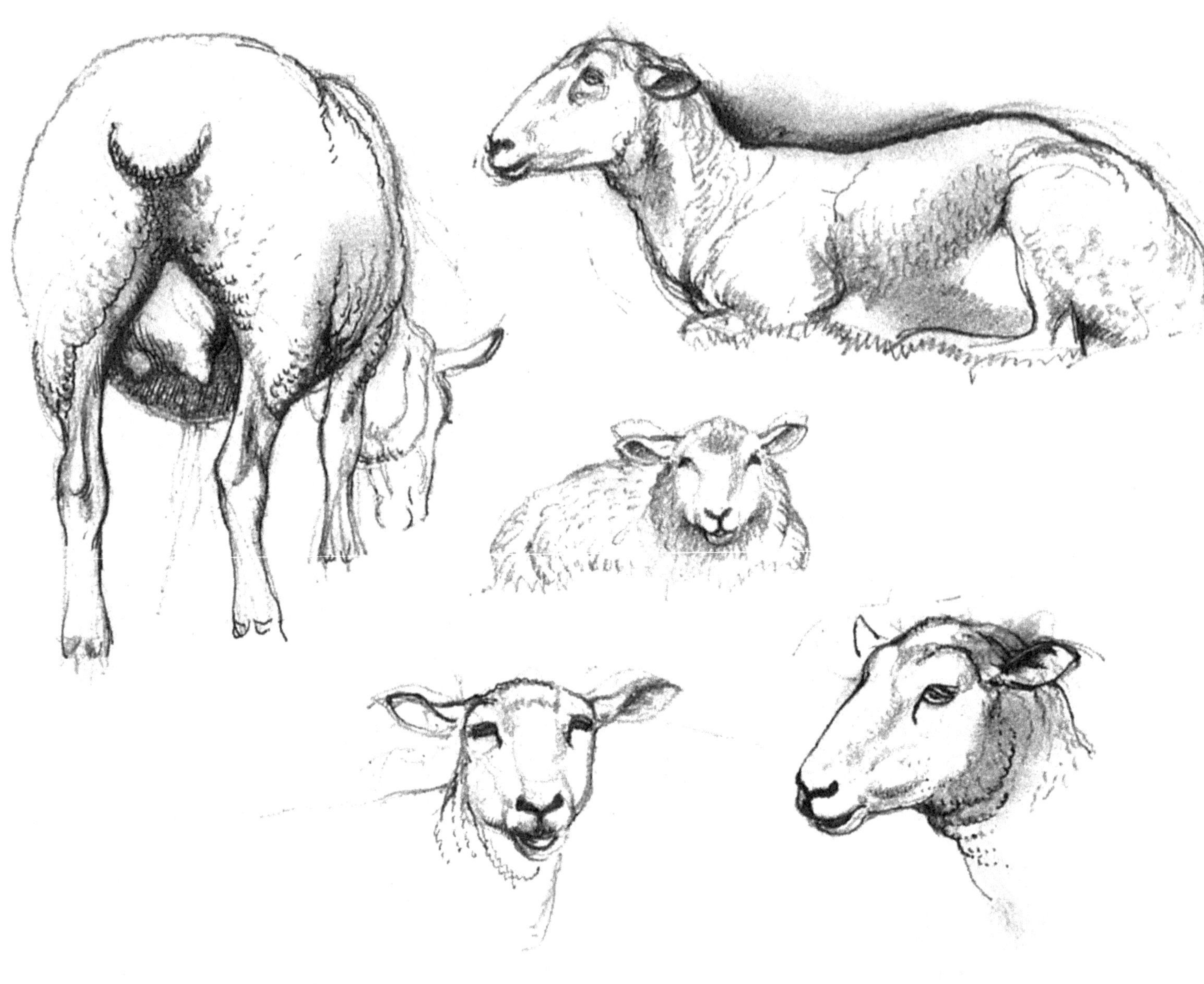

appears. This means that the length of time available for drawing the strange, unexpectedly angular shape of "nude" sheep is very limited and full advantage should be taken of it. During shearing you will see the sheep in all sorts of positions, many of them grotesque and very undignified. As a rule sheep remain quiet while the shears are at work, and this is your grand chance. Unusual views of legs and feet, the underside of jaws, chest, and belly will present themselves as the shearer turns the sheep and the fleece falls away before the shears—a fine chance to enlarge your knowledge of those parts of sheep anatomy which are normally hidden.

RECENTLY SHORN EWES

A Masham ewe with her cross-bred lamb, and, opposite, cross-bred ewes with a predominant strain of Border Leicester. Lamb in the centre.

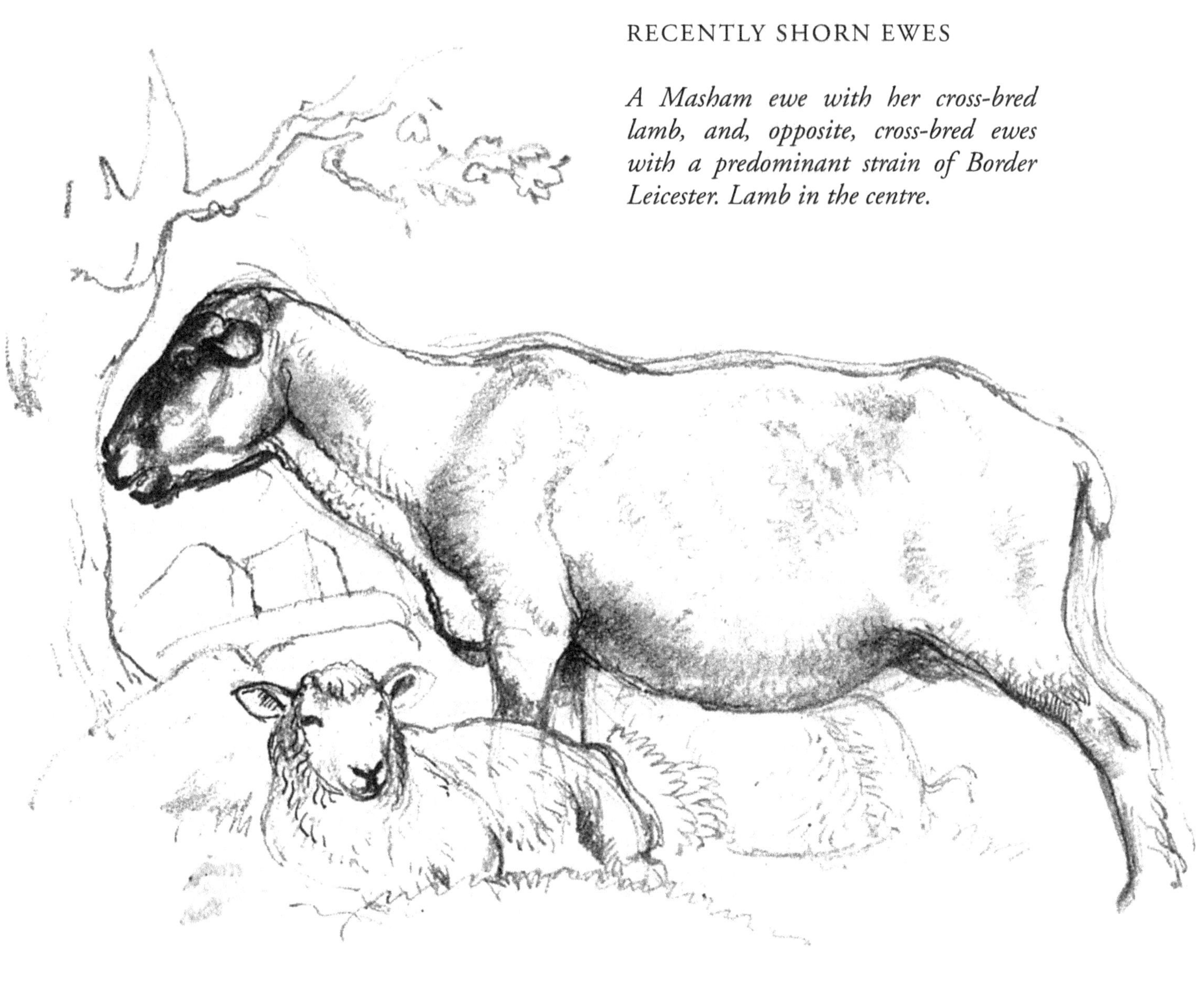

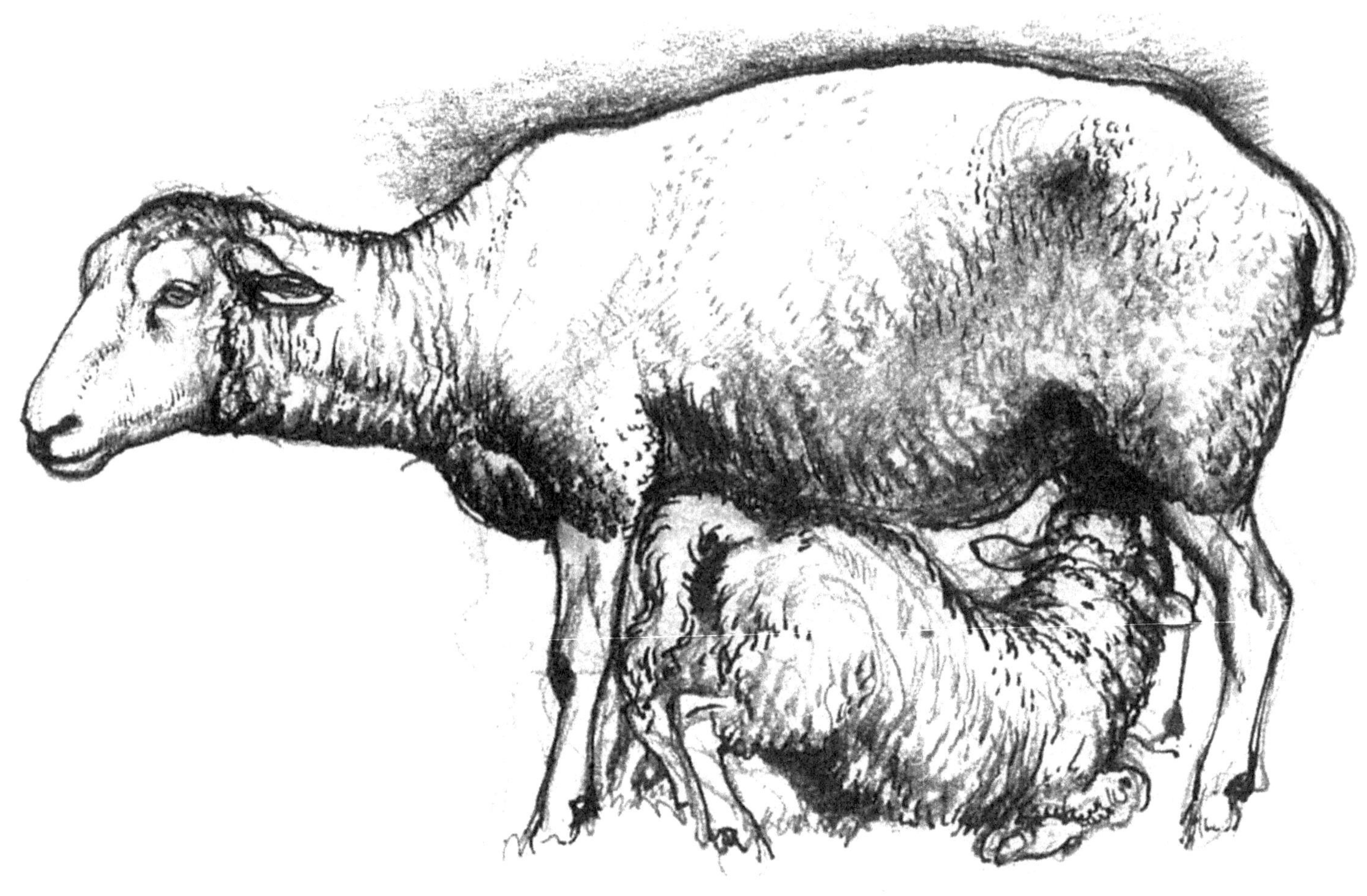

A well-grown lamb with its shorn mother.

There are also washing and dipping times to remember. On these occasions even the wildest of hill country sheep are rounded up, but both operations are more strenuous than that of shearing. However, the point to remember is, that while the dipping and washing is going on the sheep will be confined in small enclosures, and this gives you and your sketch book a chance to get to work.

Then there is lambing time, but here I beg of you to exercise the greatest care and be the soul of discretion. Always obtain permission of the farmer or the shepherd before you approach ewes that have newly-born lambs or which are near to lambing, whether they be in the lambing yards or out in the open fields. Lambing time is normally full of anxieties for the shepherd. Do not add to them.

About the breeds of sheep volumes could be written, so many and varied are they. Some are short-wooled, others long-wooled. Some have horns, others are hornless. Mountains and fells, rolling downs and lowland pastures: all have their distinctive breeds. On the whole I think my best course will be to draw a few of them so that you may have some idea of the differences in the character and shapes of the "animal with the golden hoof."

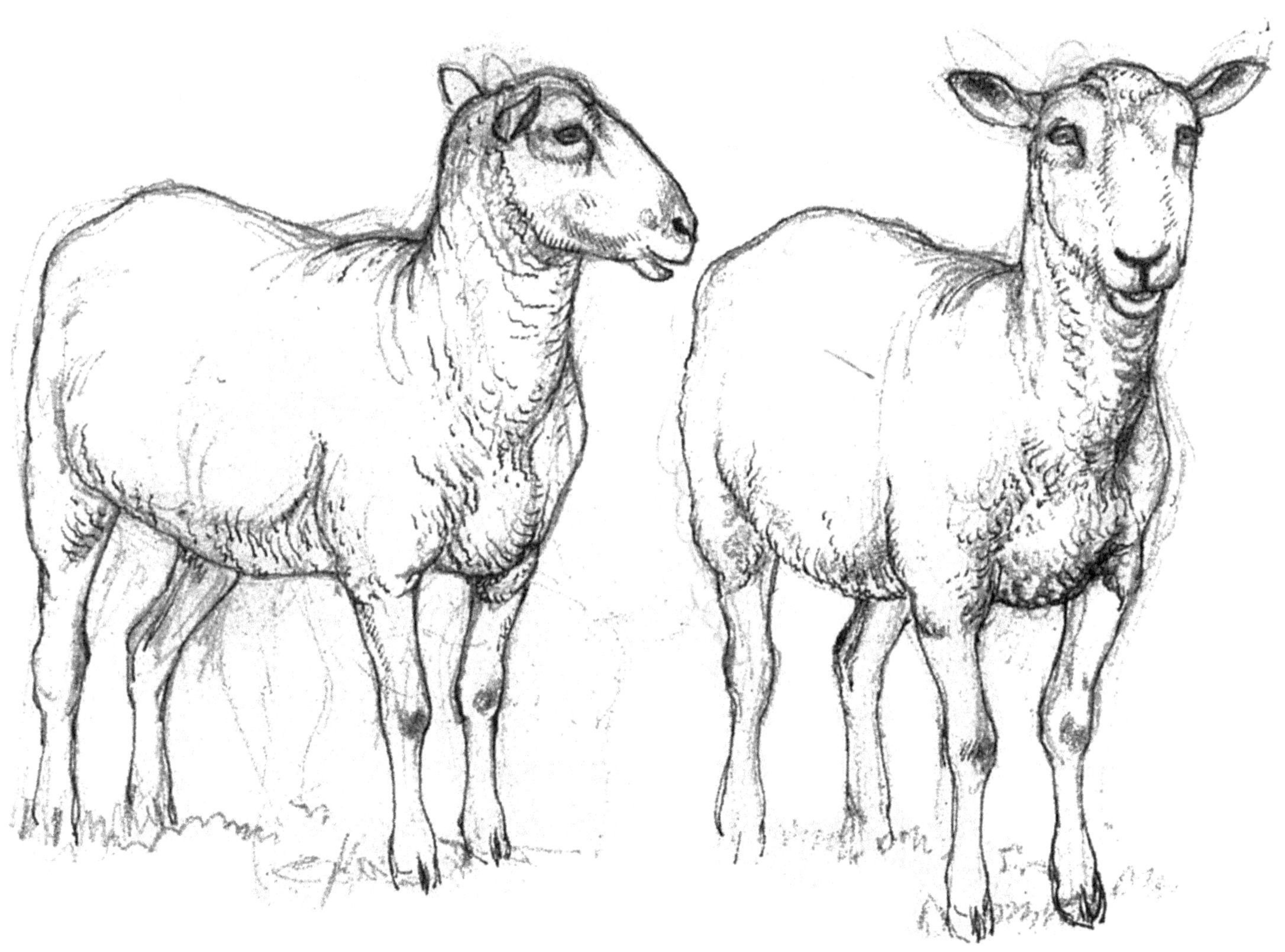

More views of sheep belonging to the same flock as those drawn on page 44. Note the "knock-kneed" front legs. These sheep are chewing their cud.

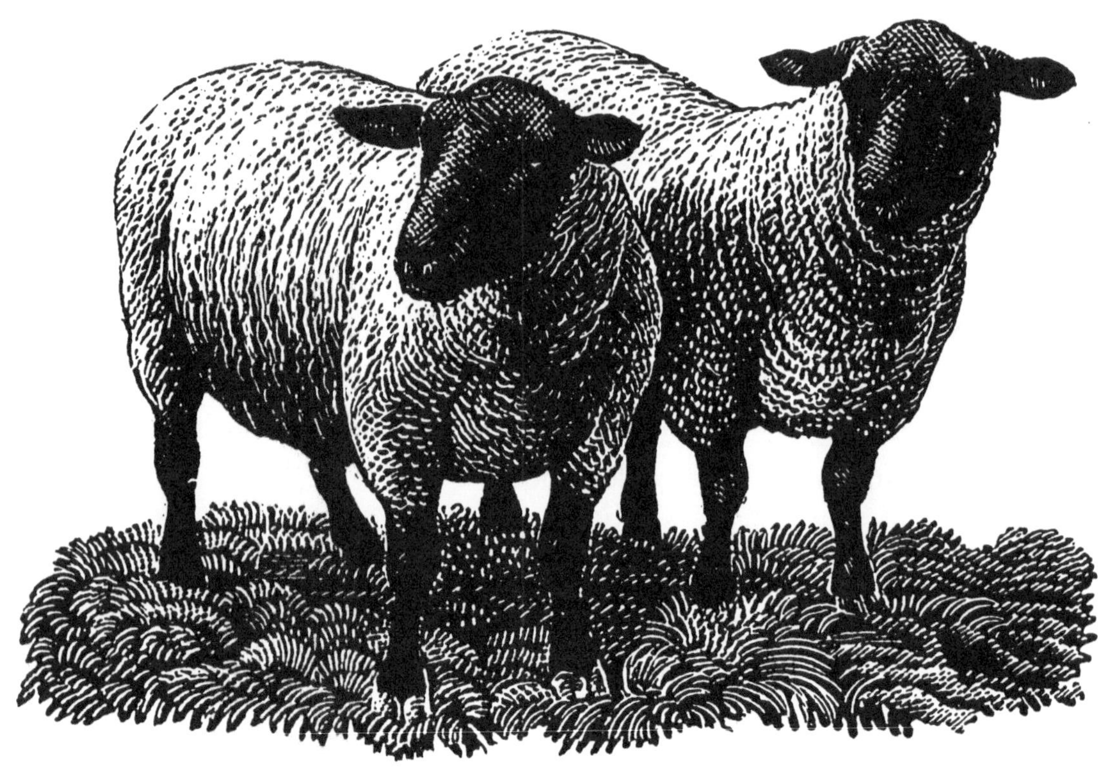

SUFFOLK EWES

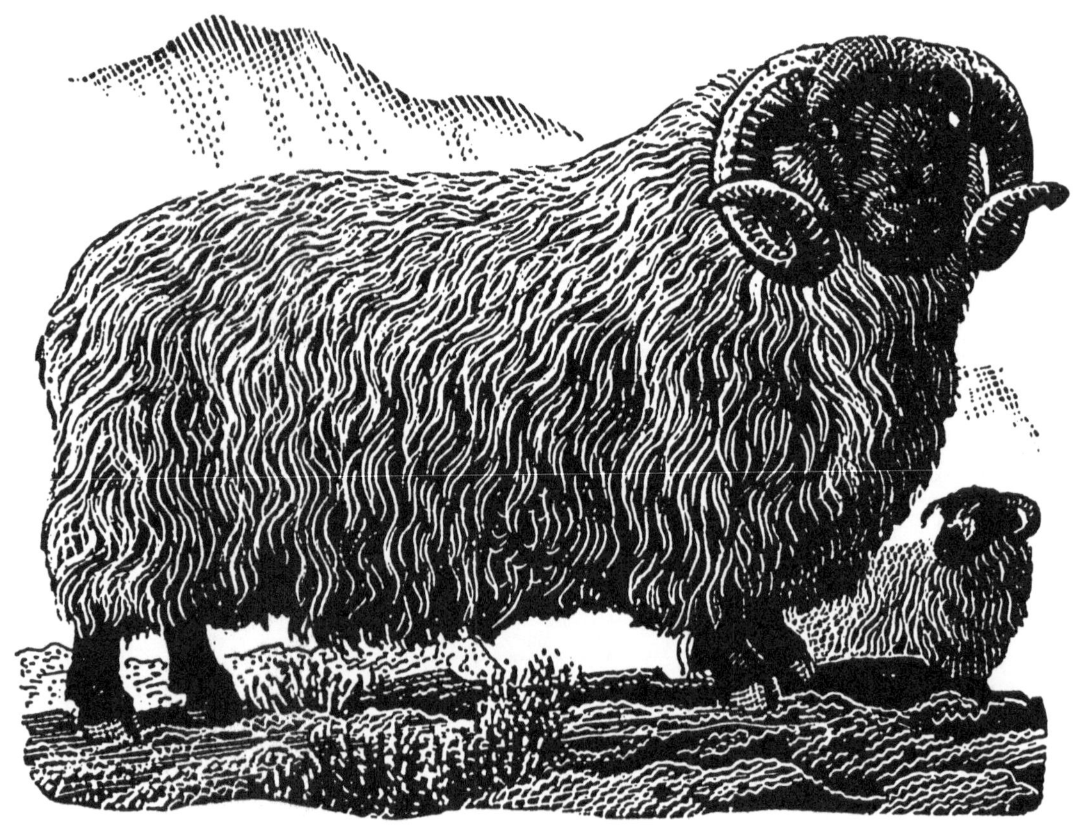

A SCOTCH BLACKFACE RAM

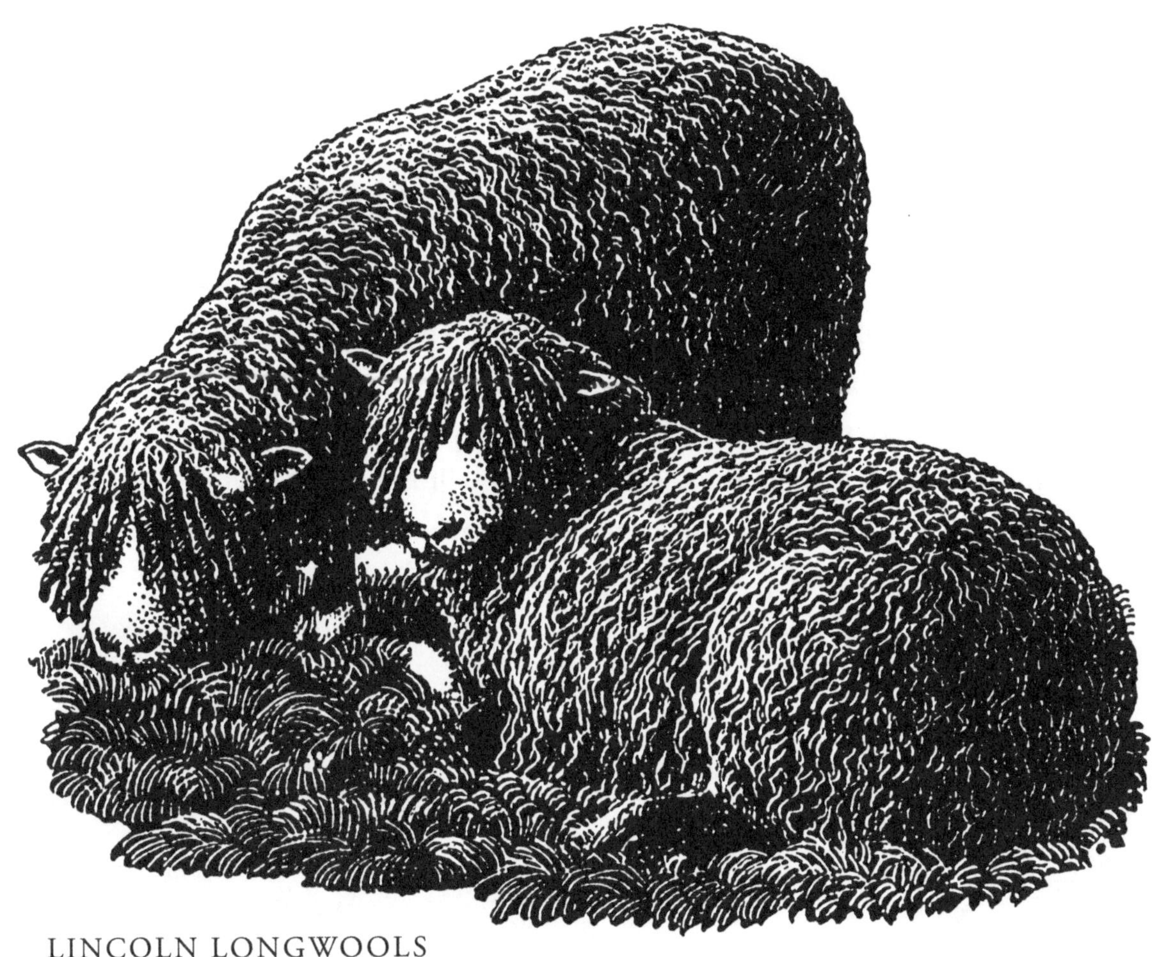

LINCOLN LONGWOOLS

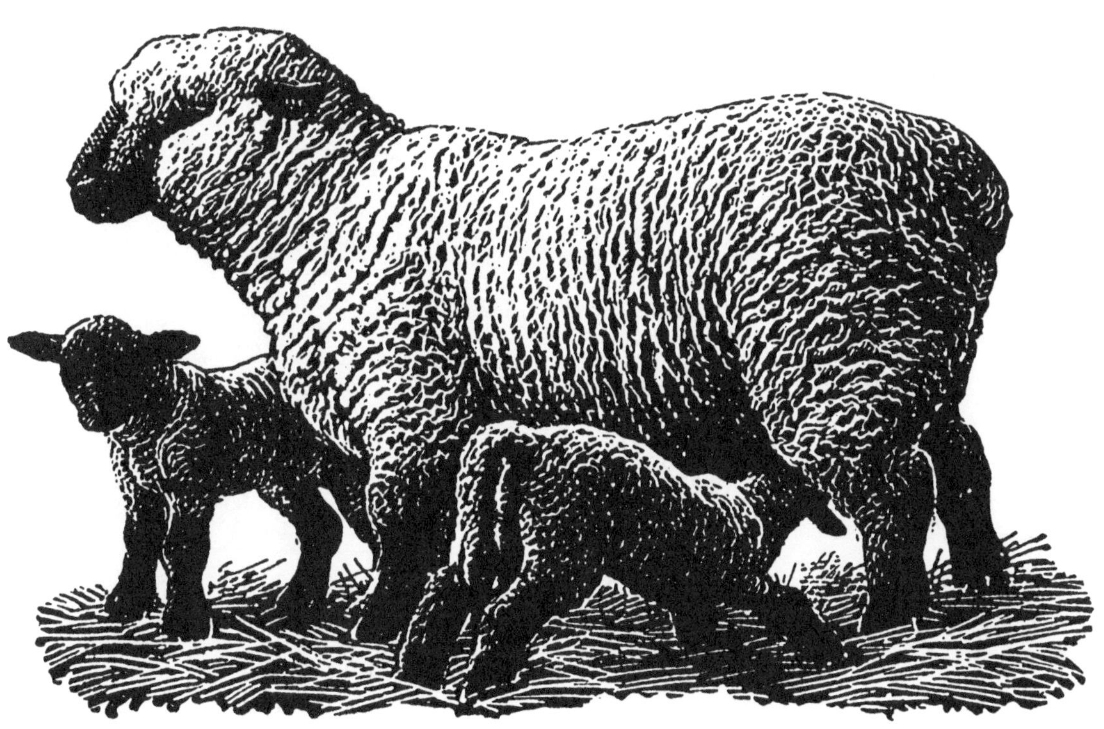

A HAMPSHIRE DOWN EWE AND LAMBS

THE FARMER'S DOG

Long before you reach the gate of the farmyard you will often be met by the farm dog, who will accompany you to the very door of the kitchen, creating a great clamour with shrill barking or fierce growling according to the nature of the beast. Usually these greetings are good tempered and are accompanied by intermittent tail wagging, but sometimes you will meet a dog which raises the hair in a ridge along the spine of its neck and back. Keep your eye on this kind!

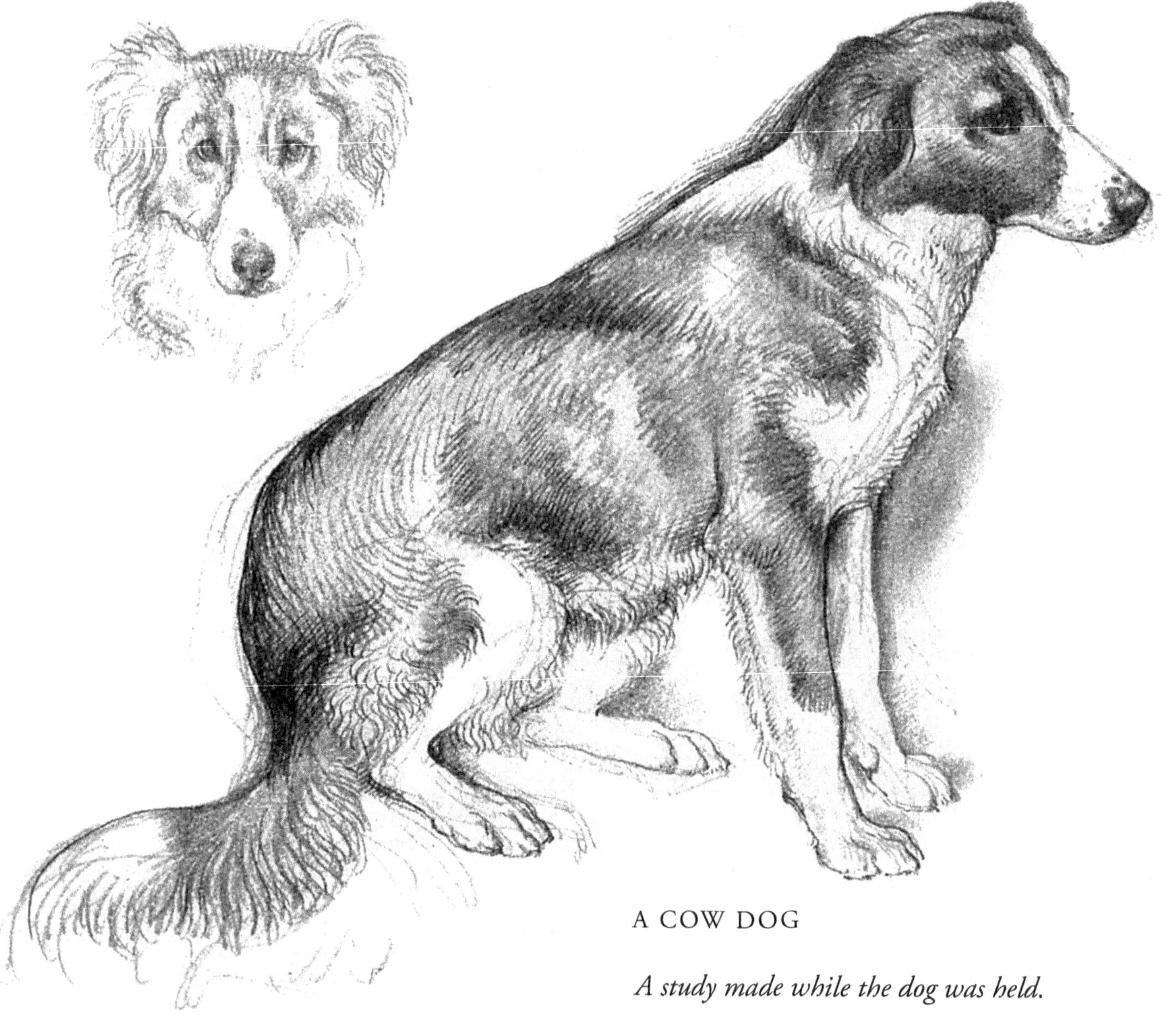

A COW DOG

A study made while the dog was held.

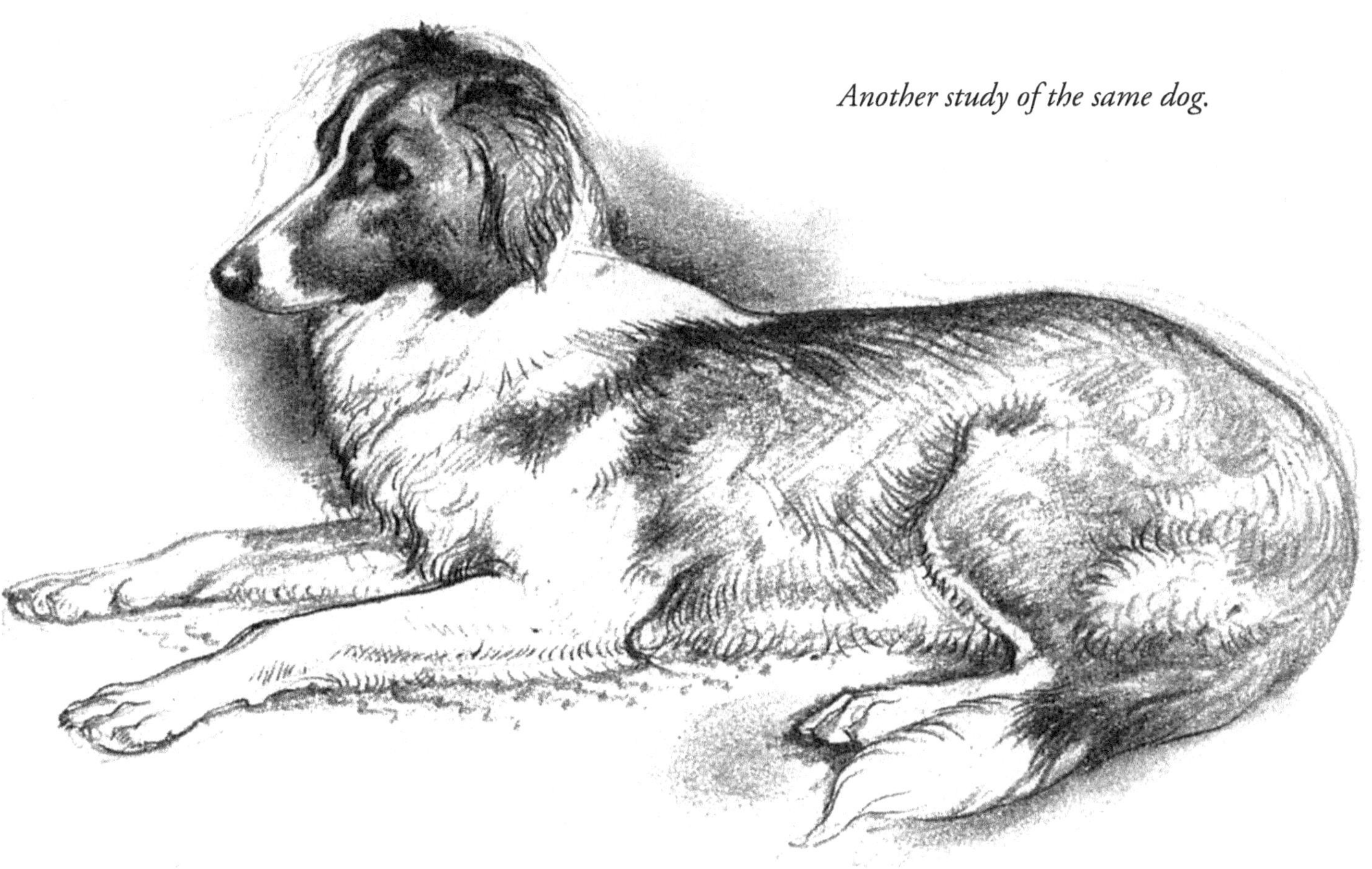

Another study of the same dog.

If you are in the habit of visiting the same farm often, the dogs will soon come to know you and there will be less barking and more tail-wagging. As they become more friendly your opportunities for drawing them will increase. They will settle down to sleep while you are about, and at other times will not object to being held by someone they know while you make careful studies. But it is their nature to be restless and alert, so do not expect them to oblige with long periods of quietness. Even when asleep they seem to have one eye open and one ear cocked, and the slightest unusual noise will bring them to their feet. Therefore, I think you ought, when drawing the dog, to concentrate on quick notes of poses and shapes, and wait until it is held or chained before doing any very close detailed studies.

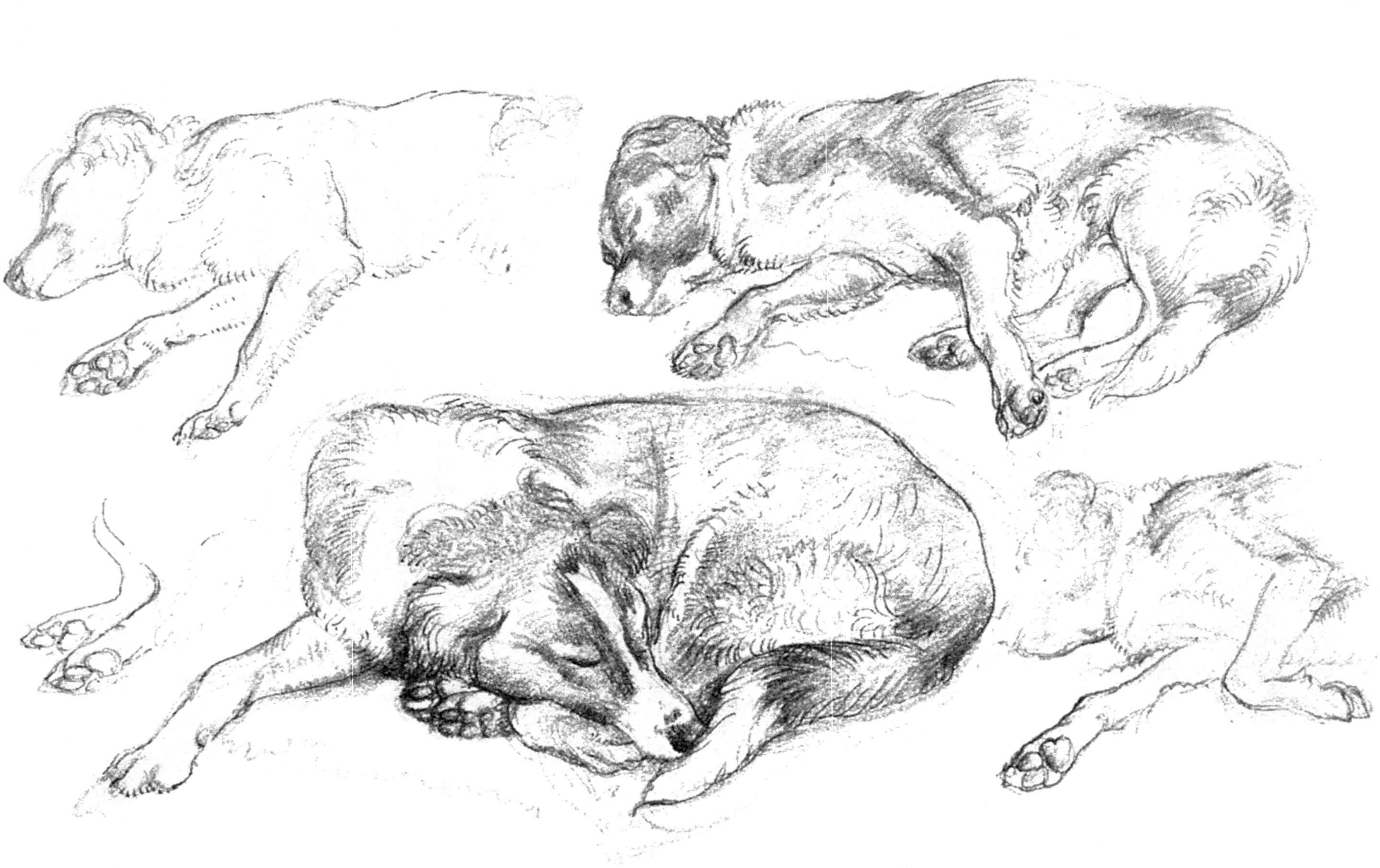

Studies of a sleeping dog.

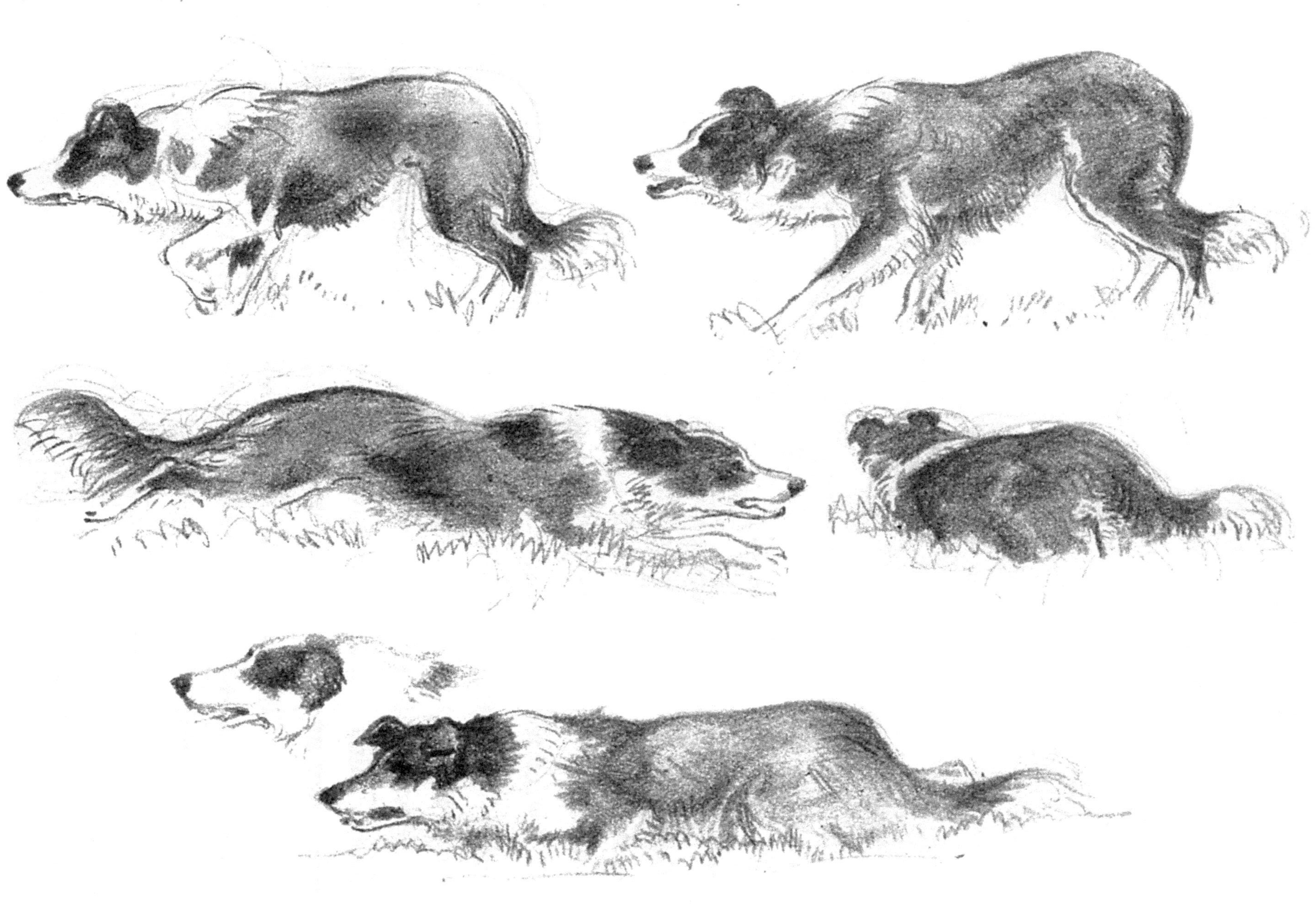

HIGHLY TRAINED SHEEP DOGS

Drawings made from memory after a visit to a sheep dog trial.

By selective breeding the farm dog has become the animal we know today—an animal obedient to man and fond of being in his company and within the sound of his voice. He can be amazingly intelligent and faithful, and is, without doubt, one of the best friends man has ever had. Watch him as he rounds up the sheep on some wild fell-side, or as he helps to pen them, sensitive and obedient to every sign from his master. Or again, when at milking time he brings the cattle up from some outlying pasture, note how he nips the heels of the laggards and heads off any beasts which attempt to stray from the road to the farmyard. What would the shepherd and the farmer do without him?

If you go among the mountains of Wales, the Lake District, or Scotland you will notice that the sheep dogs of those districts are all of the Collie breed, and very often black and white in colour. Their intelligence is astounding and their movements are a joy to watch. When working with the flock they never bark, and their tails are carried low as they ripple and flash about the hill-side. They are the essence of speed or discretion, according to the requirements of the moment.

How widely the shape of the dog differs from that of any of the other farm animals! He is carnivorous and therefore a hunter, and these characteristics have moulded his form. Centuries of domestication have not materially changed it, for the padded foot, the thin loins and the fanged jaws are all there, just as they are in the wolves, the ancient ancestors of our dogs.

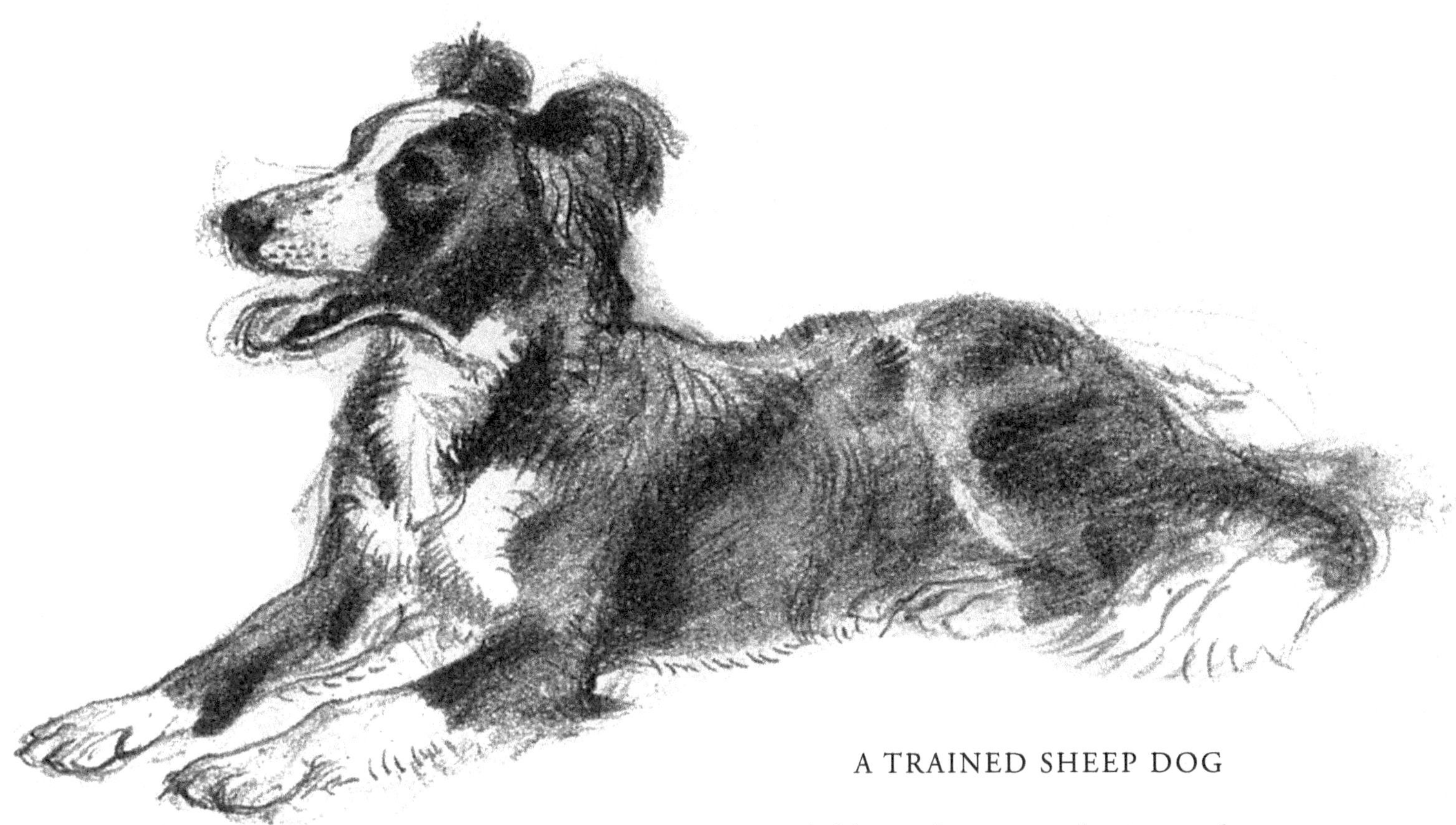

A TRAINED SHEEP DOG

Its master held it in this position by signs and slight noises until I had made my sketch.

Compared with the Sheep dog, the Cattle dog is more variable in type and colour. Usually there is a predominant strain of Collie in his make-up but other breeds also contribute to it, producing an animal whose behaviour is rather more noisy and unrestrained than is that of the "true blue" Sheep dog. He, the cattle dog, is the one who meets you at the farm gate and makes the great hullaballoo, and he can probably trace a part of his ancestry back to the old Drover's dog or Cur dog. He it was who helped the drovers, when they took their herds from the remote country districts where they had been reared, to the towns; for it must be remembered that before road and rail transport were

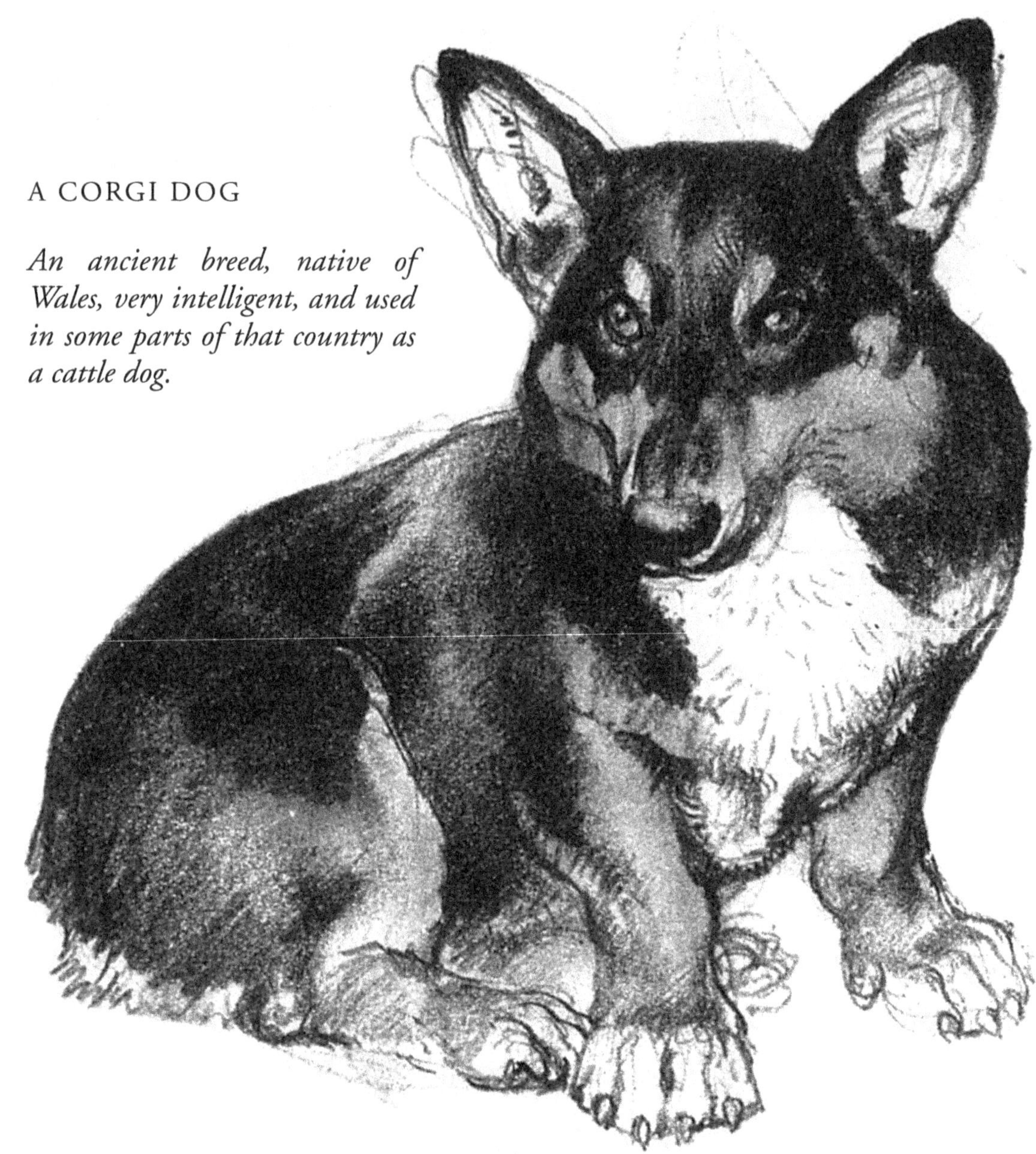

A CORGI DOG

An ancient breed, native of Wales, very intelligent, and used in some parts of that country as a cattle dog.

invented this was the only way in which cattle could be moved to the markets and slaughter houses of the towns.

No one knows the true history and lineage of the domestic dog, for in some form or other he has been connected with man since the earliest recorded times.

THE FARMYARD CAT

Where there is grain there are rats and mice, and where there are rats and mice it is fitting to have cats. Farmers are well aware of this, and often go to some trouble to obtain cats from a strain which has proved its hunting and vermin-destroying qualities. It will not, as a rule, be one of your pampered fireside pets, but a quick, active, strictly useful animal which works for its keep. It will often be lean and half wild. I remember the occasion when one of our cats had kittens in the hay of a disused loft over the pig-sties. She managed to keep the affair absolutely secret until her kittens had become agile and strong. Those kittens never became really tame, and would not approach a saucer of milk while we

Waiting among the sacks of corn for a mouse. (Farmers seem to have a special liking for tortoiseshell cats.)

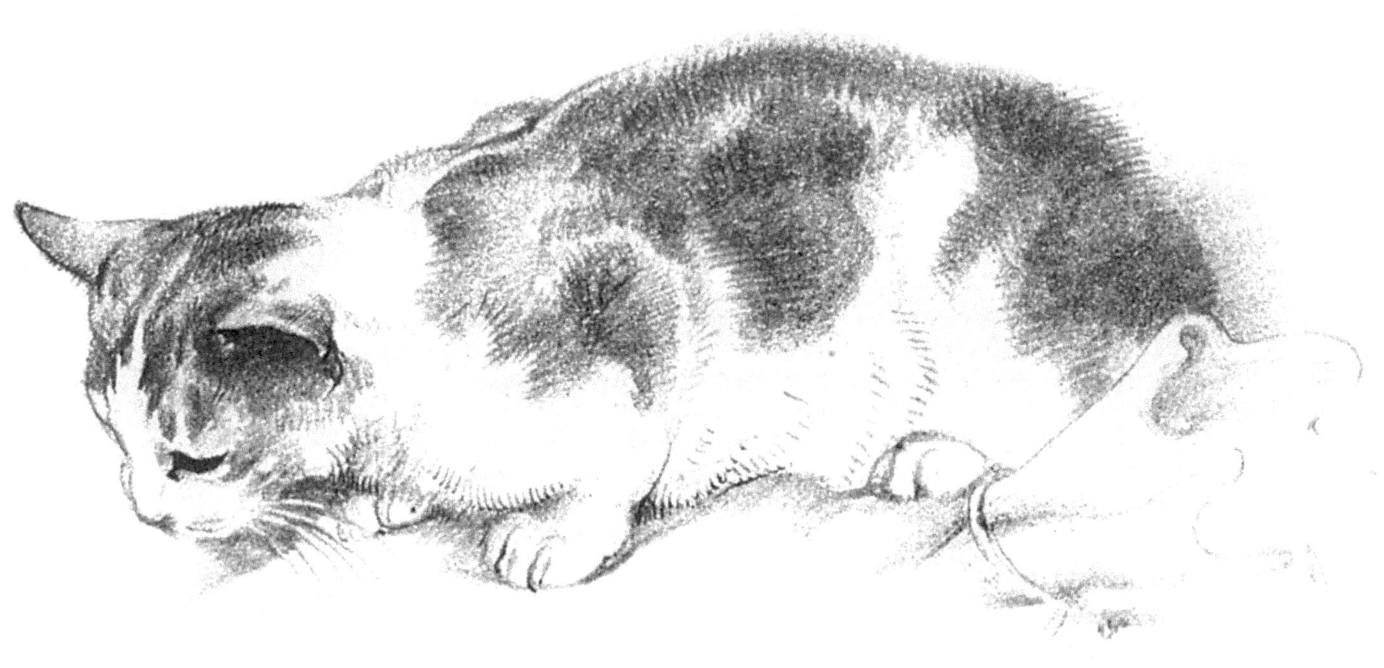

were near. As far as I know they were never handled, but they were wonderful killers of rats and mice, and would spend hours intently watching a mousehole in the shippons or would crouch patiently on the wall of the pig-sty awaiting the appearance of any rat which might venture forth to feed on the remnants of food left by the pigs in the troughs.

Farm cats are nearly always female, the wandering habits of toms not being regarded with favour by the farmer. Your drawings of them will be a case of

CAT WITH A MOUSE

(A cat usually holds its neck well erect when carrying prey.)

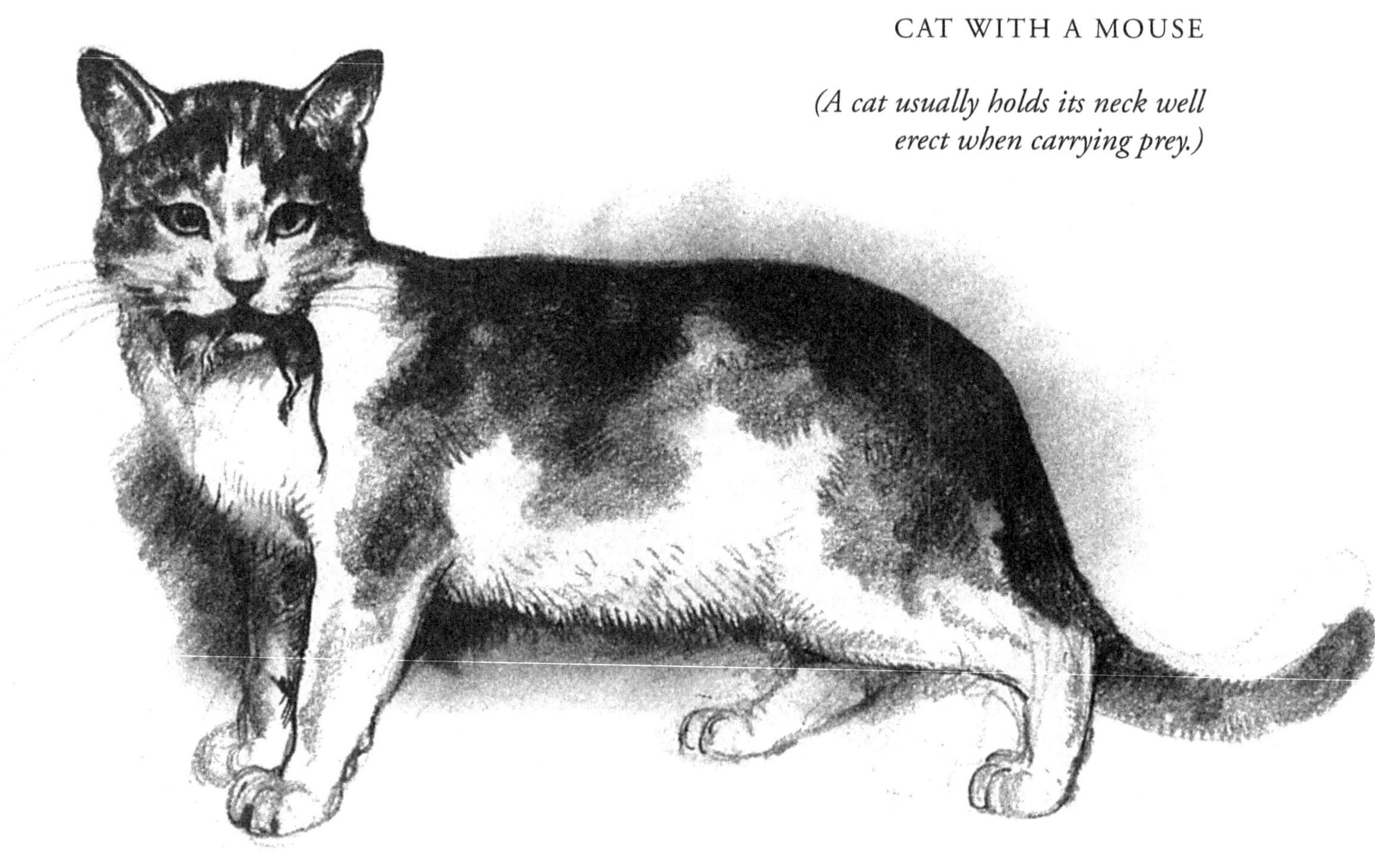

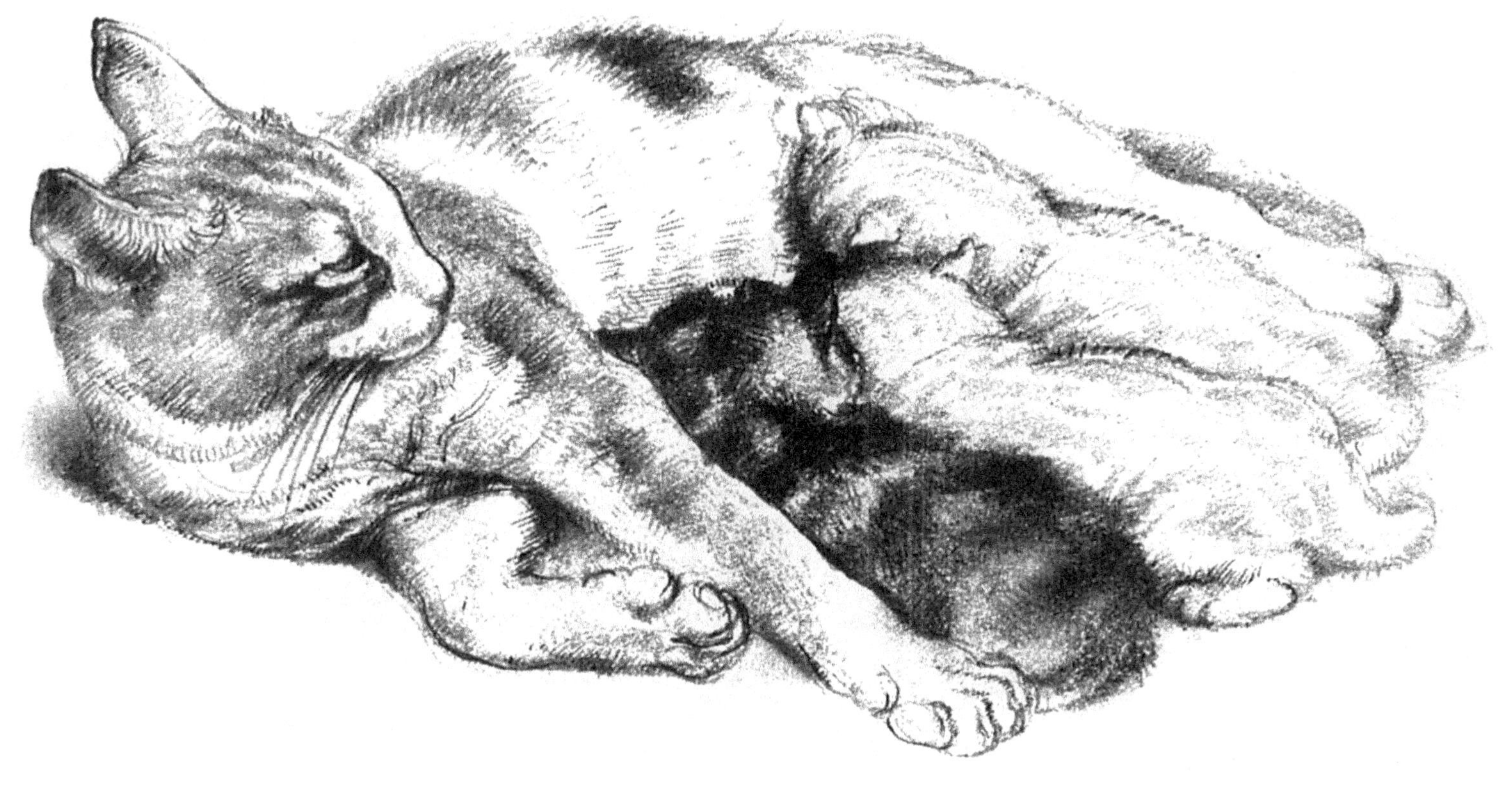

CAT AND KITTENS

"catch as catch can." However, not all of them are wild; indeed the dairy and the fireside have great attractions and if the farmer's wife is at all indulgent towards them they become as tame as other cats, and on bitter winter nights they will no doubt be found dozing in front of the kitchen fire. For the rest they go where they will and live a life of their own; but without one or two of them the farmyard scene is hardly complete.

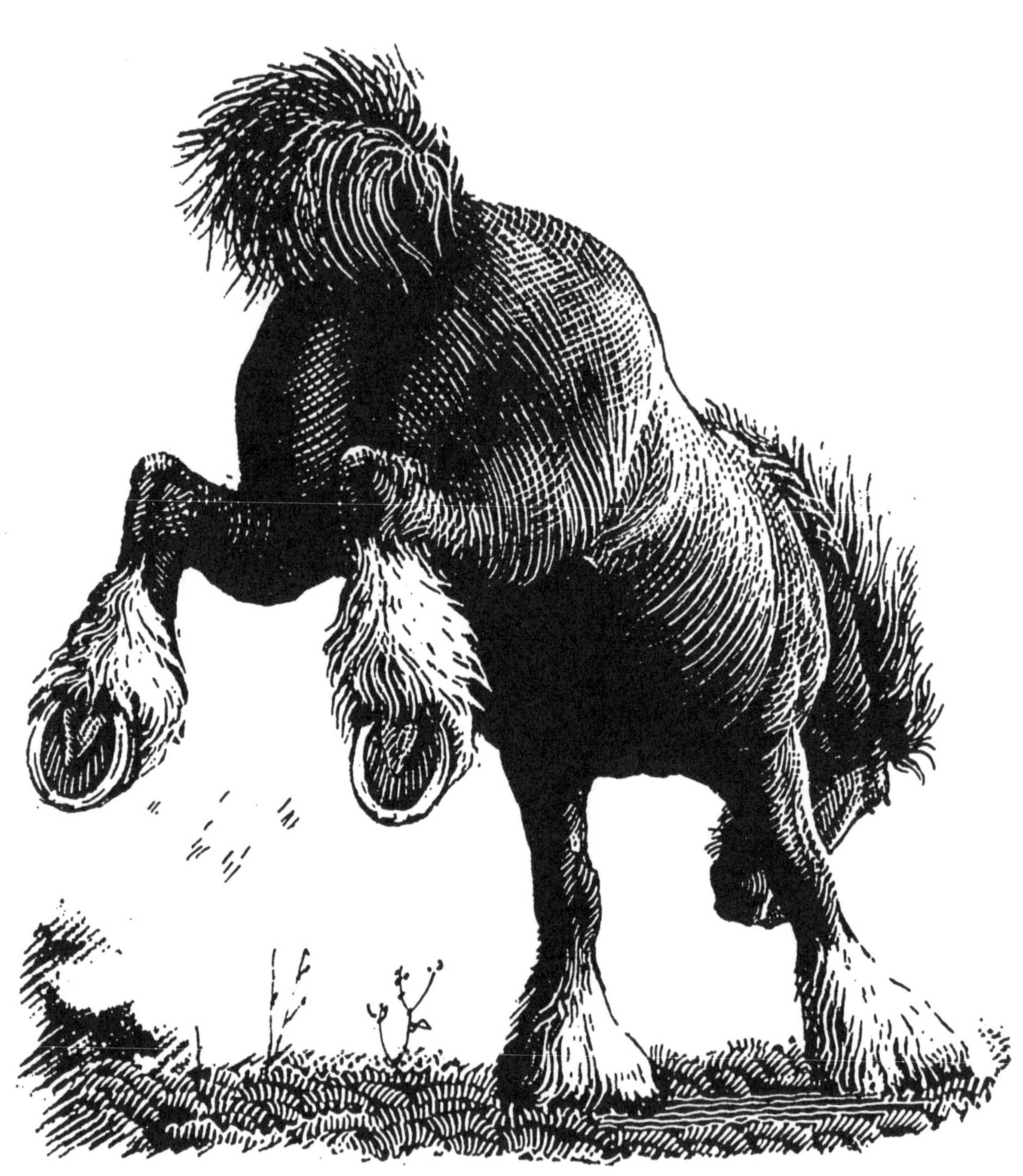

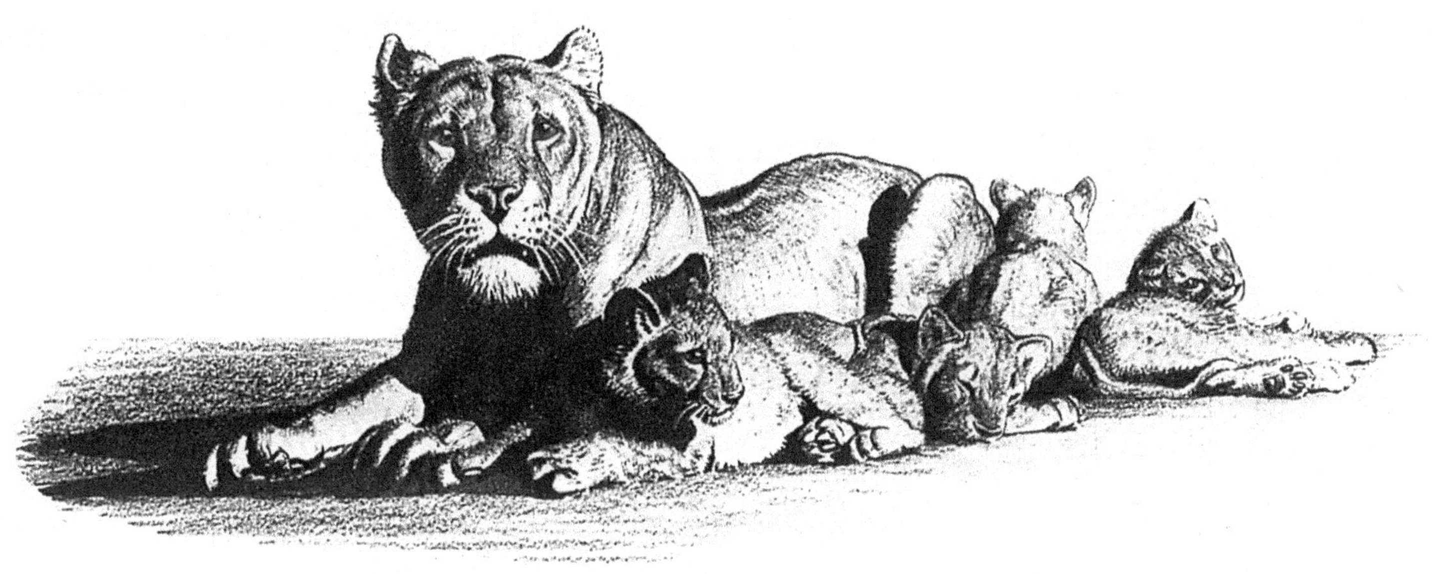

DRAWING AT THE ZOO

Raymond Sheppard

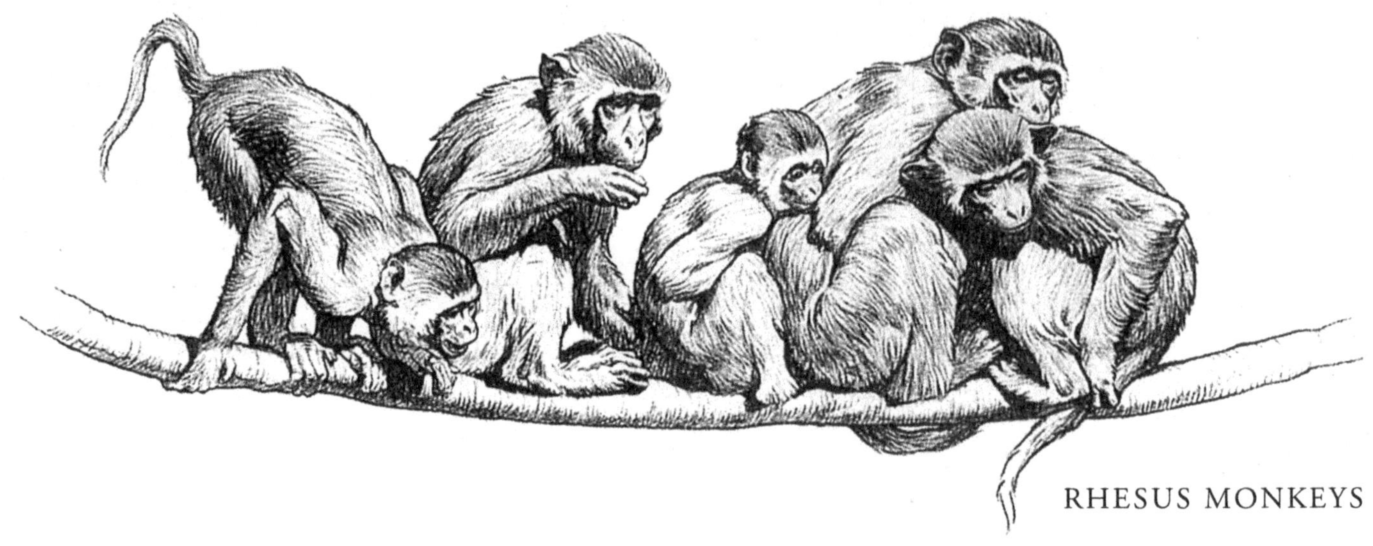

RHESUS MONKEYS

INTRODUCTION

We all like animals. Many people love them so much that they devote their lives to the exact study of animal and bird behaviour. Most of us, at one time or another, have possessed a pet—a dog or a cat—or have wished to have one. The vast crowds which daily throng the zoos of the world bear witness to the great interest animals have for us. This curiosity is aroused not only by interest in their habits and manners but also by a visual interest in animals. People go to the zoo to look at them, and derive an aesthetic pleasure from the creature's appearance.

This purely visual interest in animals goes right back to pre-historic times; to the days when the caveman, realising an animal's graphic possibilities, first scratched on bone his crude records of the chase.

The finest paintings of animals and bird life are perhaps those of the great Chinese and Japanese artists who regarded the animals, birds and insects with a sincere humility as fellow creatures inhabiting the world and worthy subjects for the brush. So many European artists have regarded the animal as subject matter of secondary importance. There have been, of course, notable exceptions among the great draughtsmen of the past. The names of Dürer, Rembrandt, Pisanello and Leonardo da Vinci spring to mind. But most of these great artists were concerned only with animals as incidentals in some larger conception of landscape or figure subject. Not so the oriental. His was an outlook at once poetic and intimate, whose technique was developed from a habit of contemplation—he observed and remembered, then swiftly his brush gave expression to the image.

Films have undoubtedly helped in the understanding of wild animals. The hours of patient waiting and watching by many modern nature photographers have brought the shy wild things to the homes of the city dwellers. The slow-motion film has shown to us all the secret of the swiftest movement. A truly balletic instrument in its revelation of rhythm.

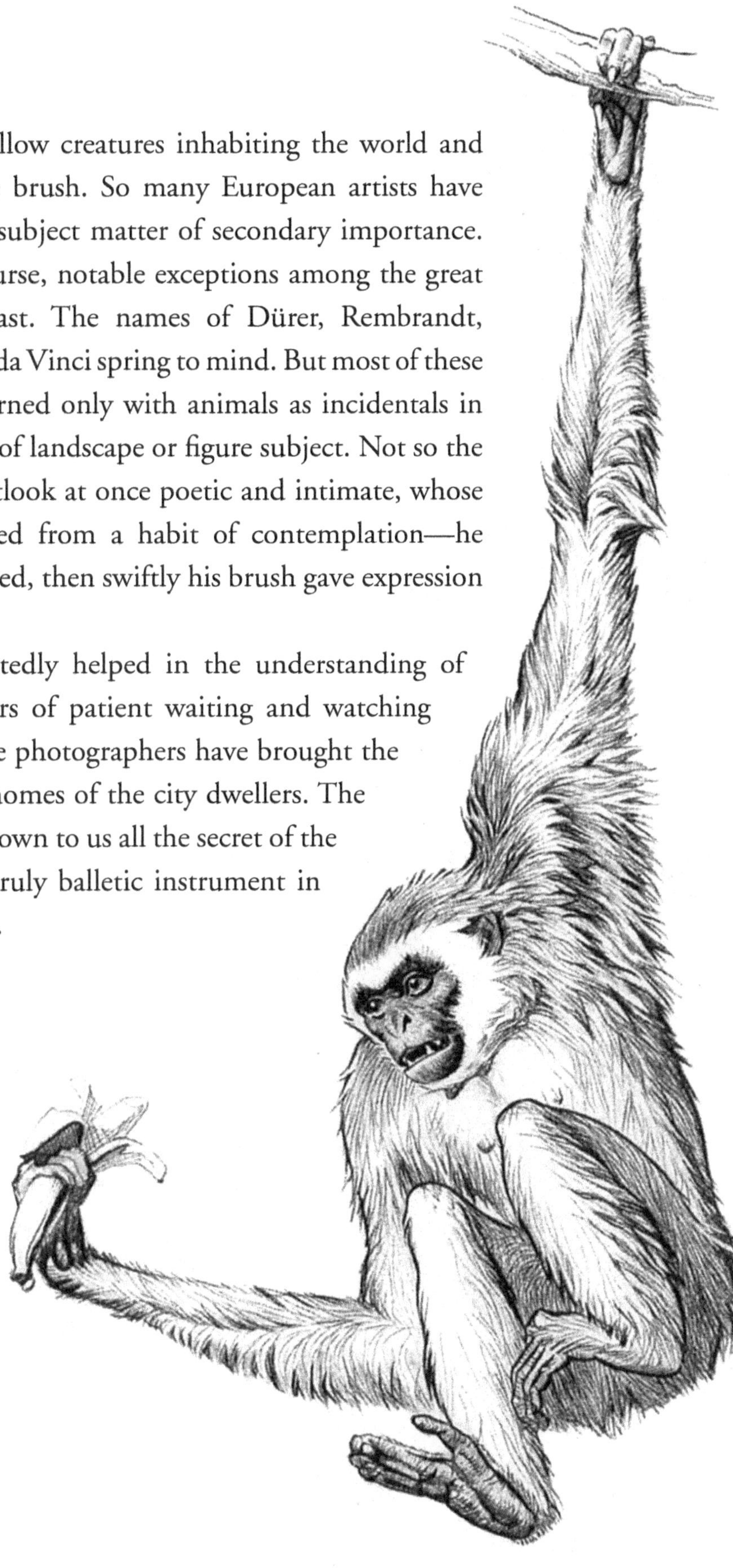

GIBBON

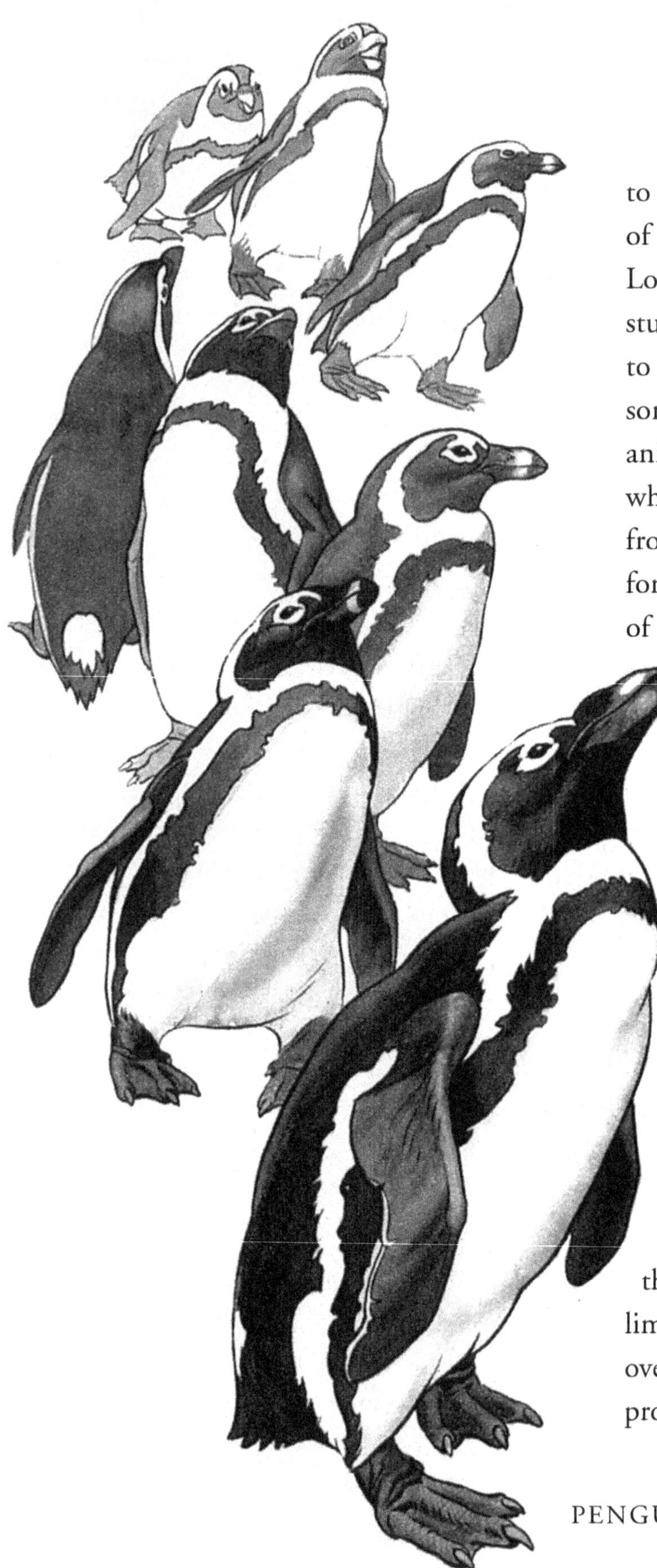

A zoo is a great place in which to draw. Such an infinite variety of models to choose from. At the London Zoo I see many artists, students and children, all trying to get something down on paper, some record or impression of an animal. The artist, of course, knows what he wants to do; the students from the various schools of art are fortunate in having the guidance of expert animal draughtsmen; but many who go there, whether adult or child, lack any expert assistance. They are frankly bewildered by many of the practical difficulties such as the jostling crowds, the movements of the animals, comments, kind or unkind, and the inevitable questions of the small boy. Now these disturbances are very real: I have been drawing at the Zoo for quite a long time and whilst I have still to overcome the major difficulties of my own limitations, I have, by experience overcome some of the practical problems involved in drawing from

PENGUINS

live animals. So in this little book I am going to tell you how I go about making my own drawings. I shall use as few words as possible, as I think my own drawings will explain themselves to you. They will, of course, show you only how *I* draw—you will evolve your own style—but we can learn much from the study of others.

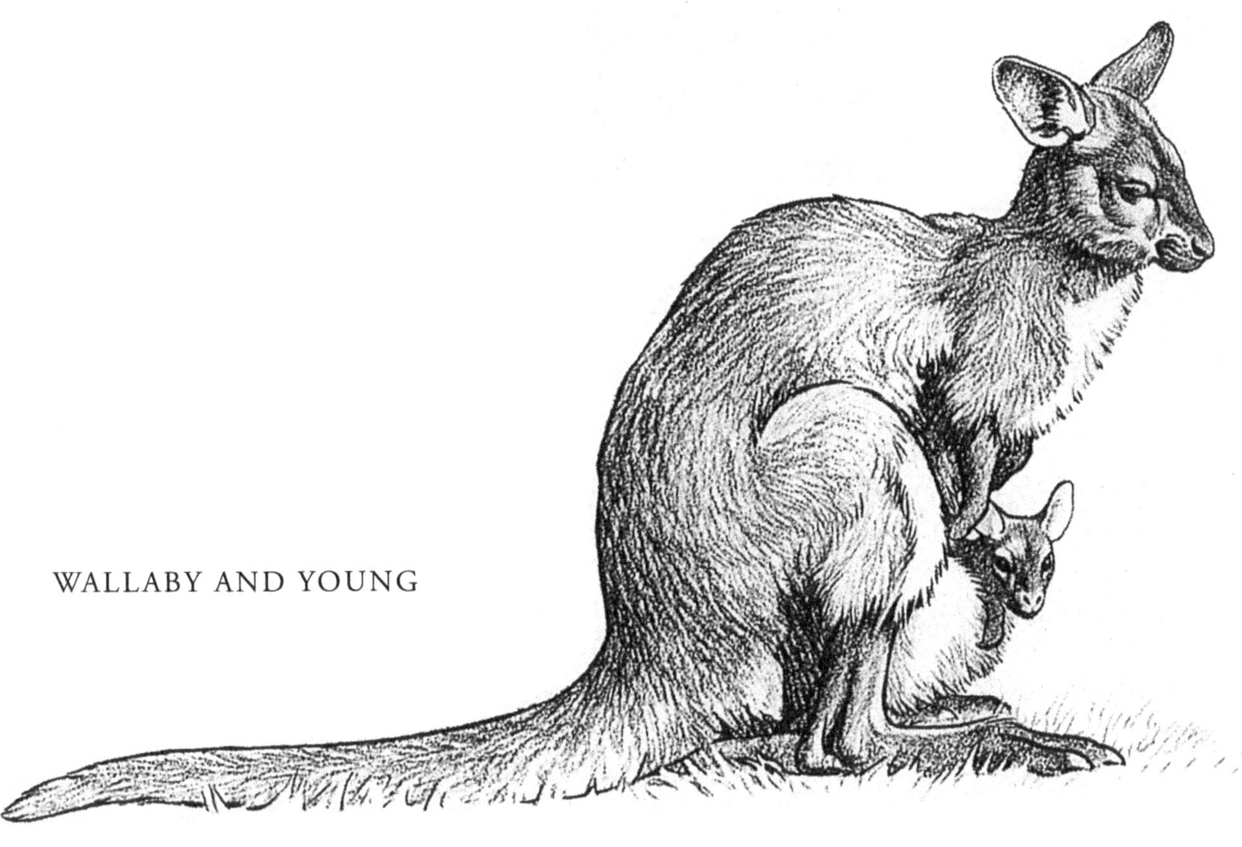

WALLABY AND YOUNG

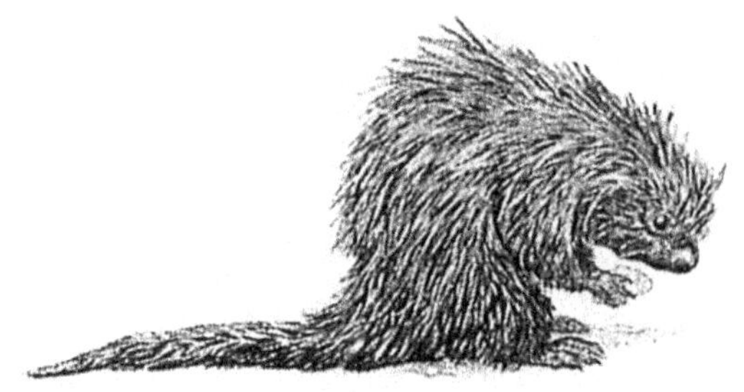

TREE-PORCUPINE

MATERIALS

What are the best materials for our purpose? I advise you to use those materials you are used to. Do not, at first, use any unfamiliar medium as it will only make difficulties. Later on, when you have gained more confidence, something new may prove to be just the stimulant you need with its suggestion of fresh possibilities. Above all, let your equipment be as light and portable as possible.

My favourite mediums are black conté chalk on a toned paper, with white chalk for the lights, or black conté or carbon pencil on cartridge. (The late Warwick Reynolds obtained wonderful effects of texture and pattern with conté on quite cheap cartridge paper.) A fairly soft pencil is almost as good.

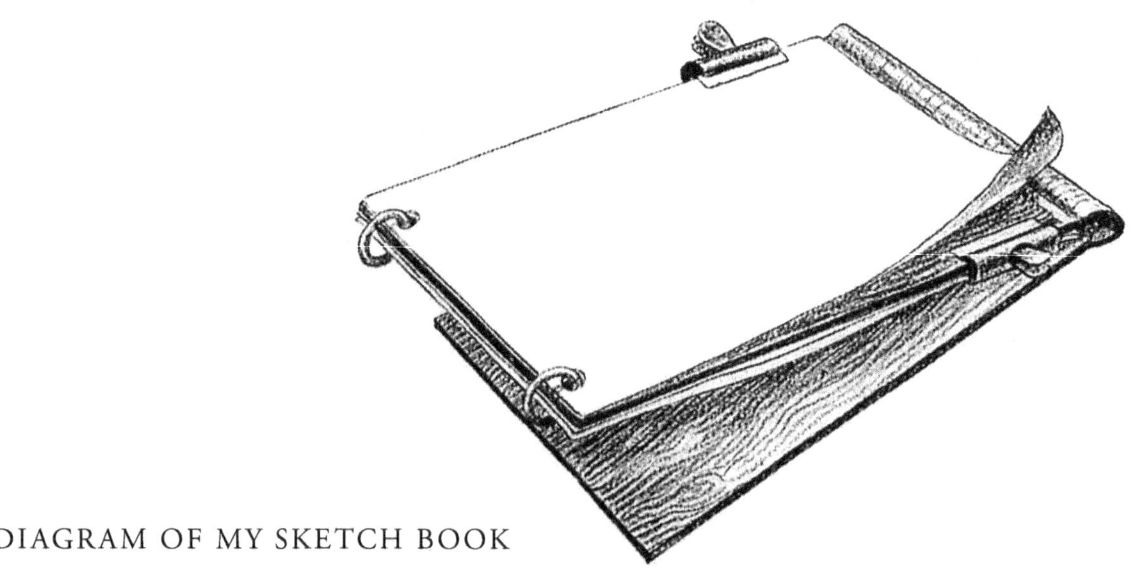

DIAGRAM OF MY SKETCH BOOK

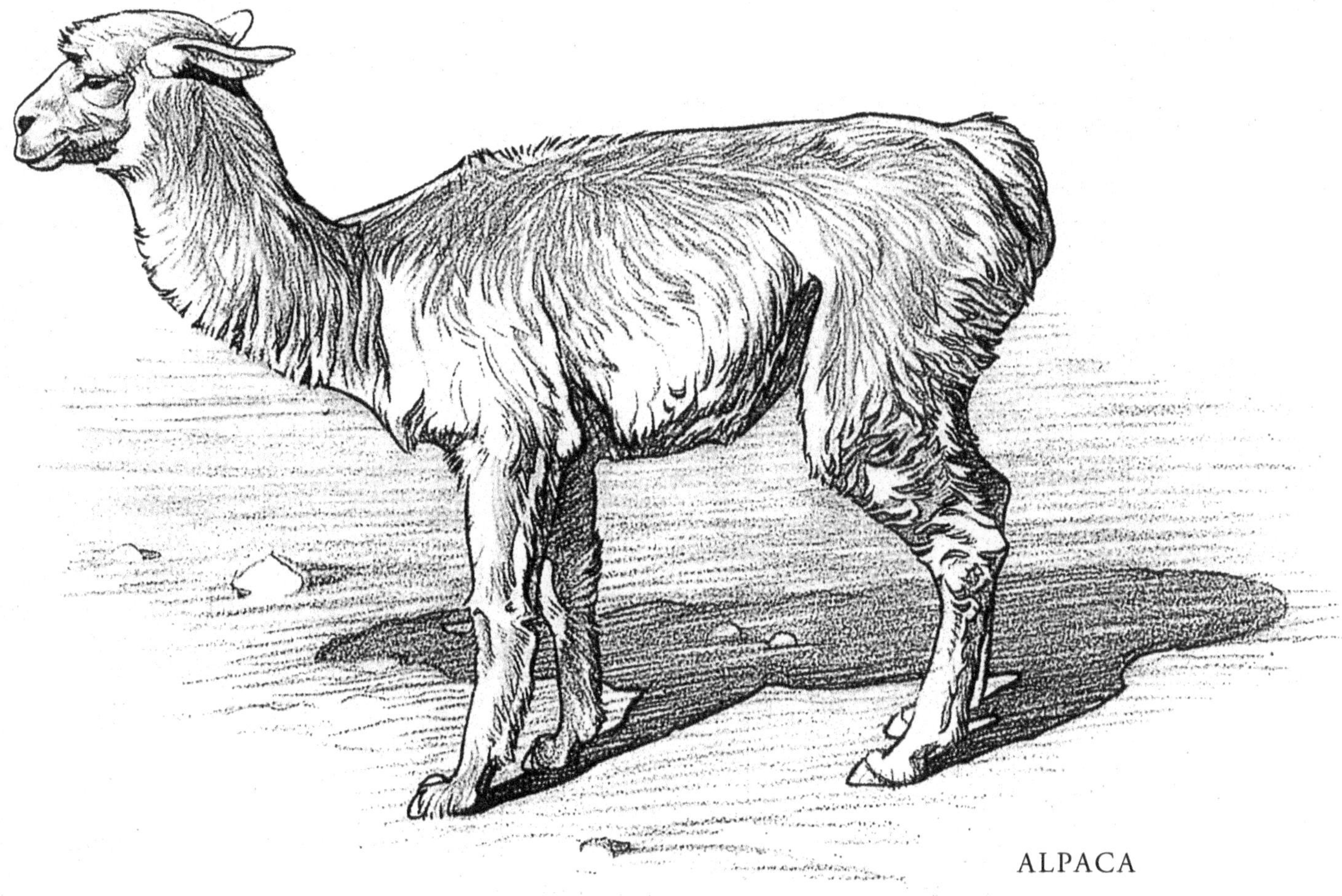

ALPACA

On page 66 there is a diagram of a sketch-book which I have made myself from two pieces of plywood hinged at one end by adhesive cloth, and with loose-leaf rings to hold sheets of paper at the other end of one of the boards. Spring clips are useful for keeping the paper clamped down when working in a strong breeze. With a book like this you can cut any paper you fancy and can carry several types at once; plain, toned, rough or smooth. The pages of the used sheets are held and protected by the overlapping back. By the way, if the animal happens to be quiet avoid making any sudden jerky movements—don't rustle your paper too much: animals are easily startled by a sudden noise.

THE METHOD OF APPROACH

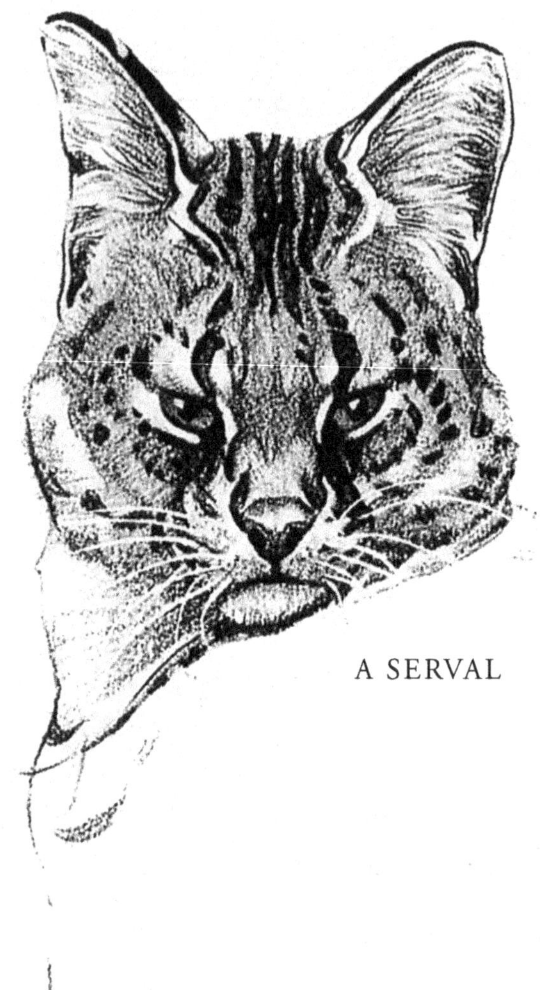

A SERVAL

Having settled the question of materials, the next problem is where to start and how to cope with an animal that is rarely still and often on the move. This latter is our most harassing and immediate problem. Most of us have learnt to draw from still objects. In the life class the model holds a pose for us, as motionless as possible, a pose to which we can constantly refer whilst drawing. I need hardly say that a different approach is necessary when drawing from an animal who rarely holds any pose for more than a minute and is just as likely to disappear entirely into some inner den or sleeping box. This vanishing trick can be very exasperating. We must just exercise patience and hope he will reappear.

Now, no one can be expected to change his habits overnight, so to start with I think it a good idea to draw from the sleeping or seated animal whenever you get the chance. At first try to get the whole animal down on paper—then make careful studies of separate details; eyes, ears, paws, etc. Consider renderings of the difficult foreshortening of limbs outstretched in slumber; all these studies will increase your knowledge. Most important of all; when you get home draw it all again from MEMORY.

Joseph Crawhall, who was greatly influenced by Chinese methods and outlook, was trained by his father from boyhood to draw from memory. In time he developed this faculty to such an extent that he

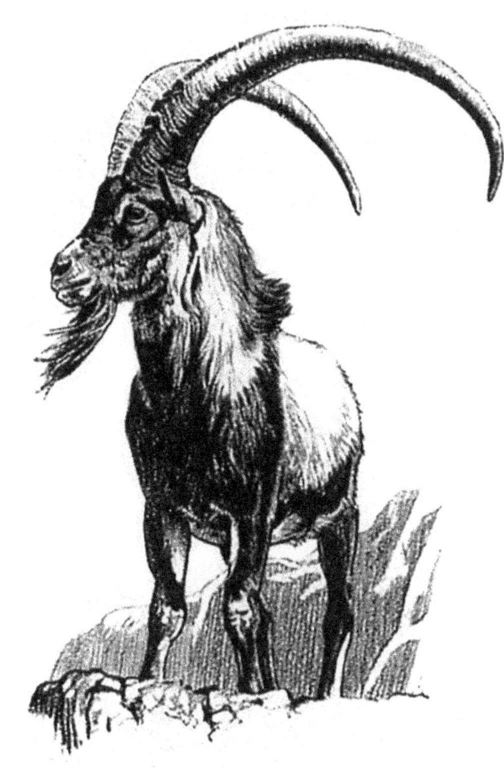

GRECIAN GOAT

GREVYS ZEBRA

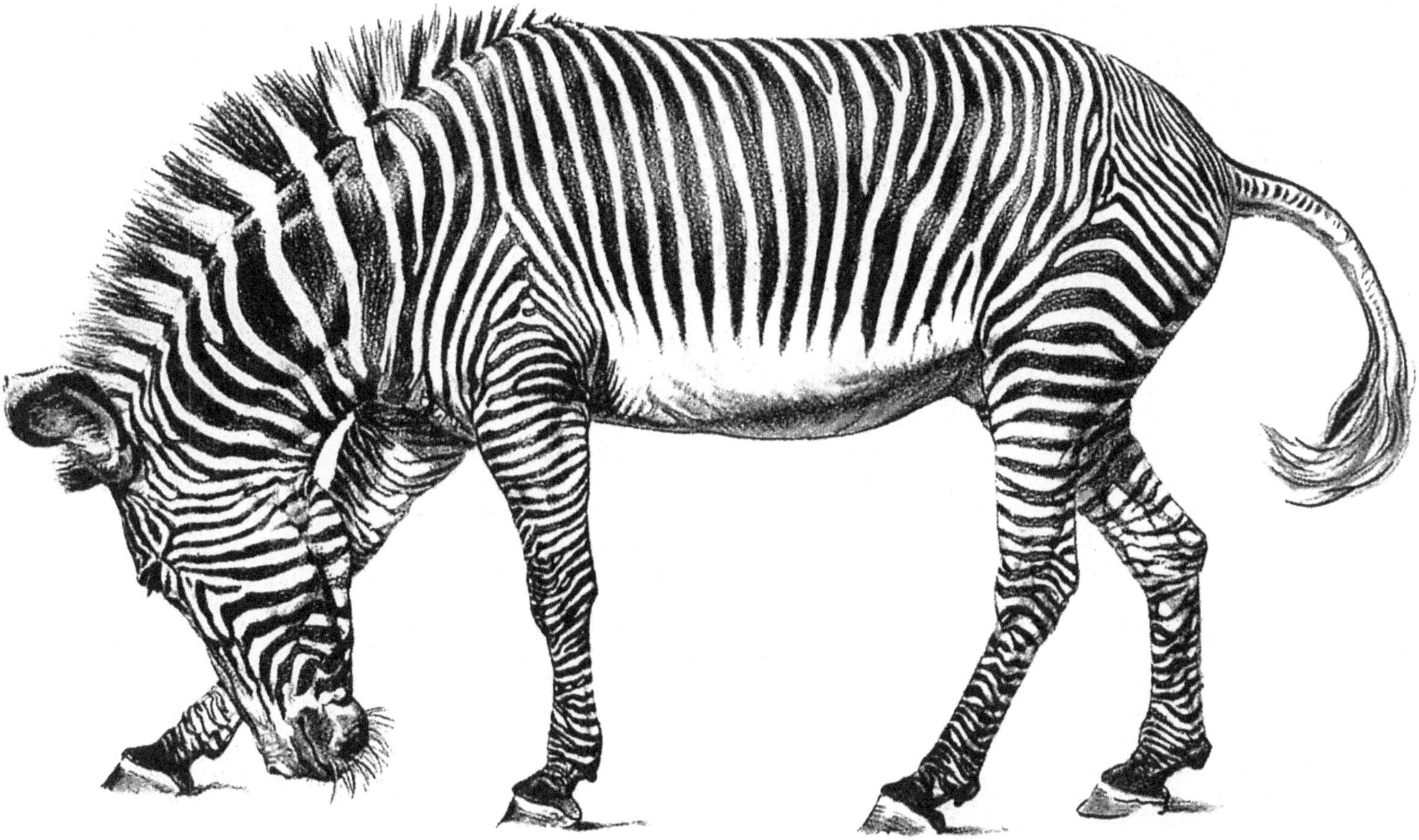

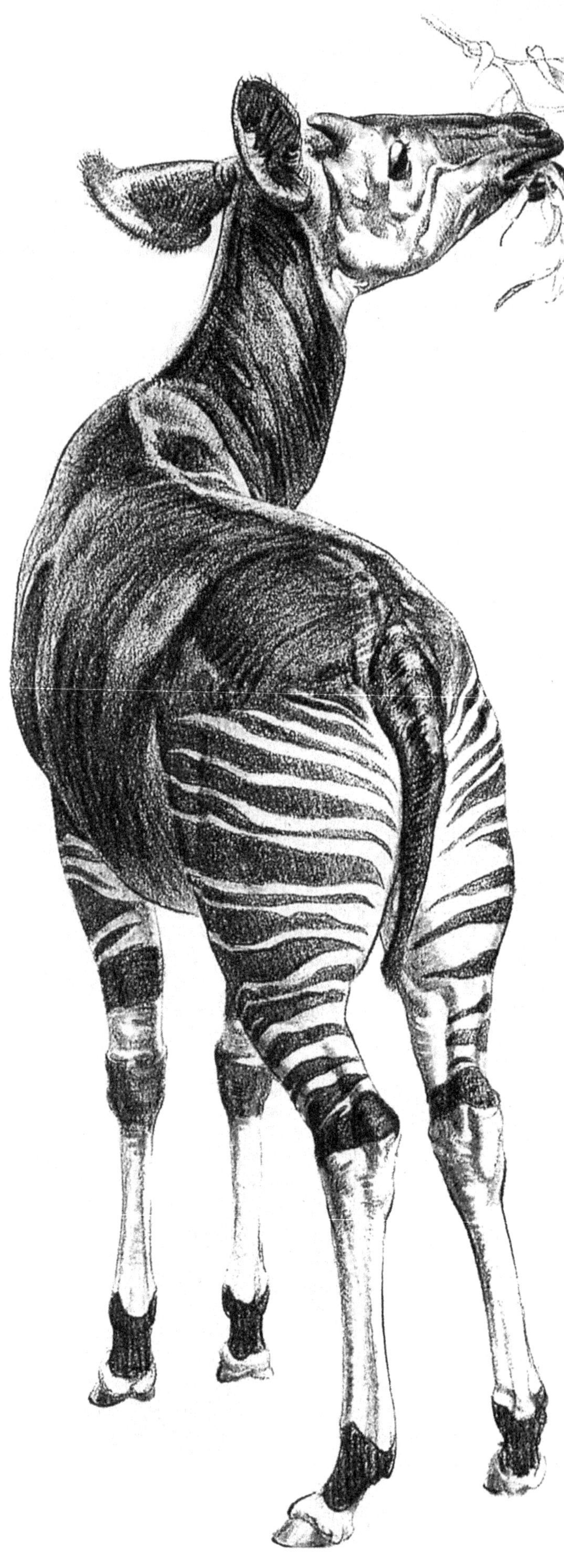

was able to memorise and depict not only the main essentials of form, but those intimate details of structure which place his bird and animal pictures amongst the finest in the world, so very alive and vital are they.

This preliminary study and memorising of details is essential if you want to build up a drawing of a leaping leopard or any other violent action which is a mere flash across the vision. The mere study of detail alone will not give you the relationships of the main masses of form and the rhythm and swing of the beast as he walks or springs.

Although we commence by drawing from the comparatively motionless, it is always with an eye for that rhythmic flow of line which can express movement. A really serious student will be well advised to study anatomy. I have found the following most helpful:—*Animal Drawing and Anatomy* by Edwin

OKAPI

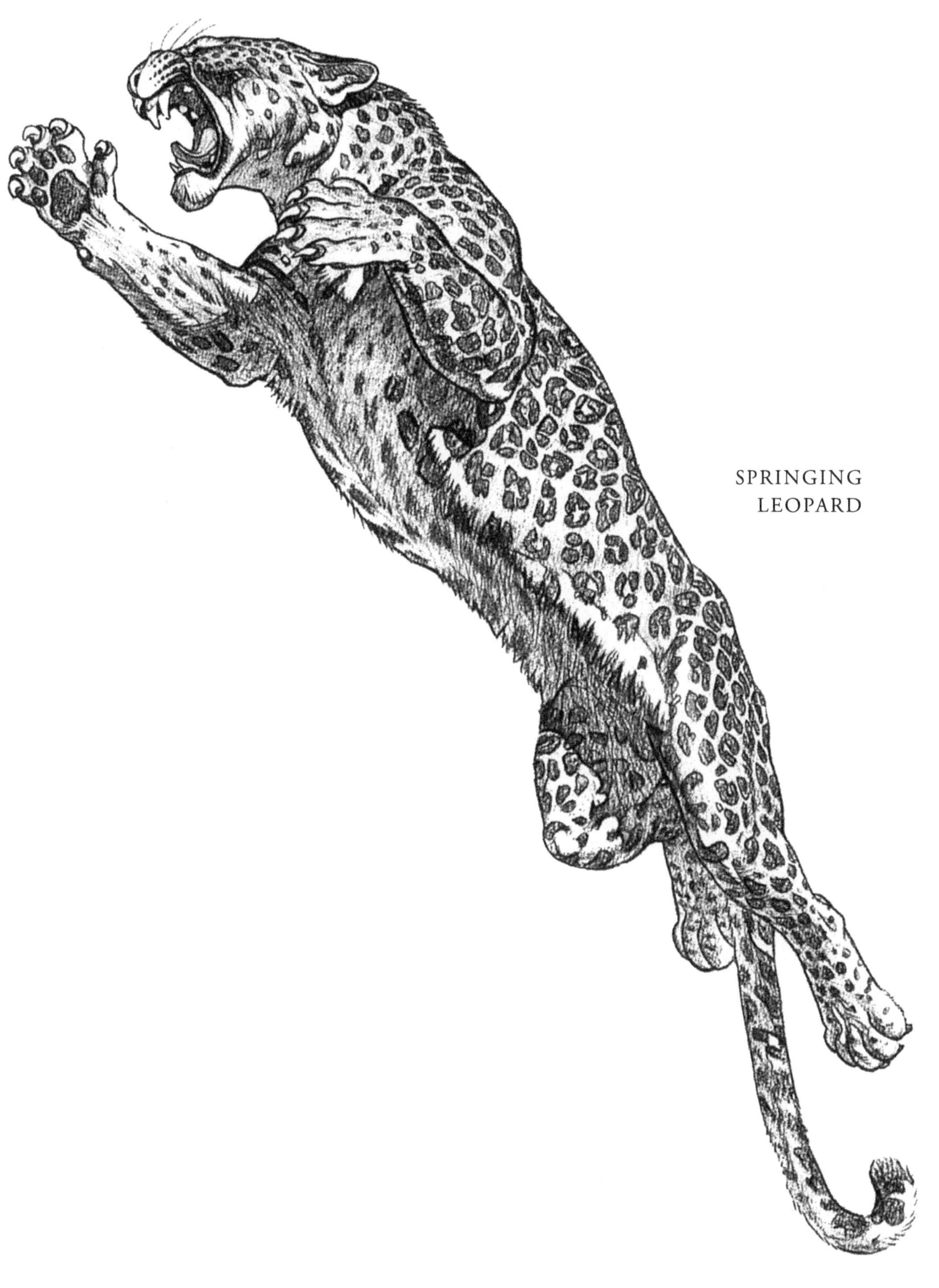

SPRINGING LEOPARD

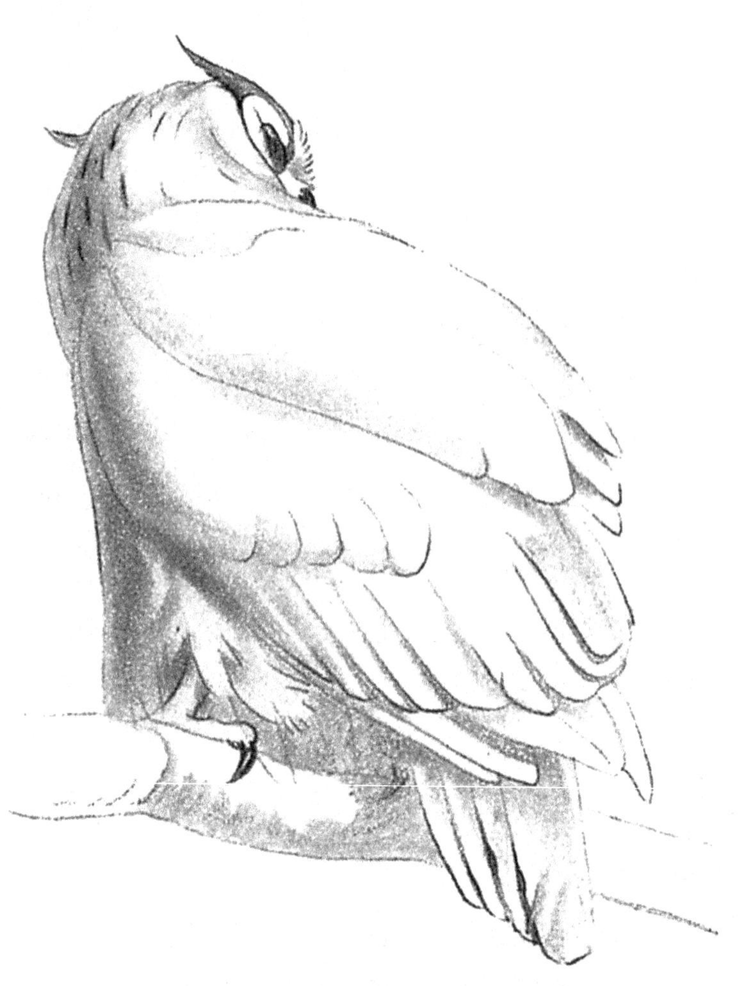

EAGLE OWL

This has been considered as a solid form with the feathers simplified into sculptural groups.

DETAILED STUDY
OF TIGER'S FOREPAW

This is the sort of careful study which will teach you a lot about the construction of an animal.

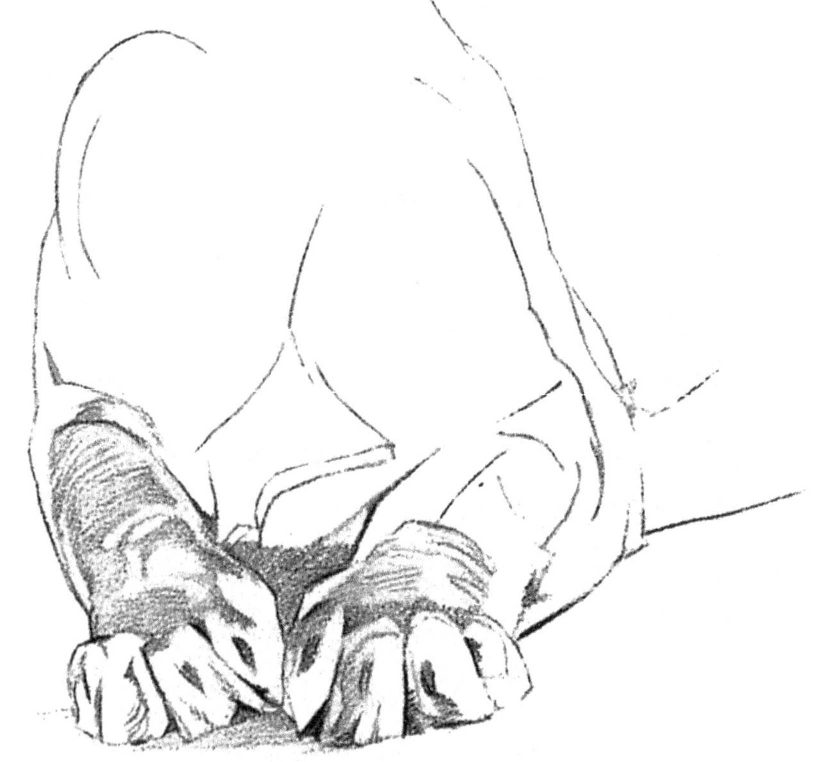

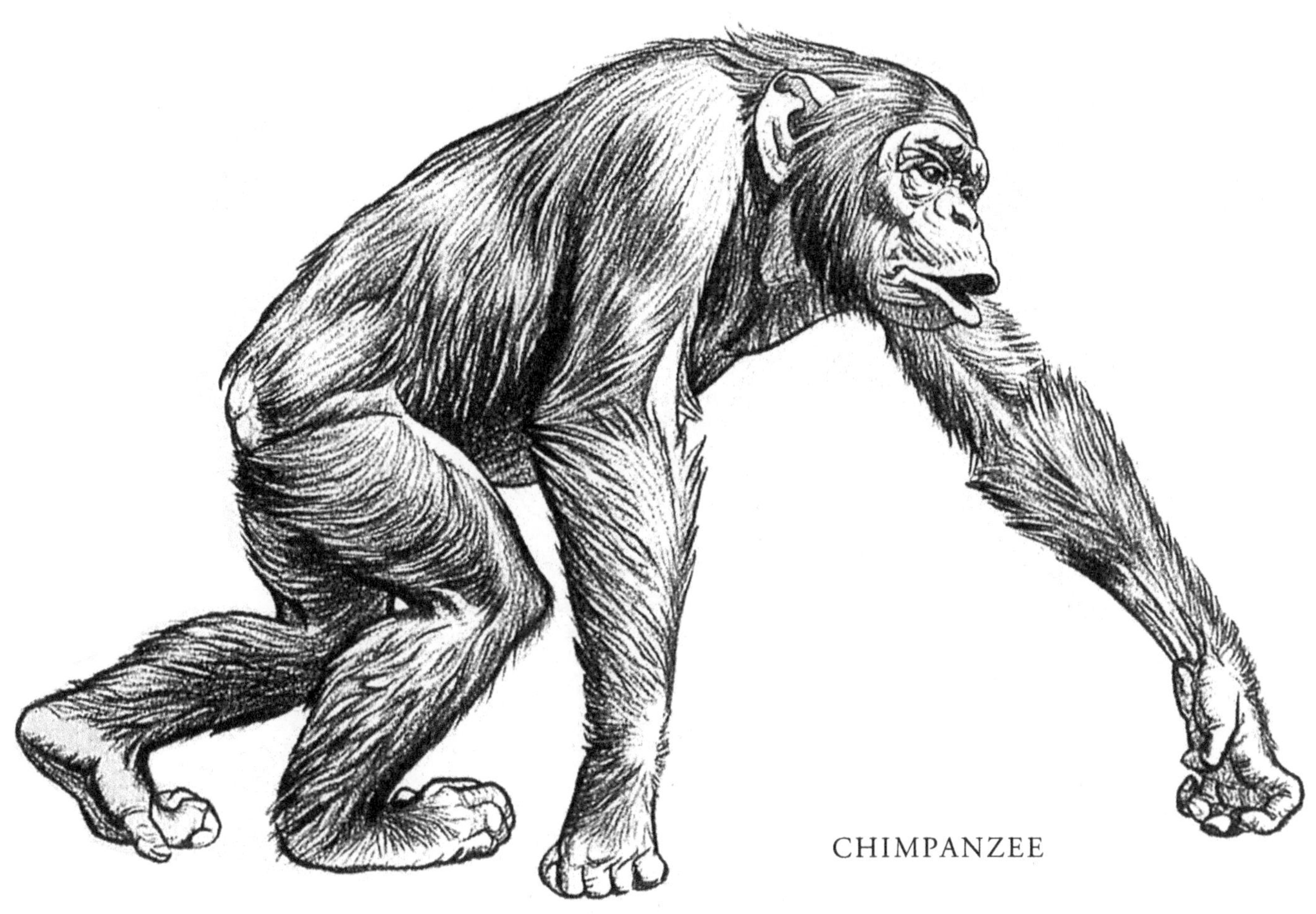

CHIMPANZEE

Noble, F.Z.S. (Batsford) and *Animal Painting and Anatomy* by Frank Calderon (Seeley-Service). Although not specifically dealing with anatomy, read also *Animal Drawing* by John Skeaping (Studio), a most stimulating and scholarly book by a great contemporary animal draughtsman.

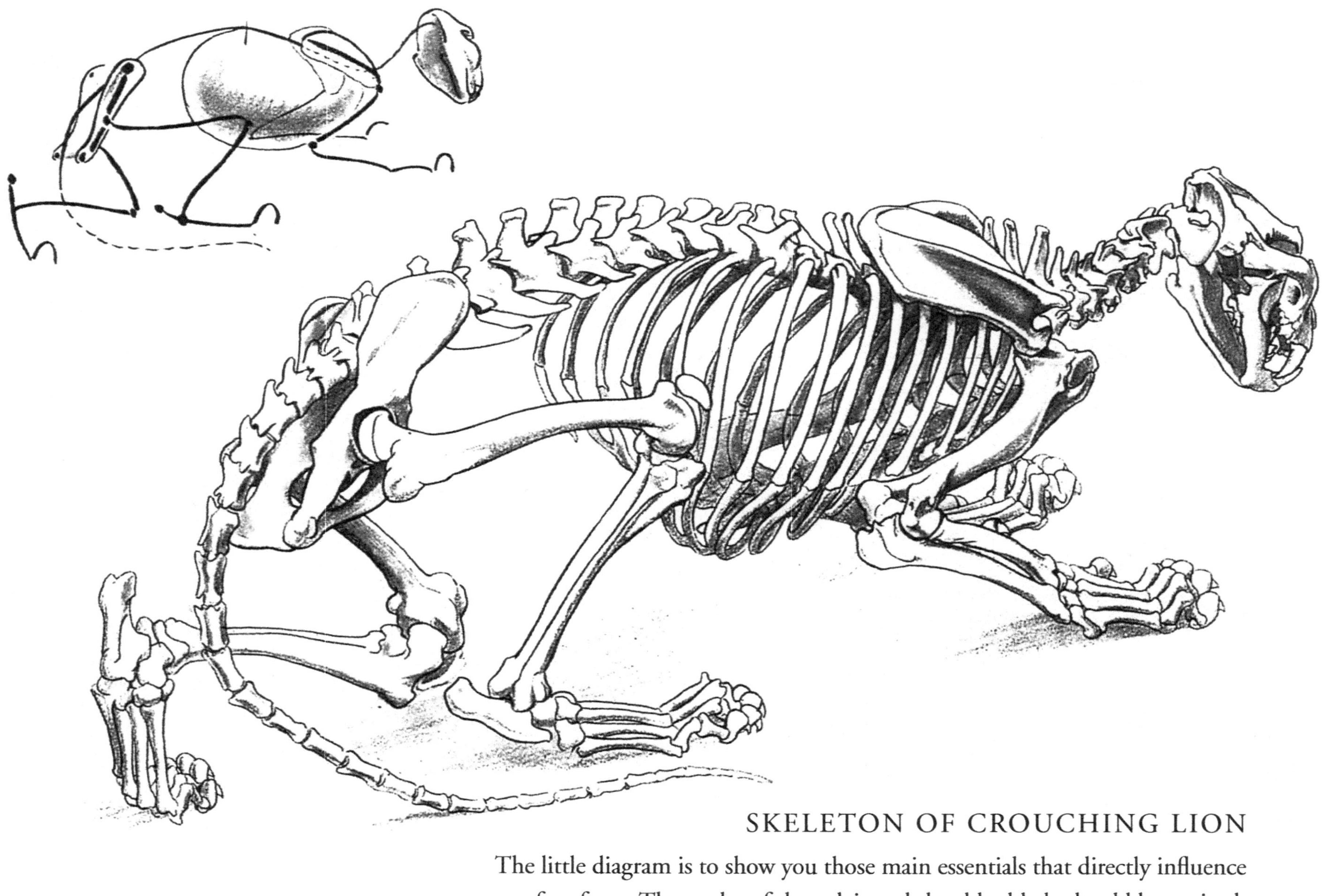

SKELETON OF CROUCHING LION

The little diagram is to show you those main essentials that directly influence surface form. The angles of the pelvis and shoulder blade should be noticed.

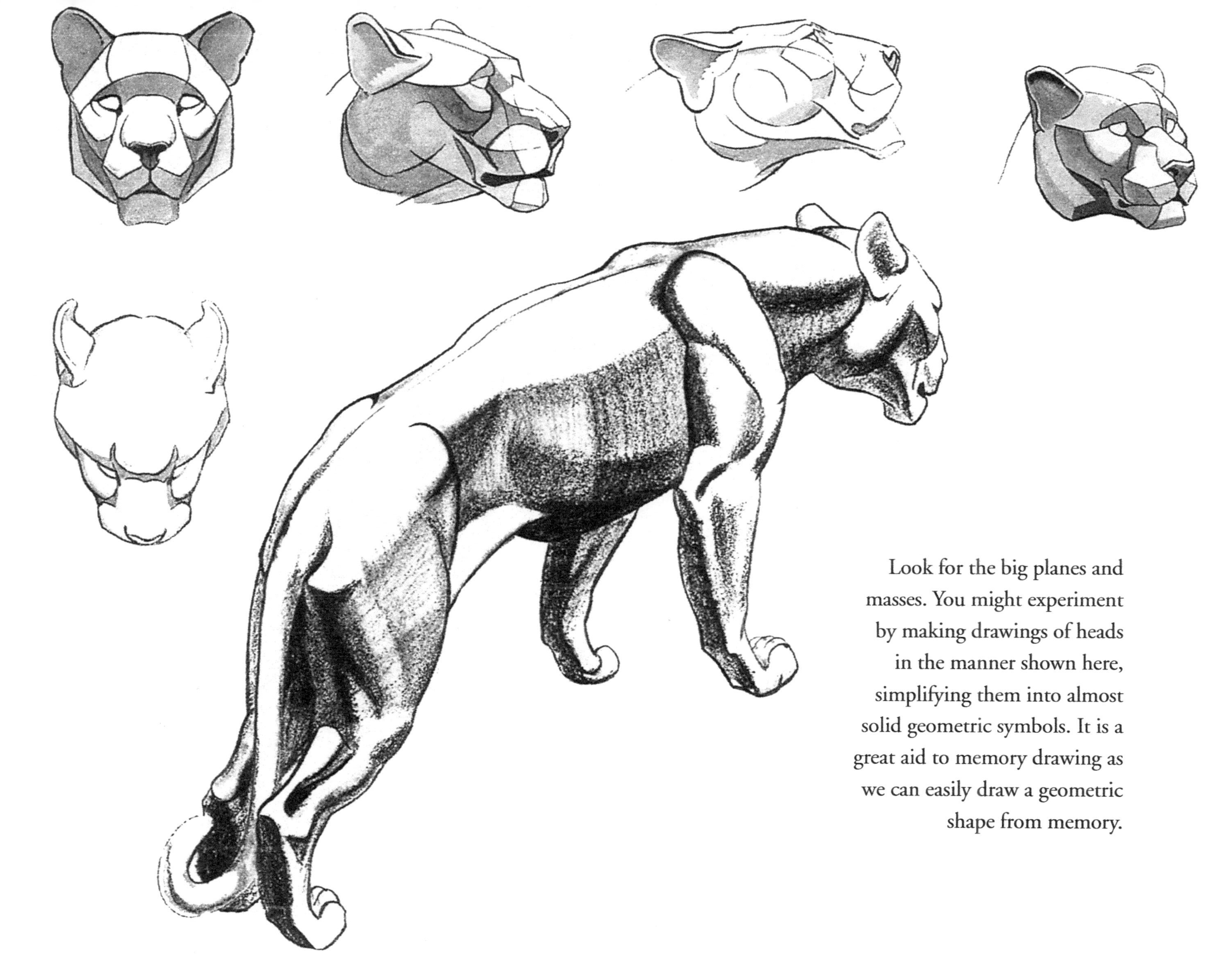

Look for the big planes and masses. You might experiment by making drawings of heads in the manner shown here, simplifying them into almost solid geometric symbols. It is a great aid to memory drawing as we can easily draw a geometric shape from memory.

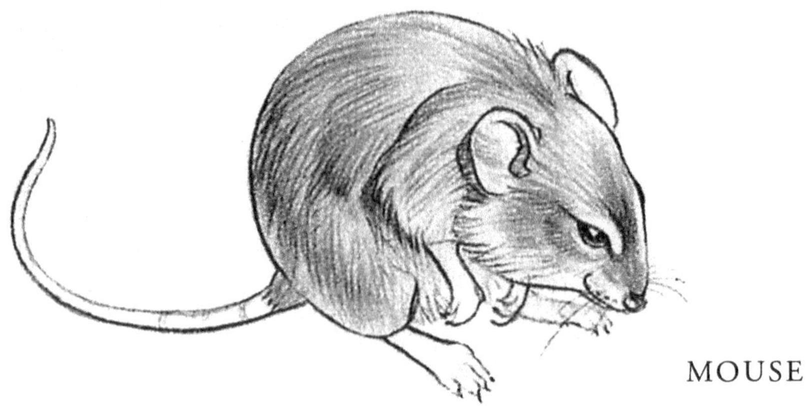

MOUSE

CONSTRUCTION

For our purpose we can consider the basic structure of all animals to be the same. I refer to the skeleton and muscular arrangement. It is the proportions of these various parts that differ, due to their being adapted for a particular use. This variation of forms due to specialisation, when properly understood, simplifies things a great deal. The mouse and the elephant, so different in size and appearance, have a similar bony framework. It is apparent, therefore, that when we understand the bone and muscle formation of one type of animal we can apply this knowledge to others.

All animal anatomy can be considered as being relevant to our own. The paws of the tiger; pads of the rhinoceros; flipper of the seal and hand of man are all specialised variations of the same thing.

On page 74 I have drawn a skeleton of a lion and on page 75 a diagram showing the main planes and masses to look for when drawing any of the larger felines. The same masses, in varying proportions, are found in most animals. However, I am not going to suggest that we start off by trying to draw such a difficult creature as a lion or leopard. We shall come to that later on. These diagrams are here for you to refer to constantly. Go for the big shapes first and the smaller details will then inevitably take their places.

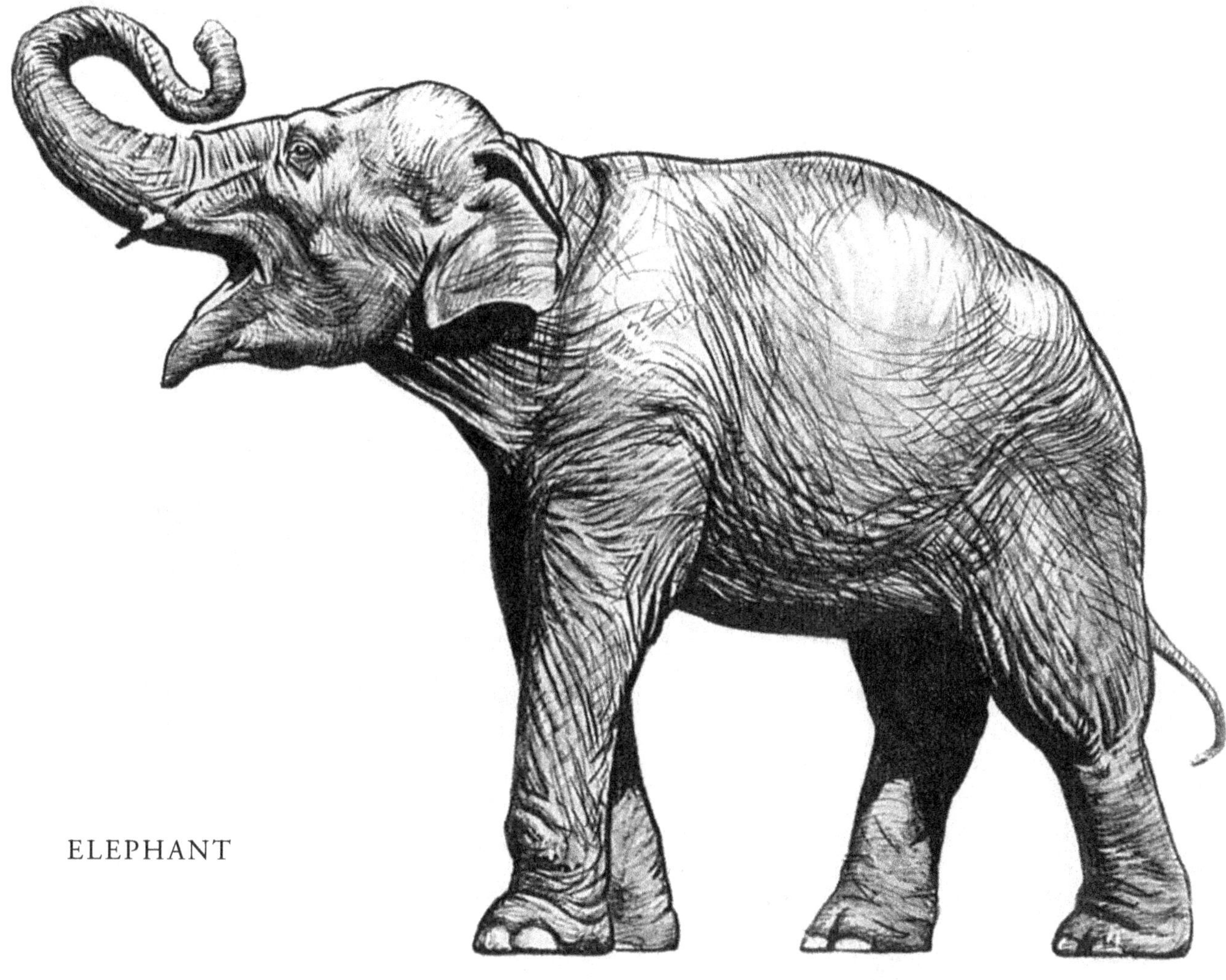

ELEPHANT

WE MAKE A START

Let us visit the reptile house where we find animals who really do keep still. The snakes are motionless as coiled rope, crocodiles and alligators lie like logs; but let us draw these lizards first because it is possible to see the whole animal at a glance. The eye does not have to travel backwards and forwards along the form as is the case with the larger crocodile. It is so much easier when we can take in the entire form in one eyeful.

Even such an immobile creature as a lizard is given to sudden spasms of agility followed again by a lifeless freezing so do not start drawing right away but take a good look at your subject. Study its shape carefully, see how quaintly its legs bend in seeming double-jointure; how the sweep of its long tail continues up the spine and neck, flows through the turn of its head with all the grace of a slender branch bent with the weight of blossom, a long rhythmic line. Now draw rapidly in long lines containing the essence of form, let your lines follow through as a golf club completing its own arc after the ball has been struck. Try to feel the rhythmic flow of line before and after your pencil leaves the paper. The drawings on this and the next page may show you what I mean.

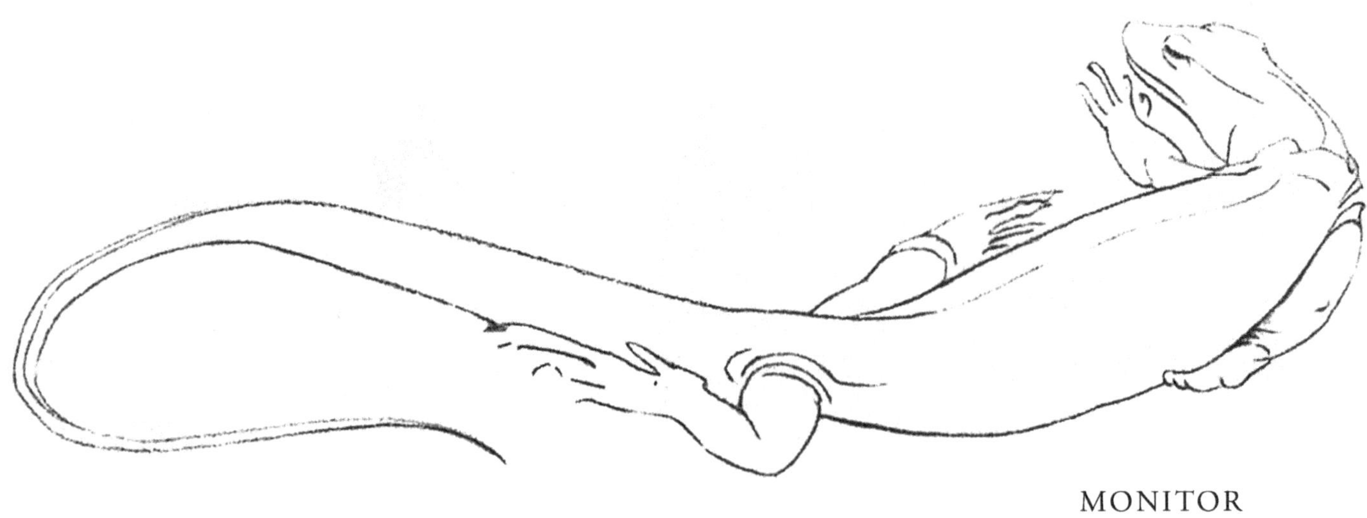

MONITOR

STUDIES OF IGUANA

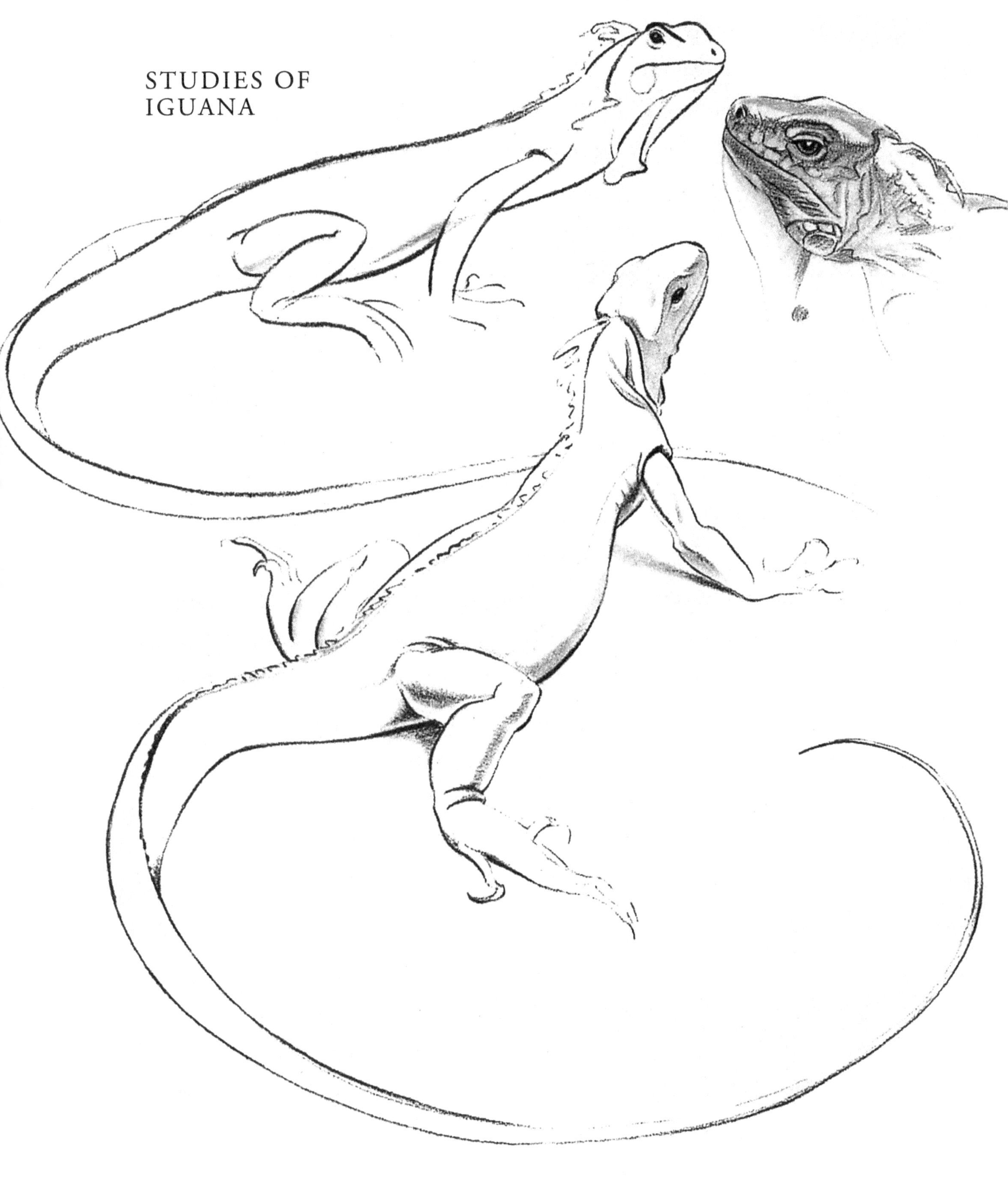

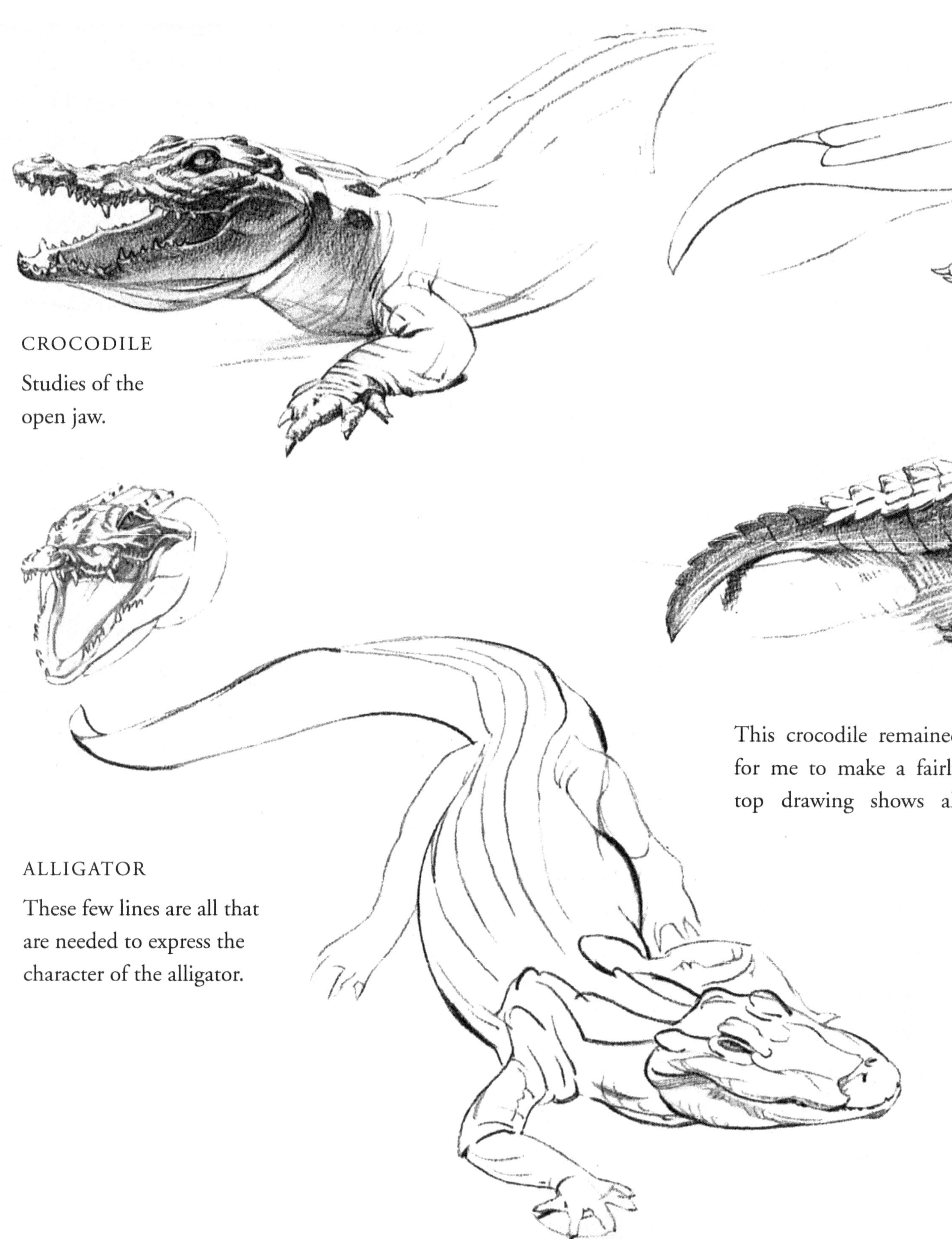

CROCODILE

Studies of the open jaw.

This crocodile remaine[d] for me to make a fairl[y] top drawing shows a[...]

ALLIGATOR

These few lines are all that are needed to express the character of the alligator.

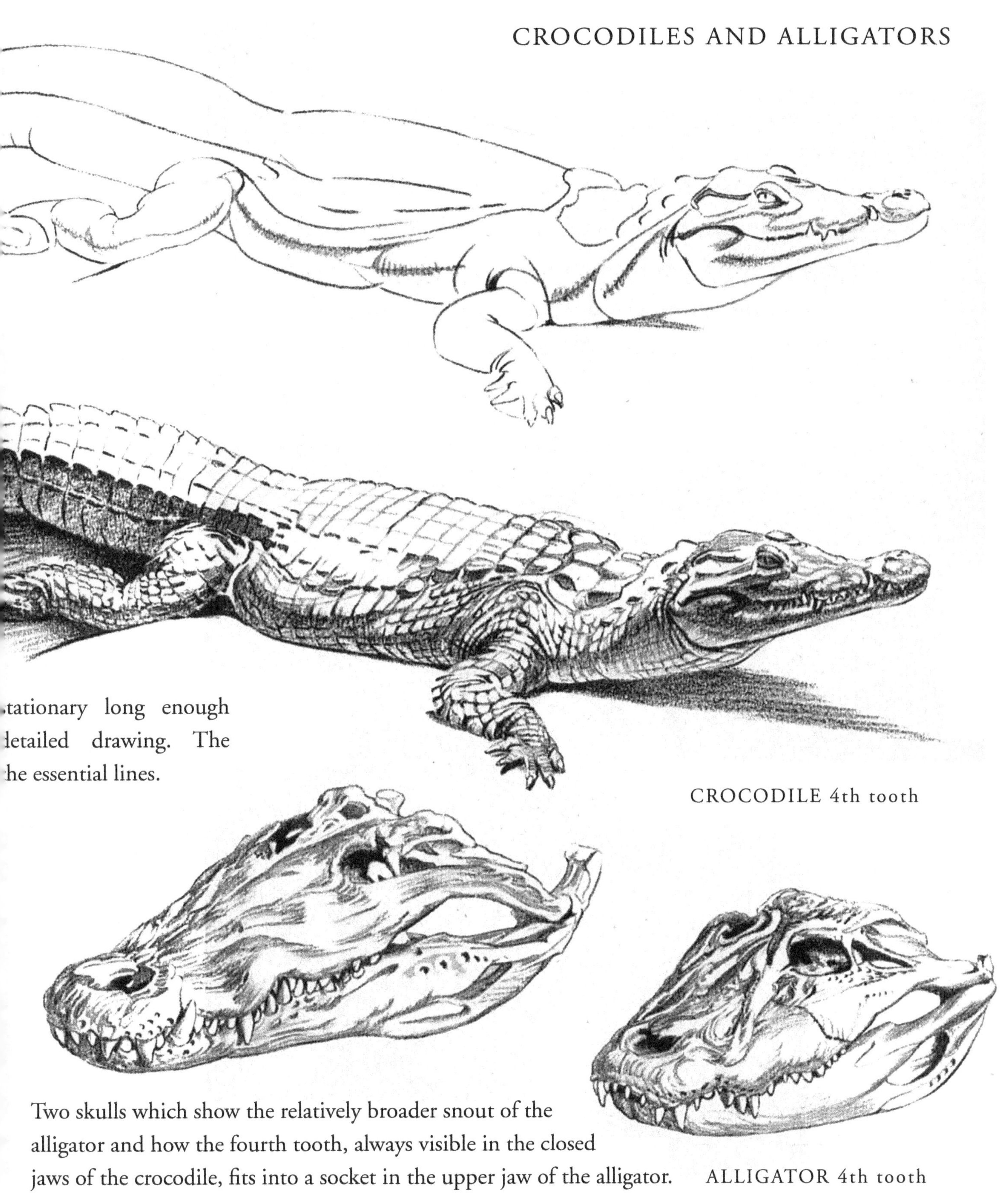

ꞏtationary long enough
ꞏletailed drawing. The
ꞏhe essential lines.

Two skulls which show the relatively broader snout of the alligator and how the fourth tooth, always visible in the closed jaws of the crocodile, fits into a socket in the upper jaw of the alligator.

HIPPOPOTAMUS AND RHINOCEROS

Two hippos basking in the late afternoon sun gave me an opportunity to make these studies on toned paper with black and white chalk. Although such an ungainly beast I enjoyed drawing his full rich forms. A good subject for a beginner because his form is large and simple to realise. All the real interest is in the head and feet.

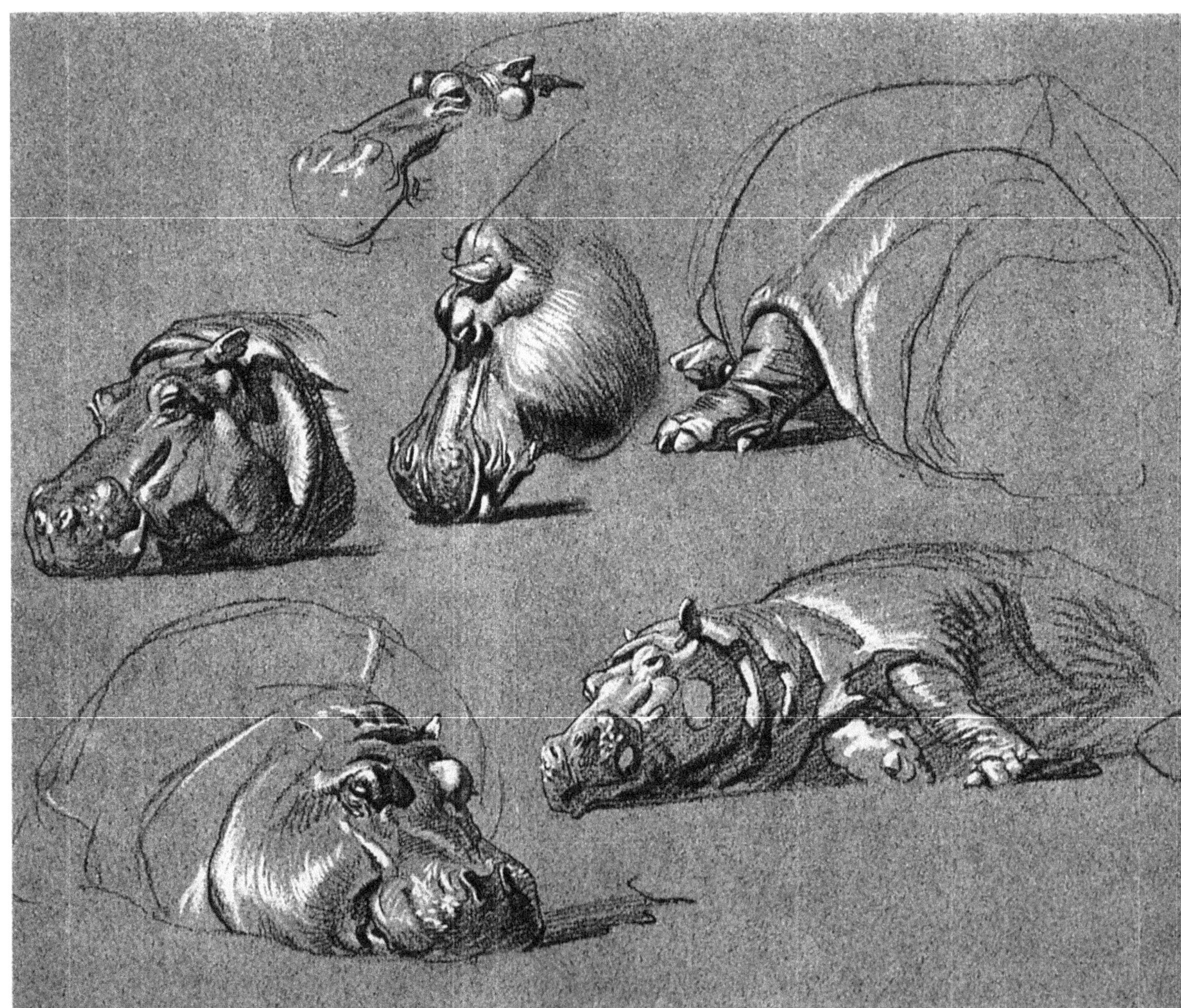

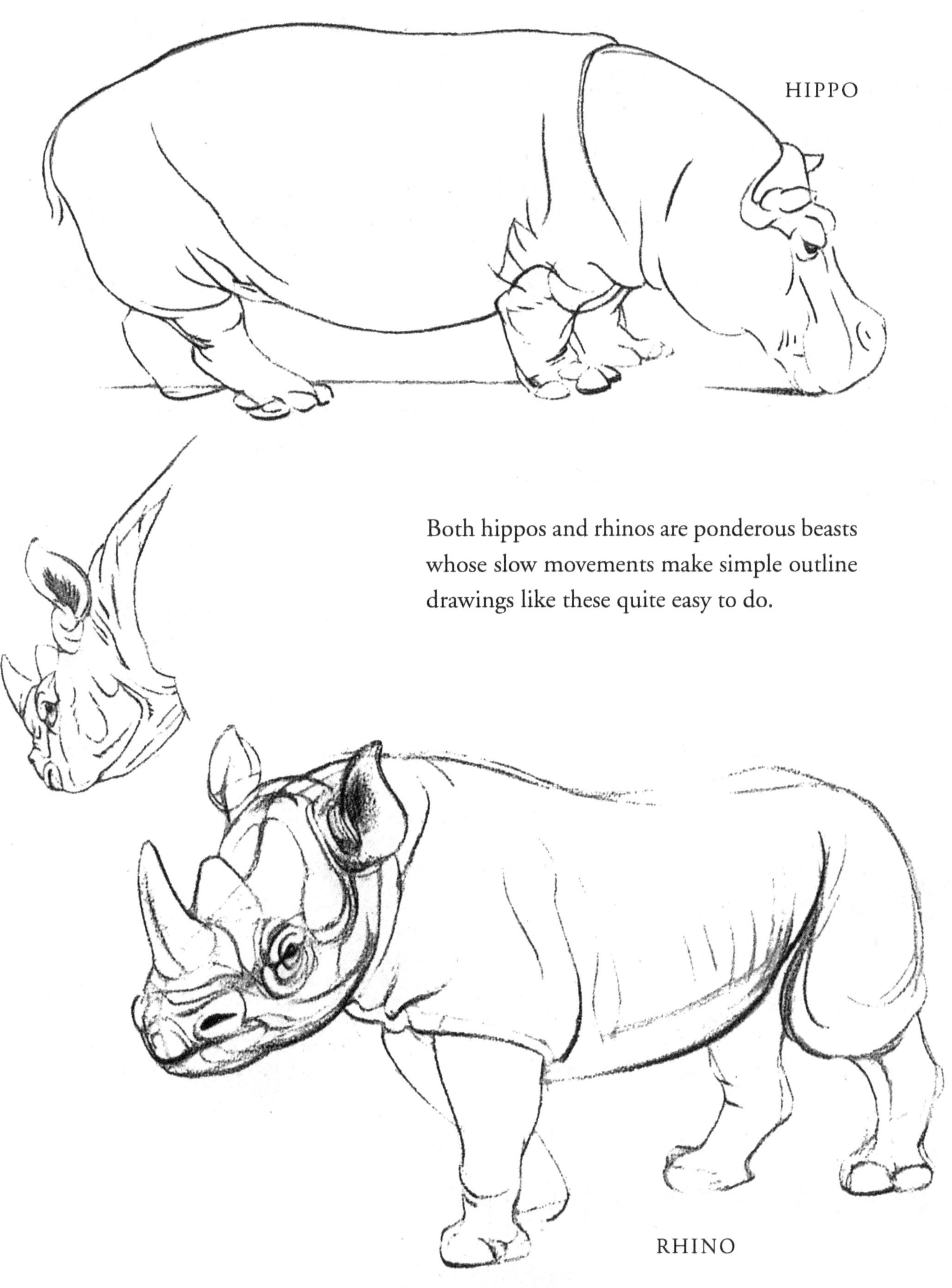

Both hippos and rhinos are ponderous beasts whose slow movements make simple outline drawings like these quite easy to do.

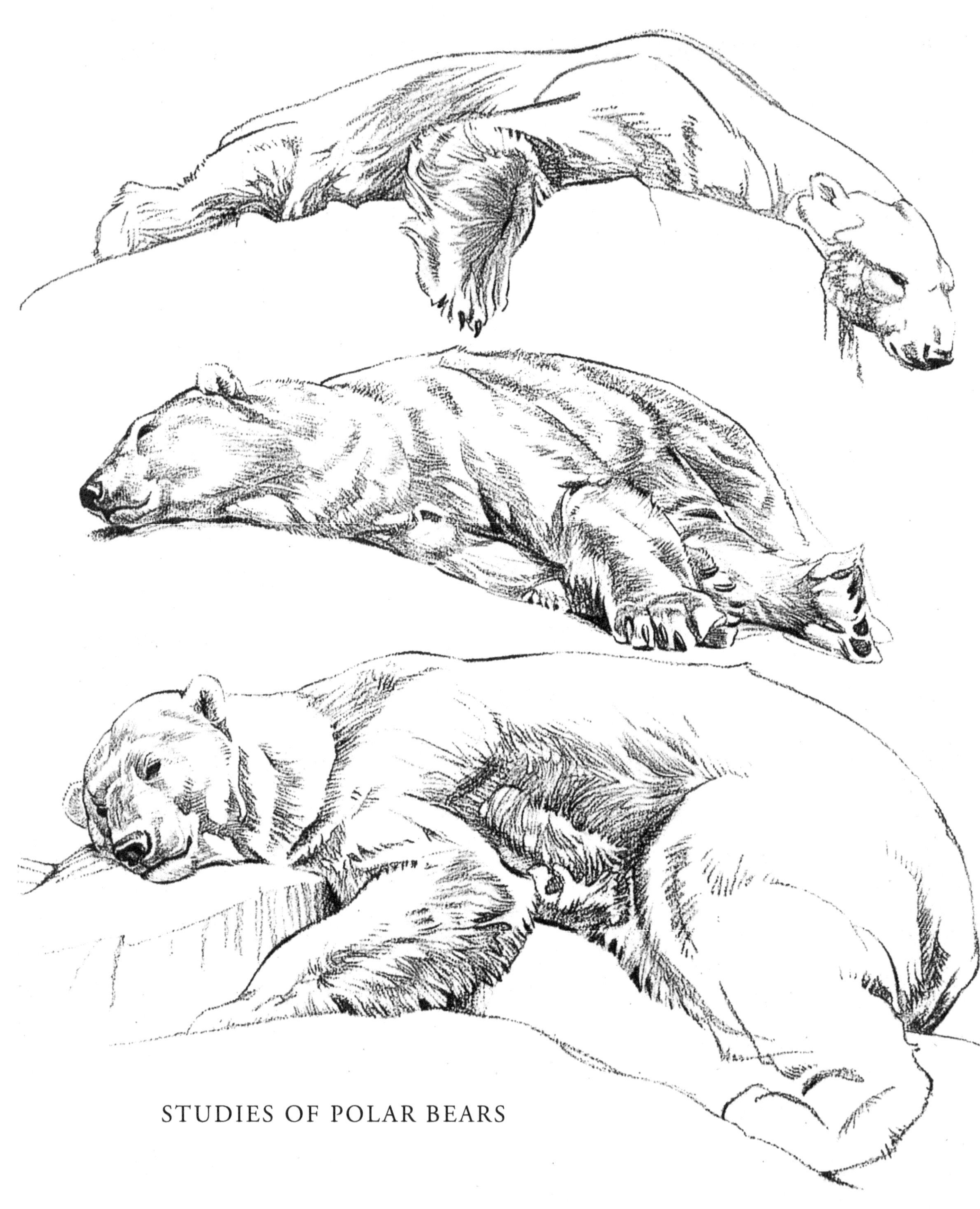

STUDIES OF POLAR BEARS

After you have drawn these polar bears enjoying a sunbath, you will know quite a lot about their shape. Watch them when they walk about and when they pause either to sit down or have a drink. Try and get down on paper with those same long selective kind of lines you used in drawing the lizards. It doesn't take many lines to summarise such momentary pauses. Just a few in the right place.

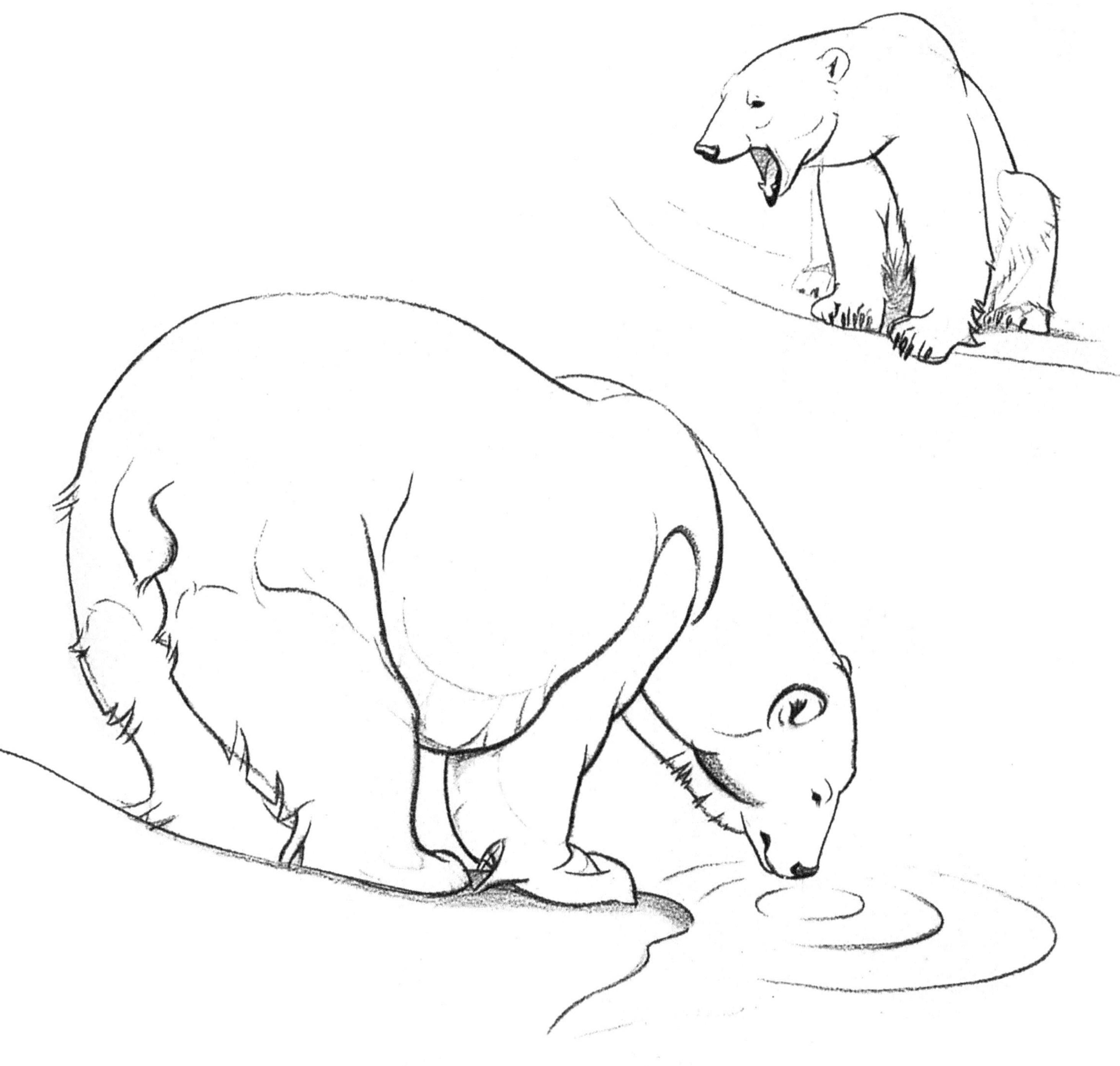

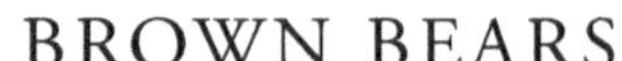

BROWN BEARS

These are a little more active. Use a blunt piece of charcoal or conté and go for the main masses and shapes quite freely. You will get breadth of treatment in this way. So far I have encouraged you to depict only seated animals, or at the most active, these pauses between movements. I shall come to real animal action in a page or two.

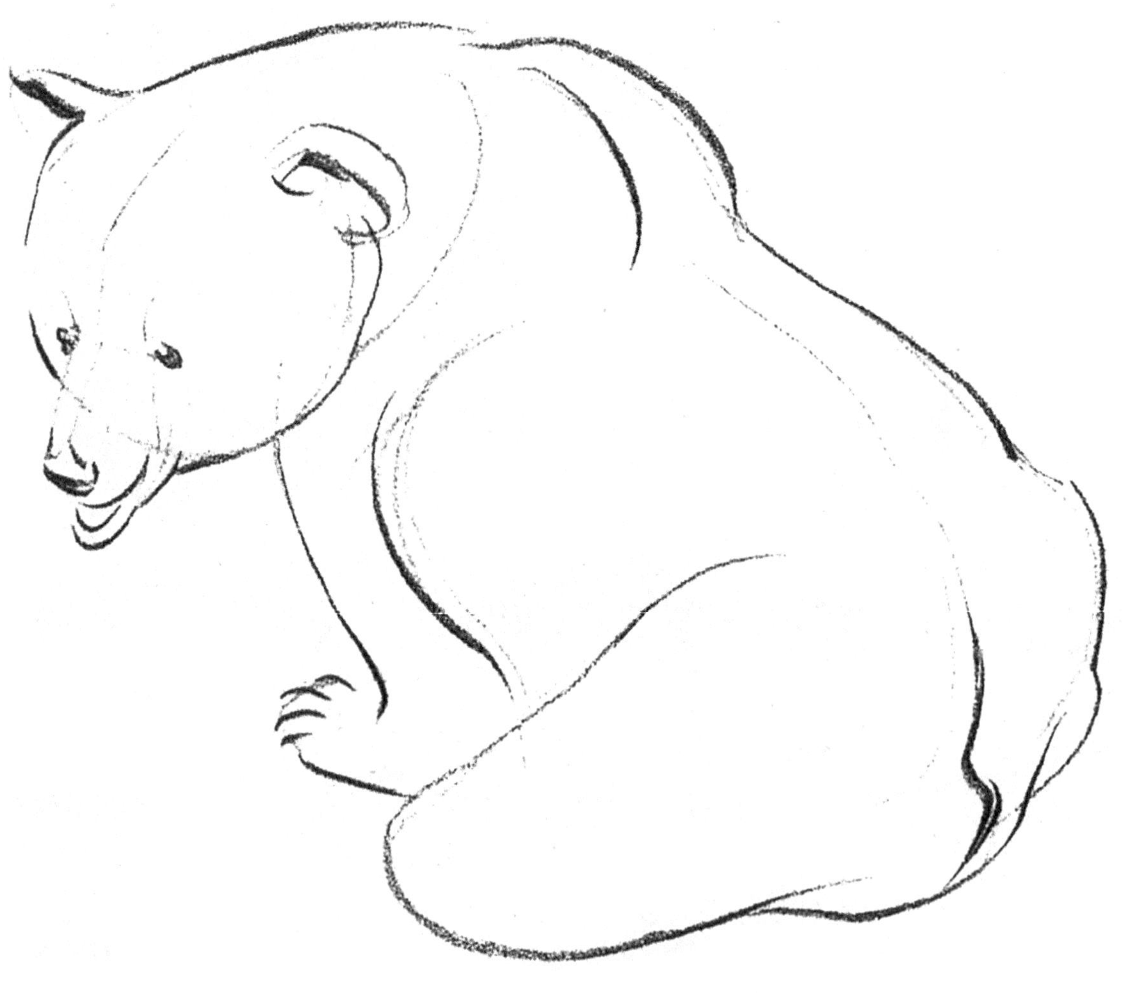

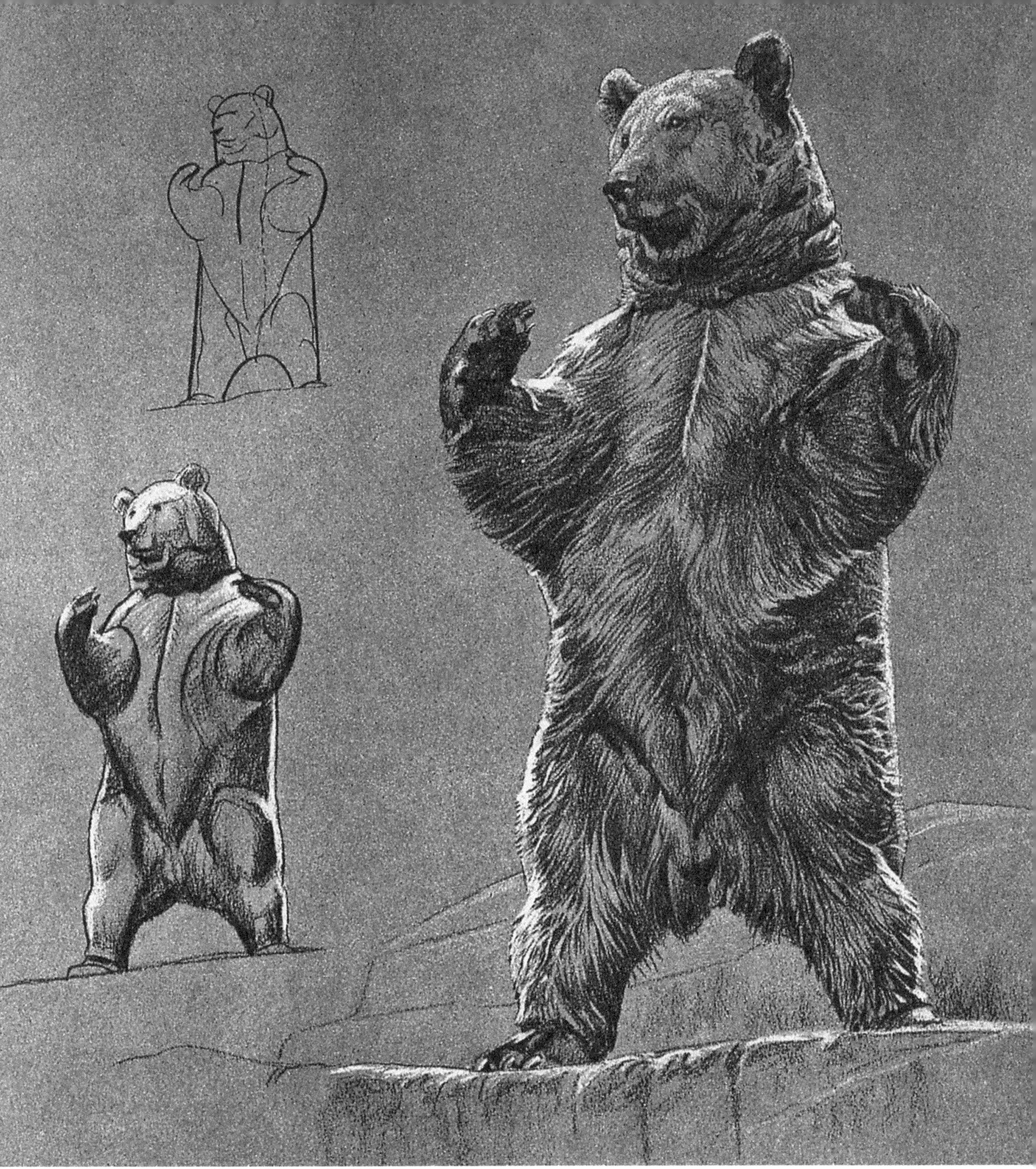

A more ambitious drawing. This chap loves standing up and begging for buns. A friend armed with a good supply is a useful ally. The small diagrams show how to begin and the big shapes to look for.

DRAWING THE TIGER AND LIONESS

Of all the large cats, the tiger is my favourite. What a splendid model he makes either asleep or resting. Seize every opportunity to depict any unusual attitude such as the one on this page of a tiger resting on his back. It gives you such valuable information about foreshortened form.

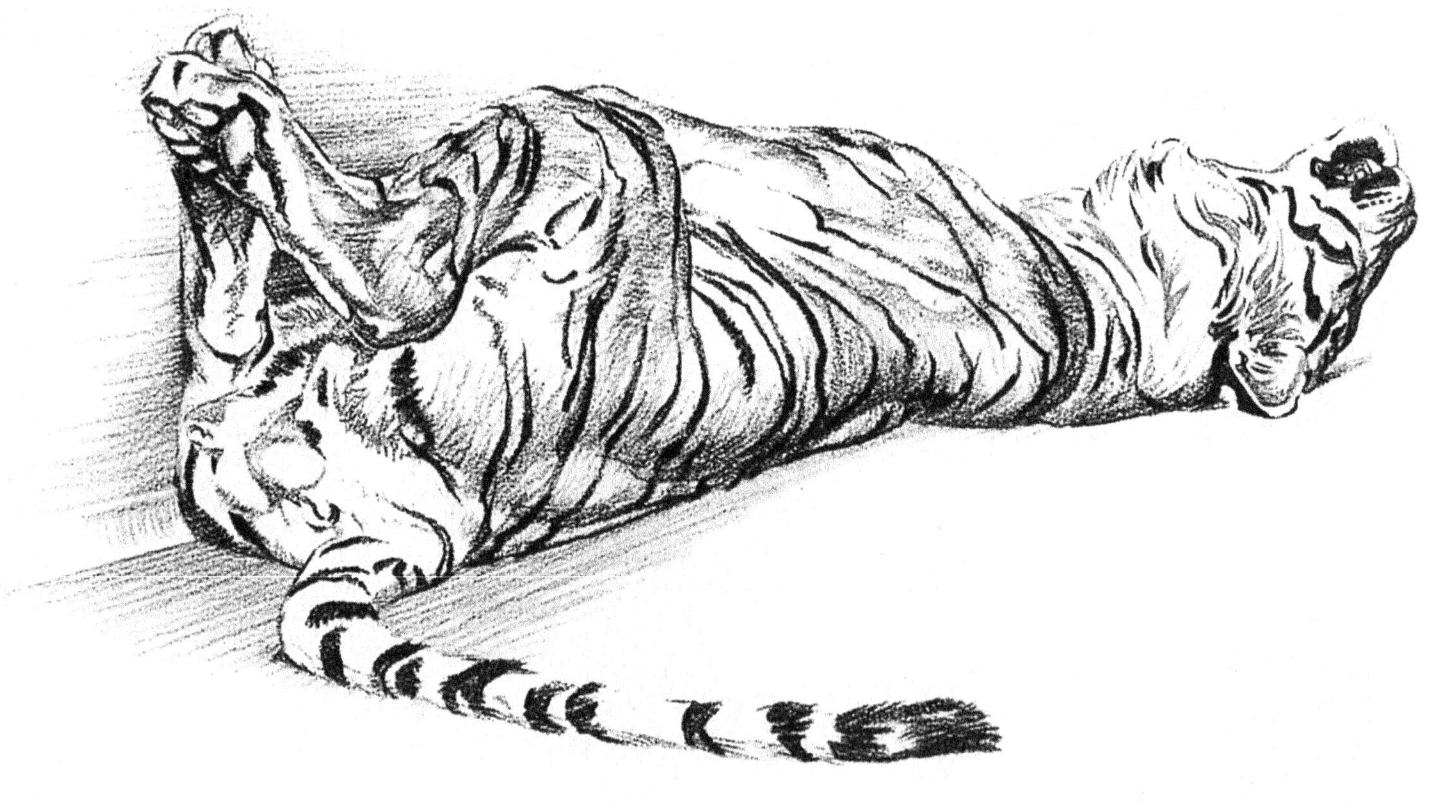

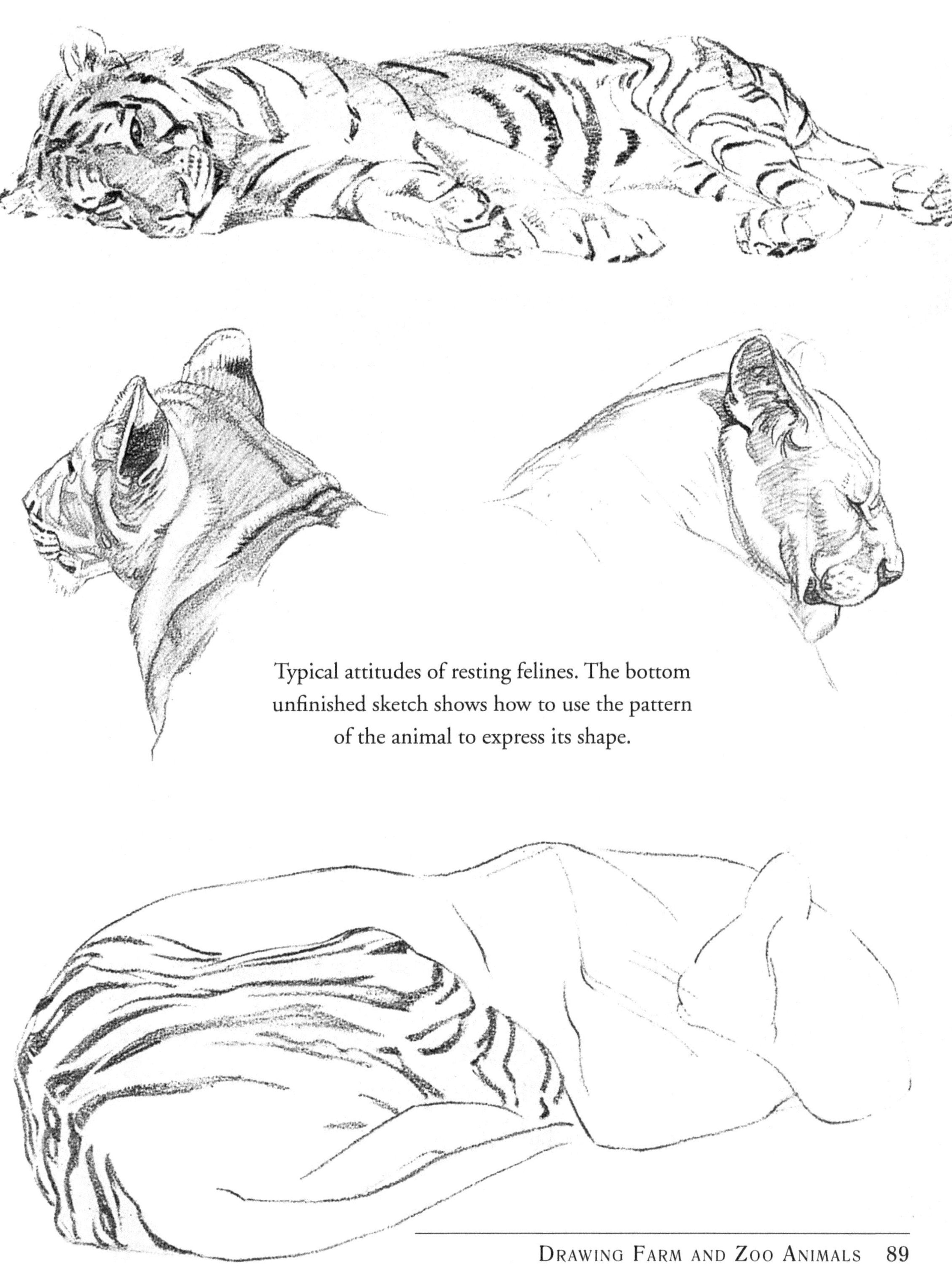

Typical attitudes of resting felines. The bottom unfinished sketch shows how to use the pattern of the animal to express its shape.

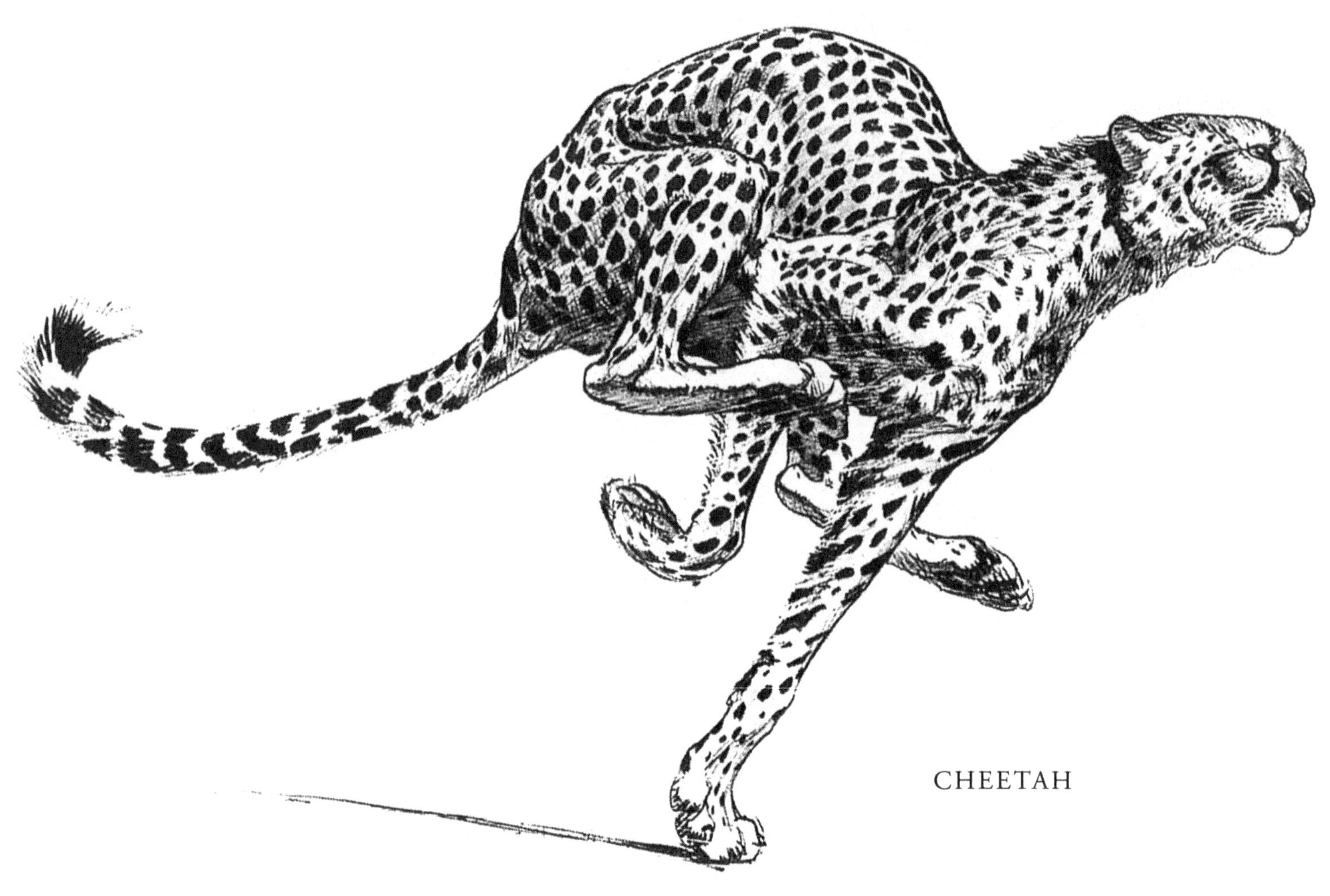

CHEETAH

ANIMAL MOVEMENT

We come now to that most exciting sort of animal drawing—animals in action. Some actions, like that of the cheetah running at top speed can only be drawn from memory, using previous knowledge, experience and imagination. The study of slow-motion films can be very helpful, so much better than a still photograph which 'freezes' the animal without showing that continuous flow of movement so lovely in the living creature. The photograph shows one instant of one phase of action. Your drawing can do more. It must suggest both the phase that precedes and that which follows an action. One drawing may contain several phases of action. It can never be photographically accurate if it is to show real movement.

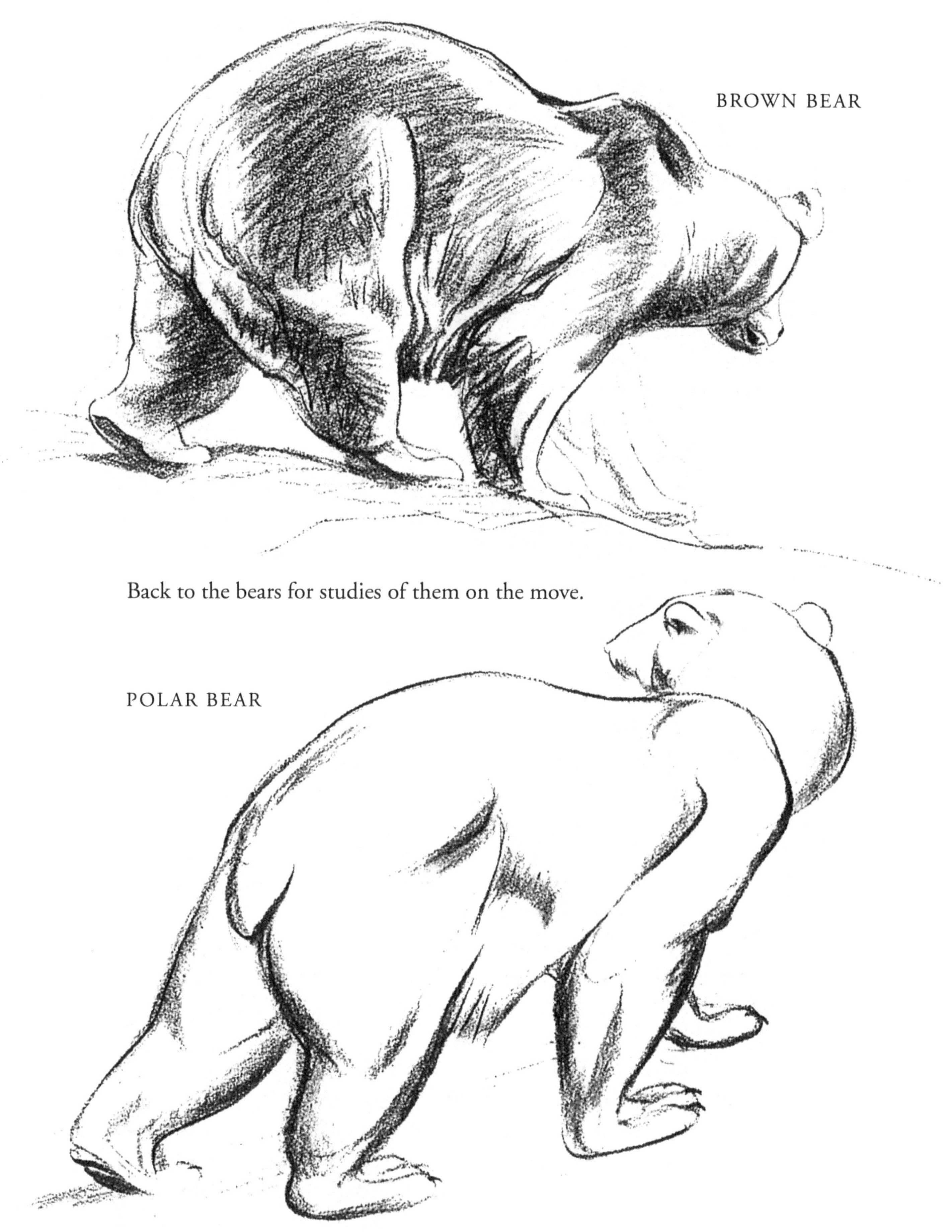

BROWN BEAR

Back to the bears for studies of them on the move.

POLAR BEAR

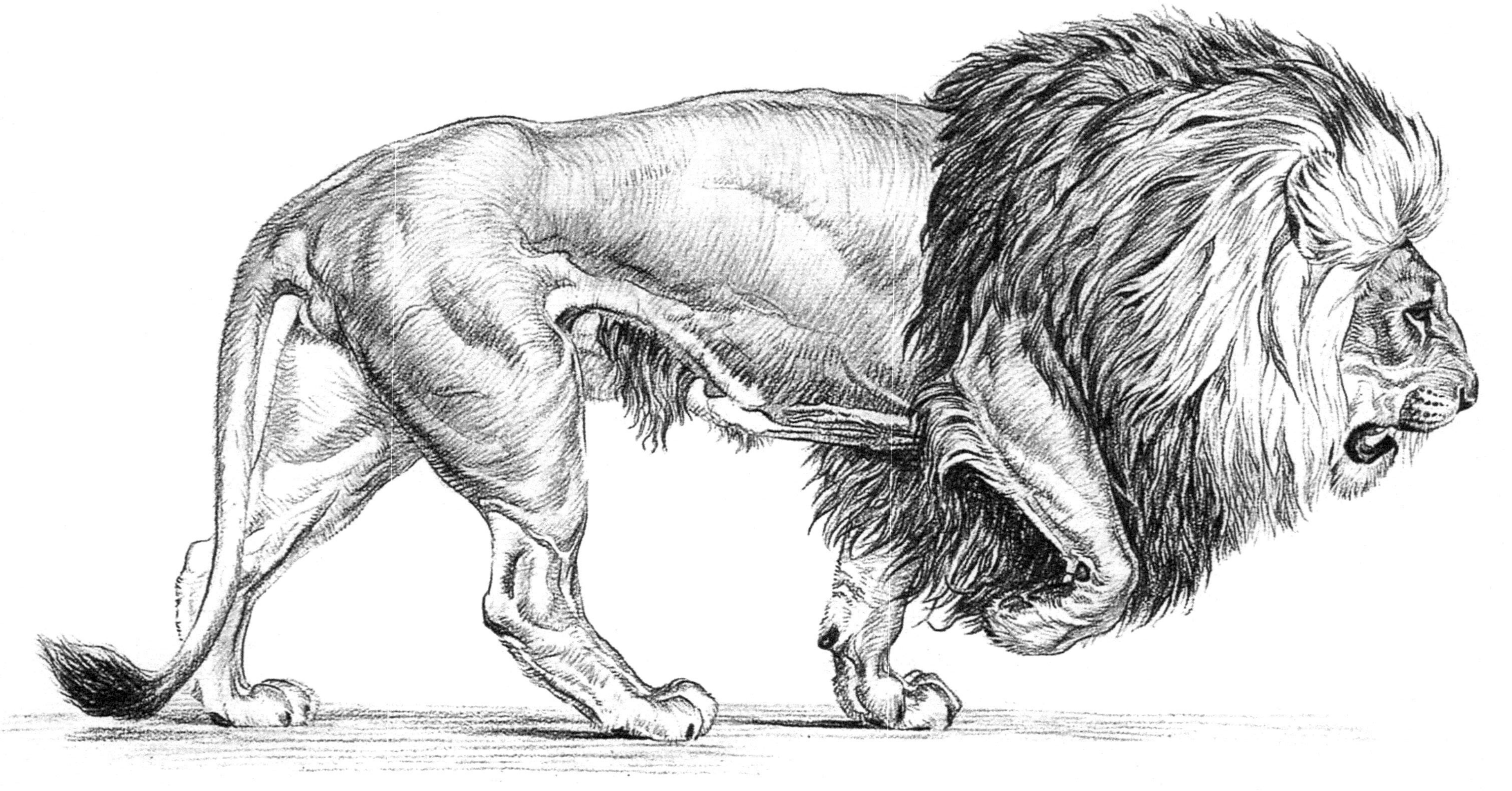

THE LION WALKS

You may now feel confident enough to attempt a drawing such as the lion walking. In the diagram I have shown in heavy black the lines that I feel contain the rhythms of the walk. The lighter pencillings indicate points of structure.

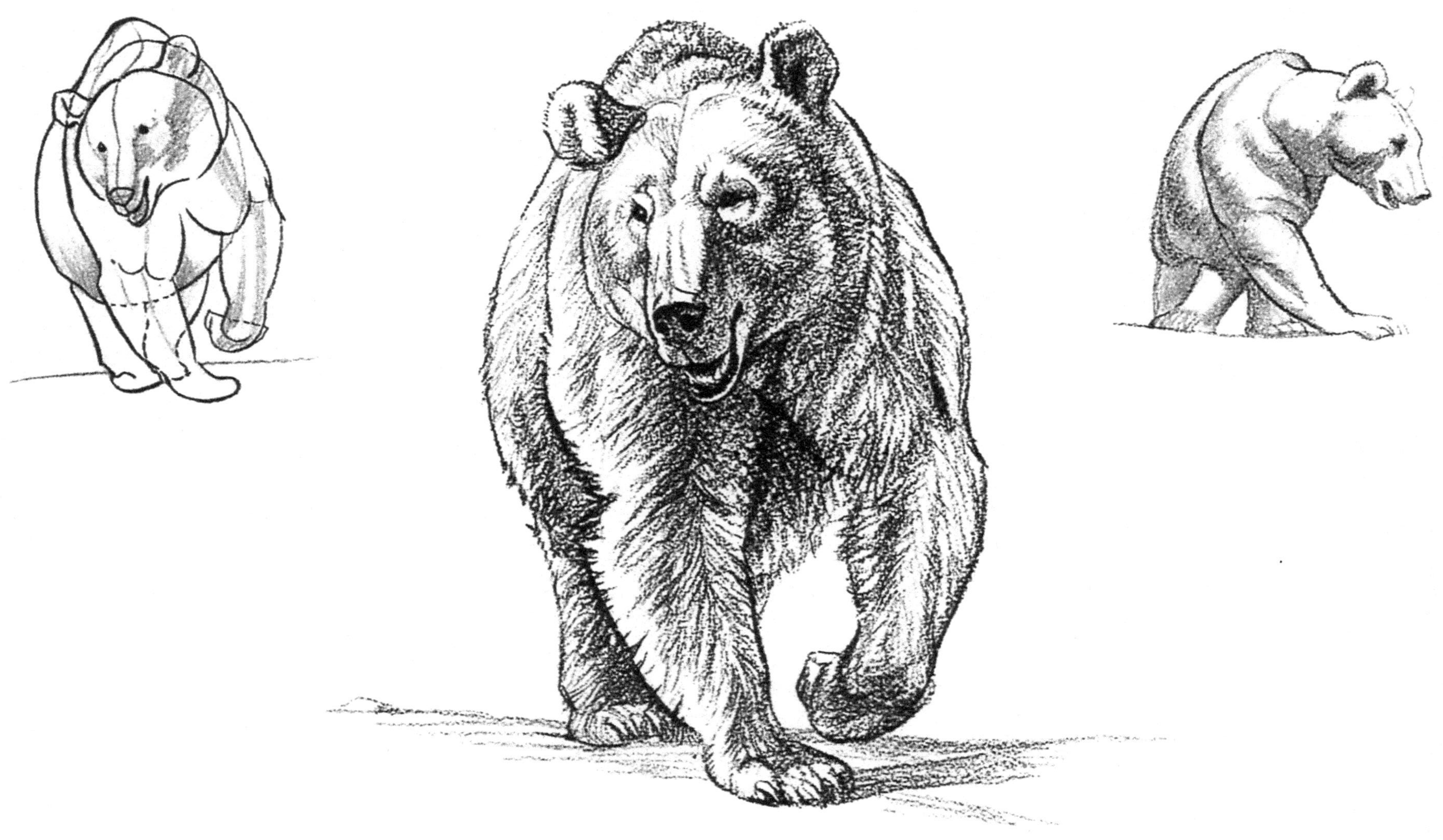

This old Syrian bear proved to be a more difficult subject but he kept on walking round in a circle long enough for me to make a fairly sustained study. The small diagram in the top left-hand corner shows a way of realising the rather extreme foreshortening by considering the forms to be moulded in some transparent substance and then drawing the overlapping forms. Top right shows a violent opposition of form when he decided to turn in the opposite direction.

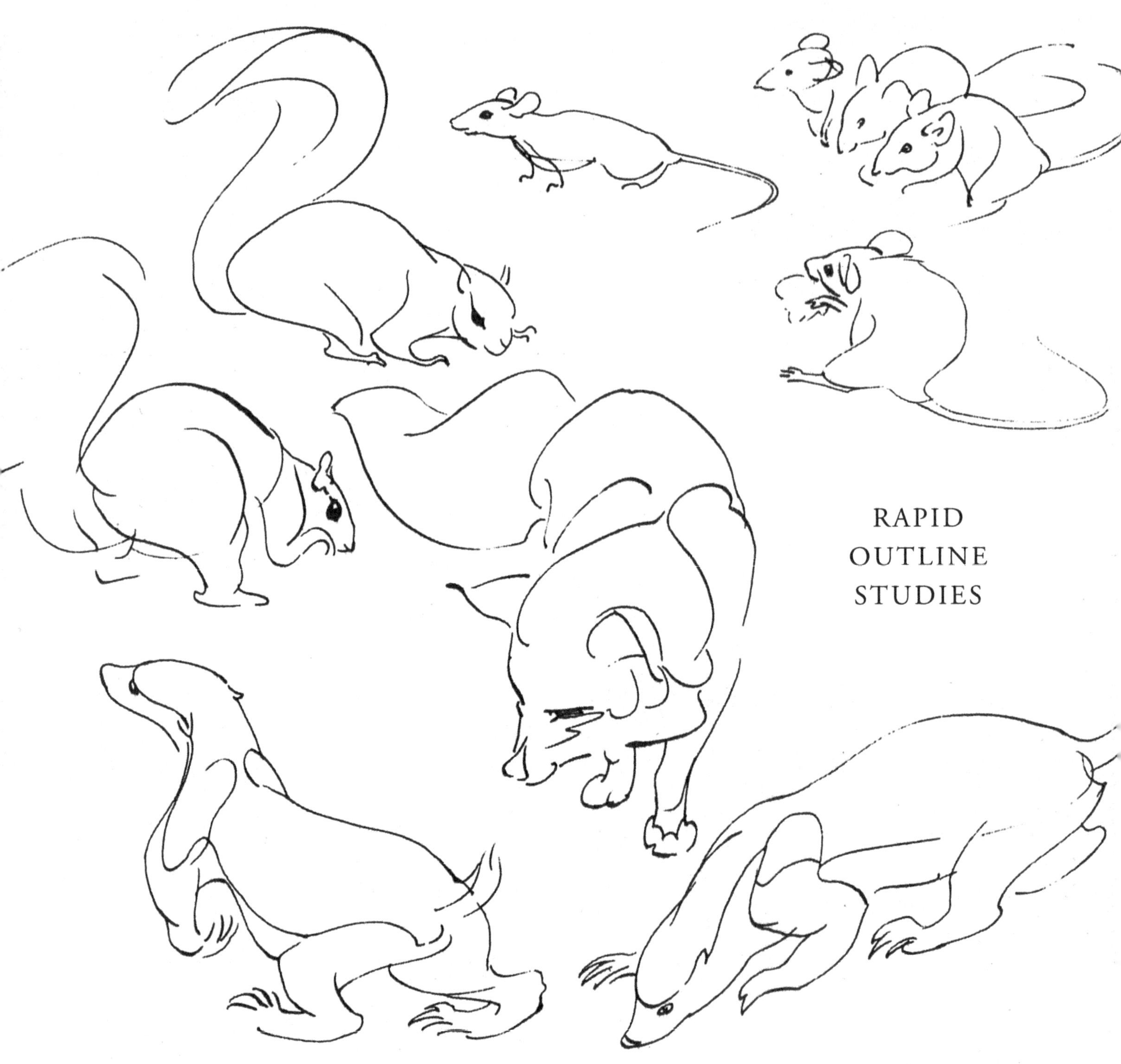

RAPID OUTLINE STUDIES

Try drawing quickly and freely with a fountain pen. Make many such drawings. In this way you will get a fluent style. Observe the animal steadily for some time and then, without looking up from your paper, draw the whole animal as rapidly as possible with as long and continuous a line as possible. By doing so you have to ignore details and concentrate on main characteristics.

THE PANDA This lovable animal is an ideal subject from which to make outline studies.

When you get home you can fill in the black pattern with a brush.
Better still try and draw him again from memory.

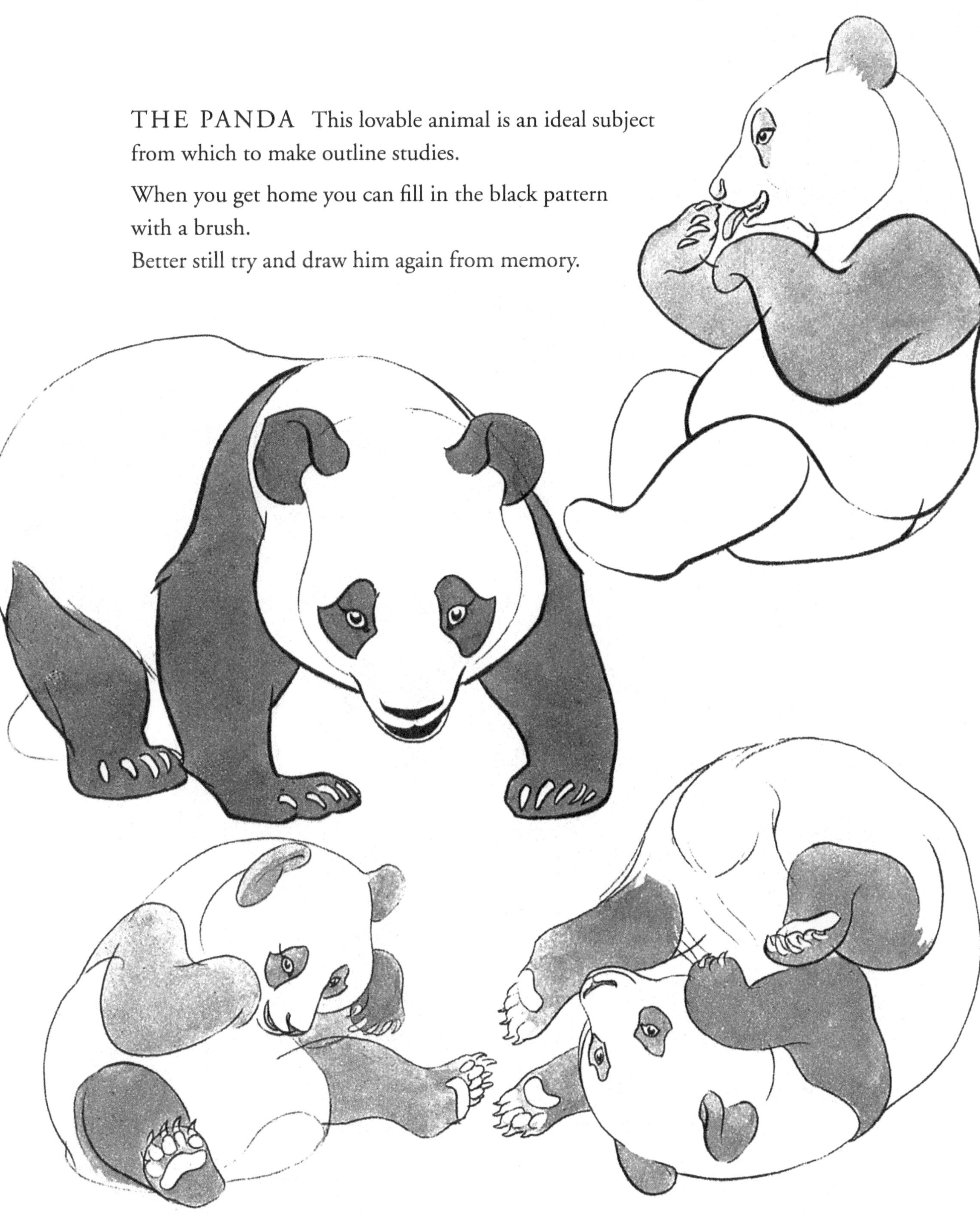

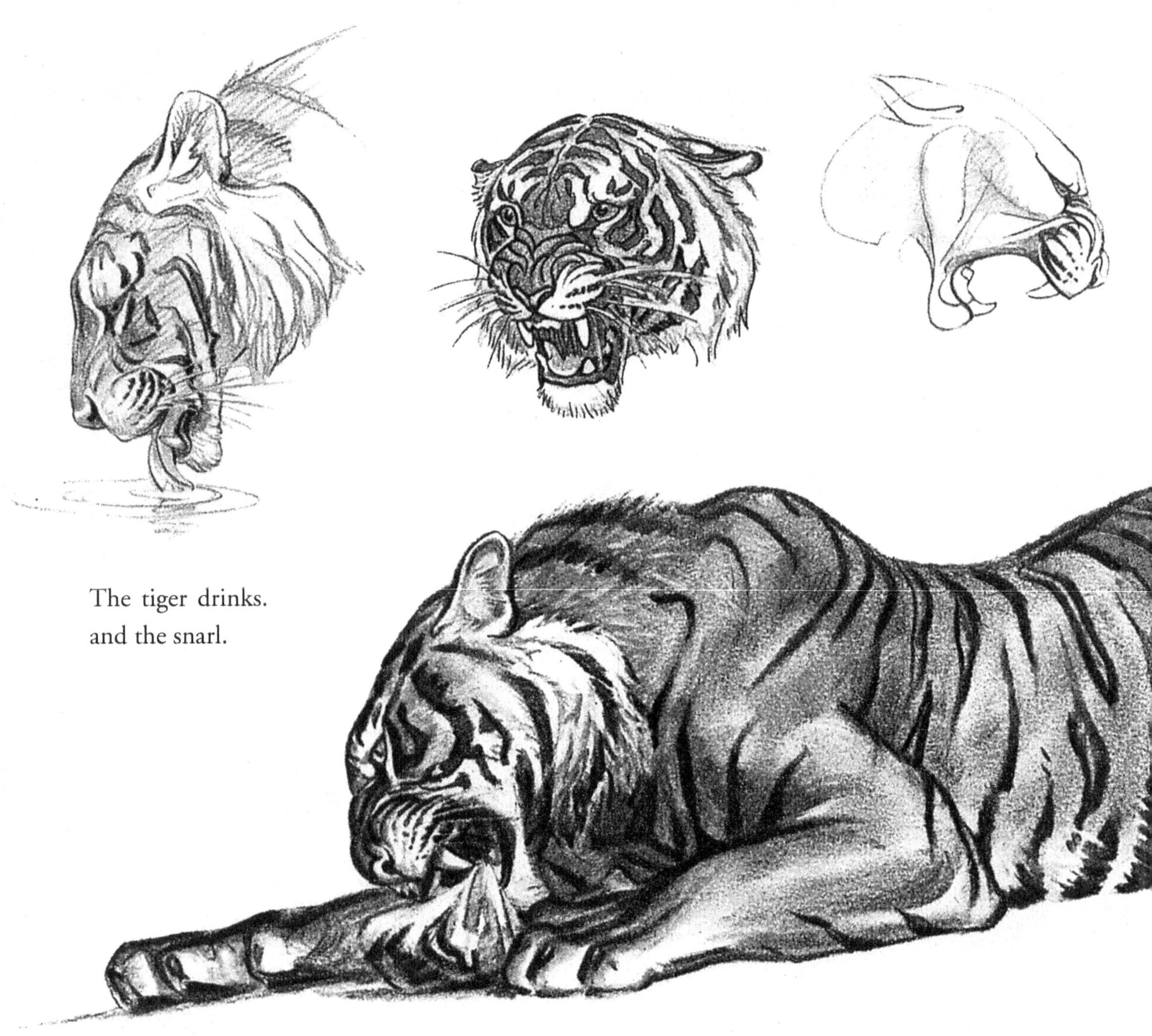

The tiger drinks.
and the snarl.

THE TIGER DINES

The animals know when feeding time approaches and get very animated as they run excitedly up and down their cages. This excitement is infectious and one works with breathless speed to get down on paper something of the real litheness and supple grace.

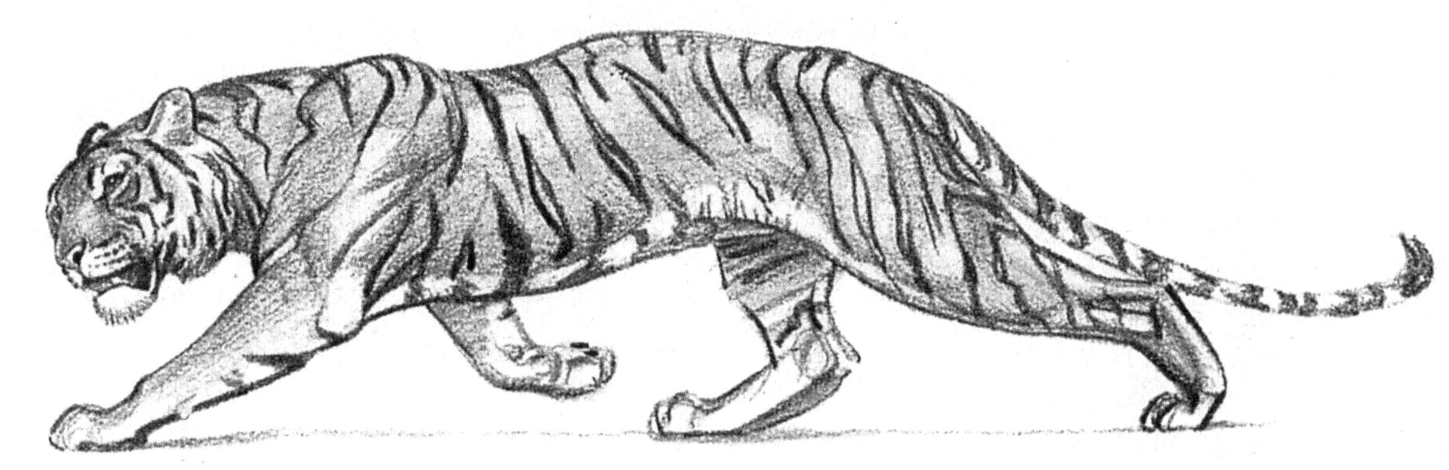

A memory drawing of the tiger running up and down in anticipation of his meal. The large study of the feeding animal was drawn in charcoal. In the lower study I drew mainly the lines of pattern on the animal.

GIBBONS

The Zoo's trapeze artists who seem to fly through the air, so effortless is their swing. Your drawings should echo this fluent flow of line. Note the great length of the arms and the quaint way they are held when walking on the ground.

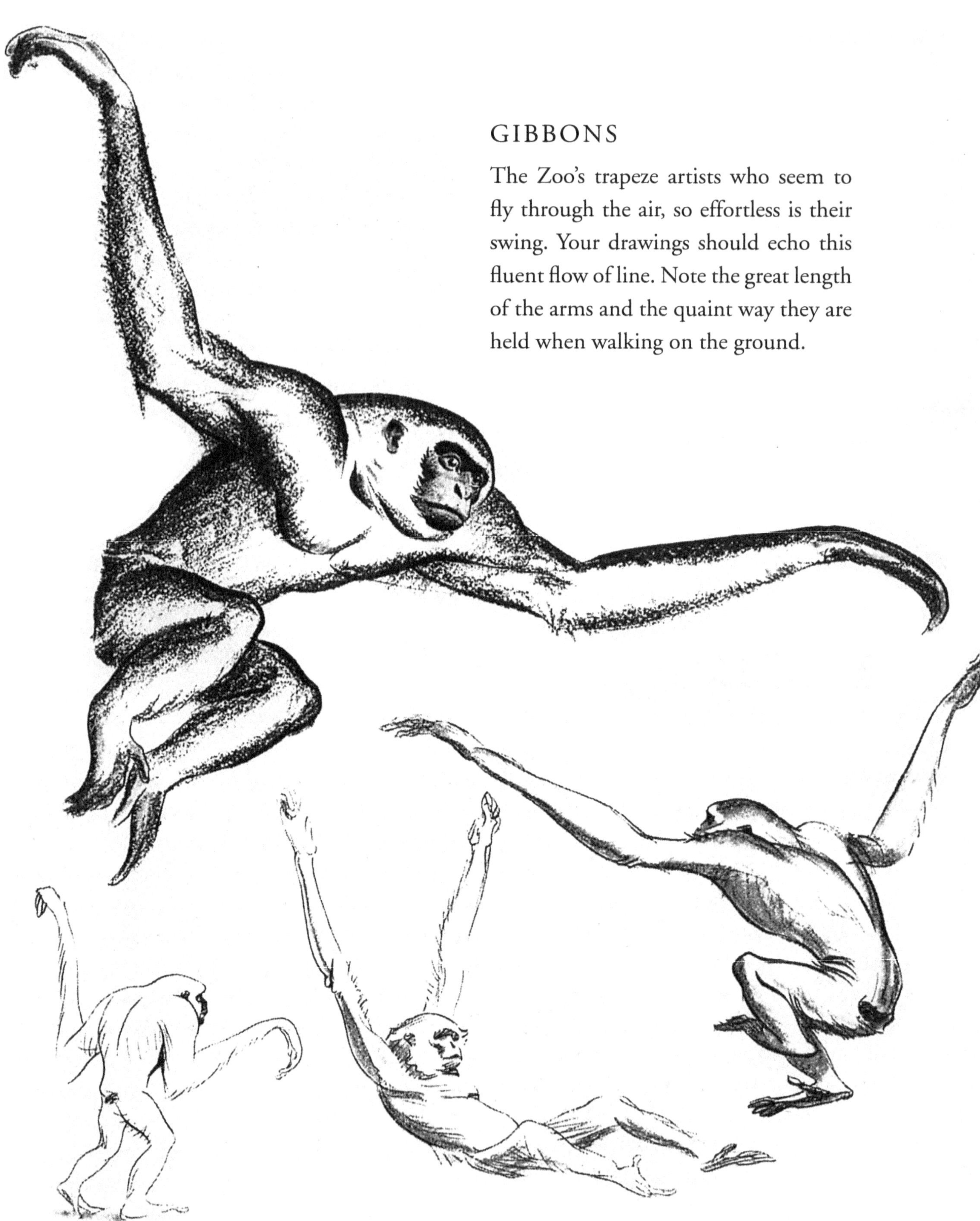

THE CHIMPANZEE

A droll clown whose near-human antics are an endless source of pleasure, and how he enjoys an audience! The young ape on the pole posed most obligingly for me.

I have tried to show how the face can be symbolised by emphasising the rhythmic relationship of the features. You'll enjoy yourself drawing these fellows.

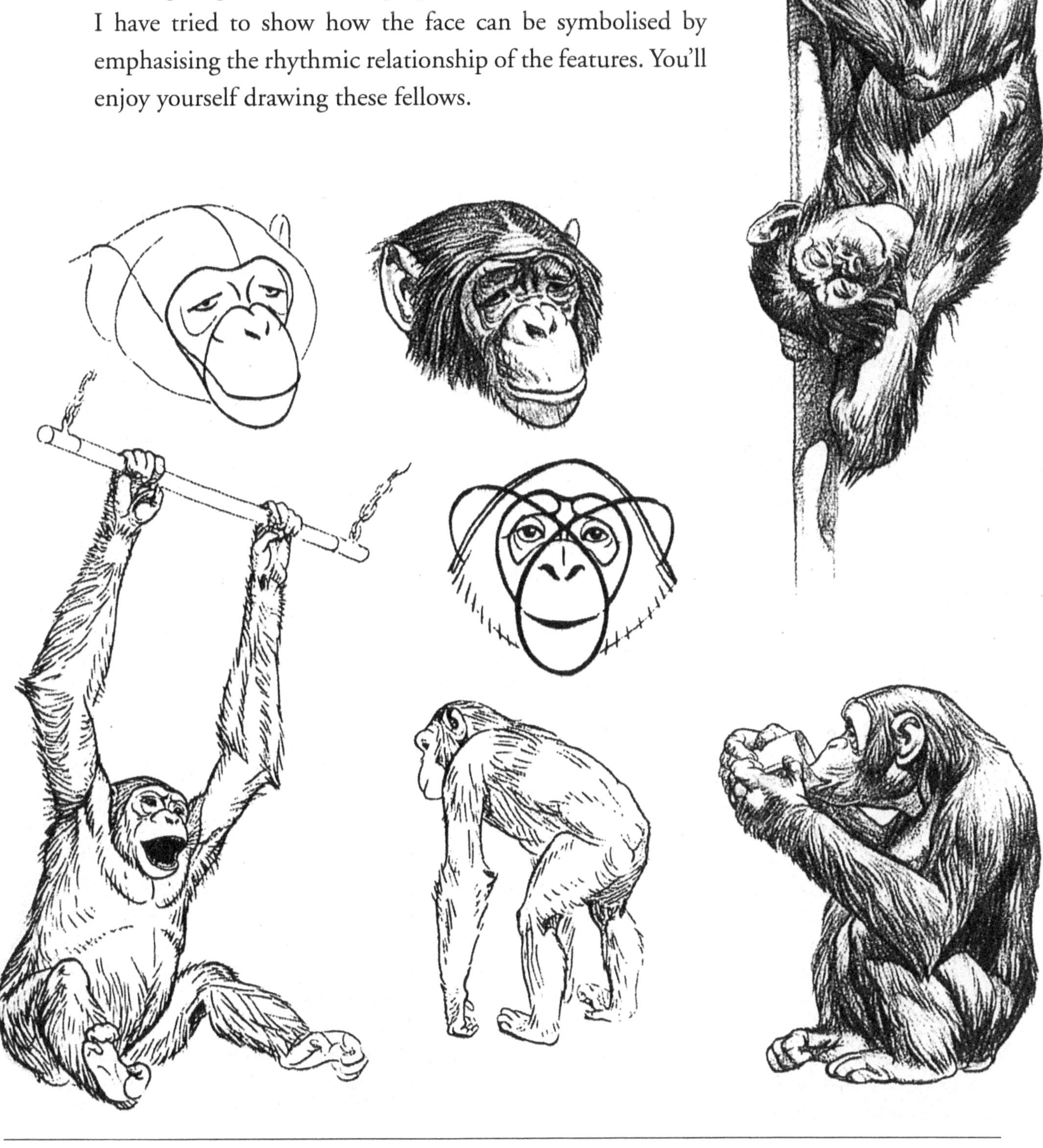

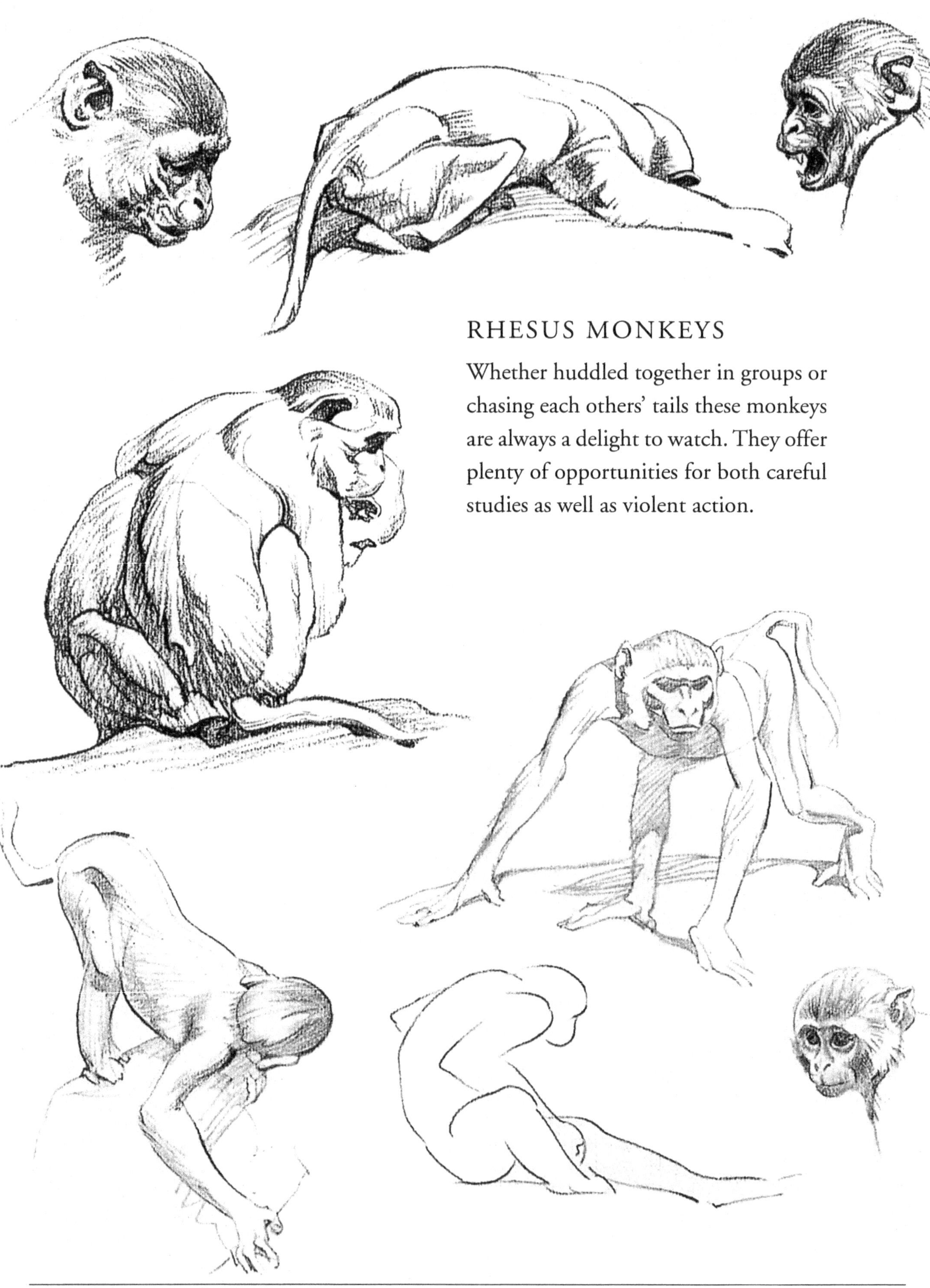

RHESUS MONKEYS

Whether huddled together in groups or chasing each others' tails these monkeys are always a delight to watch. They offer plenty of opportunities for both careful studies as well as violent action.

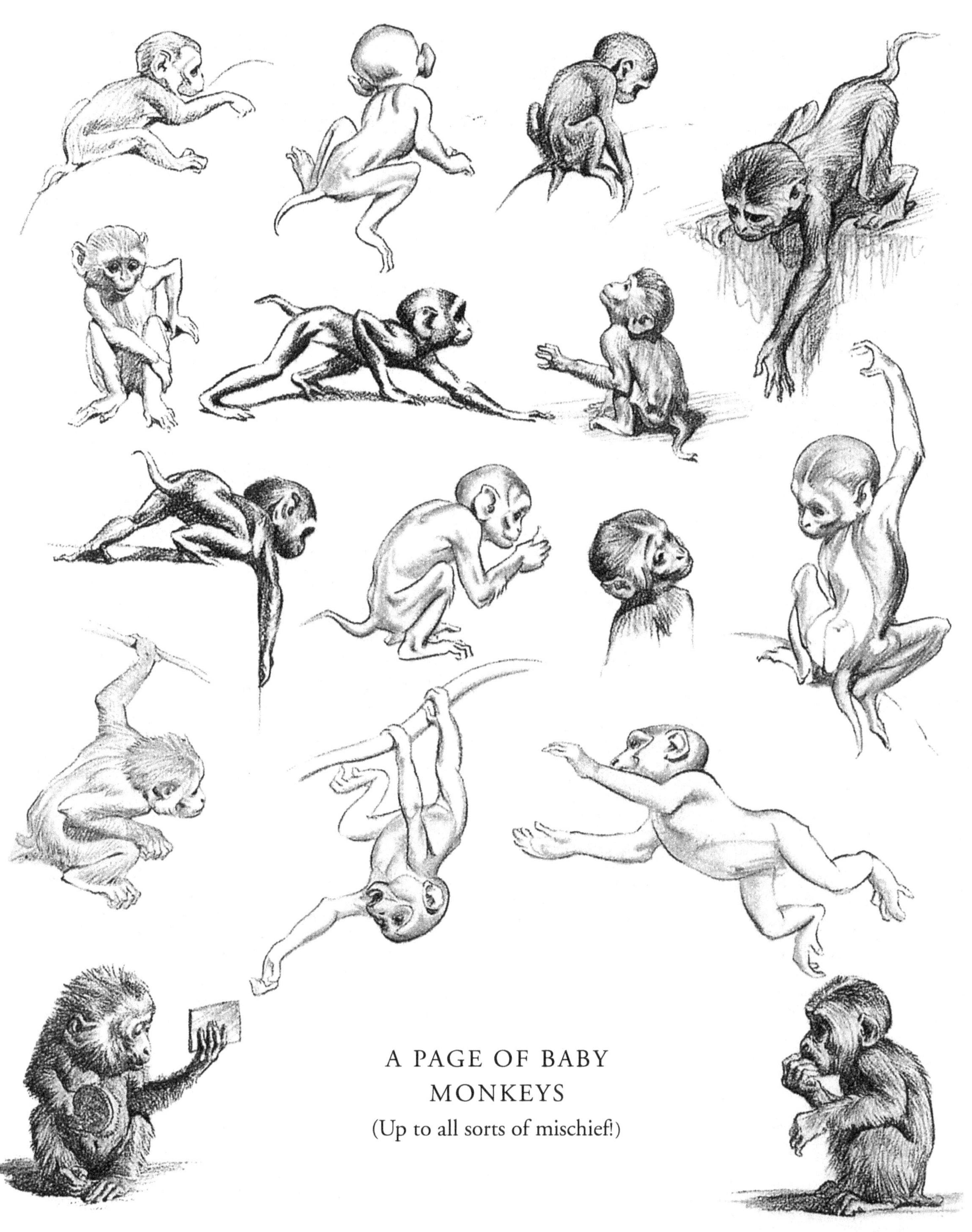

A PAGE OF BABY MONKEYS
(Up to all sorts of mischief!)

DRAWING ZOO BABIES

These are everybody's favourites. Emphasise those special characteristics which make them so appealing. The lion cubs' large fluffy paws and wistful regard; baby bears' woolly animation with twinkling beads for eyes, the fawns' large melting eyes and feylike leggy elegance.

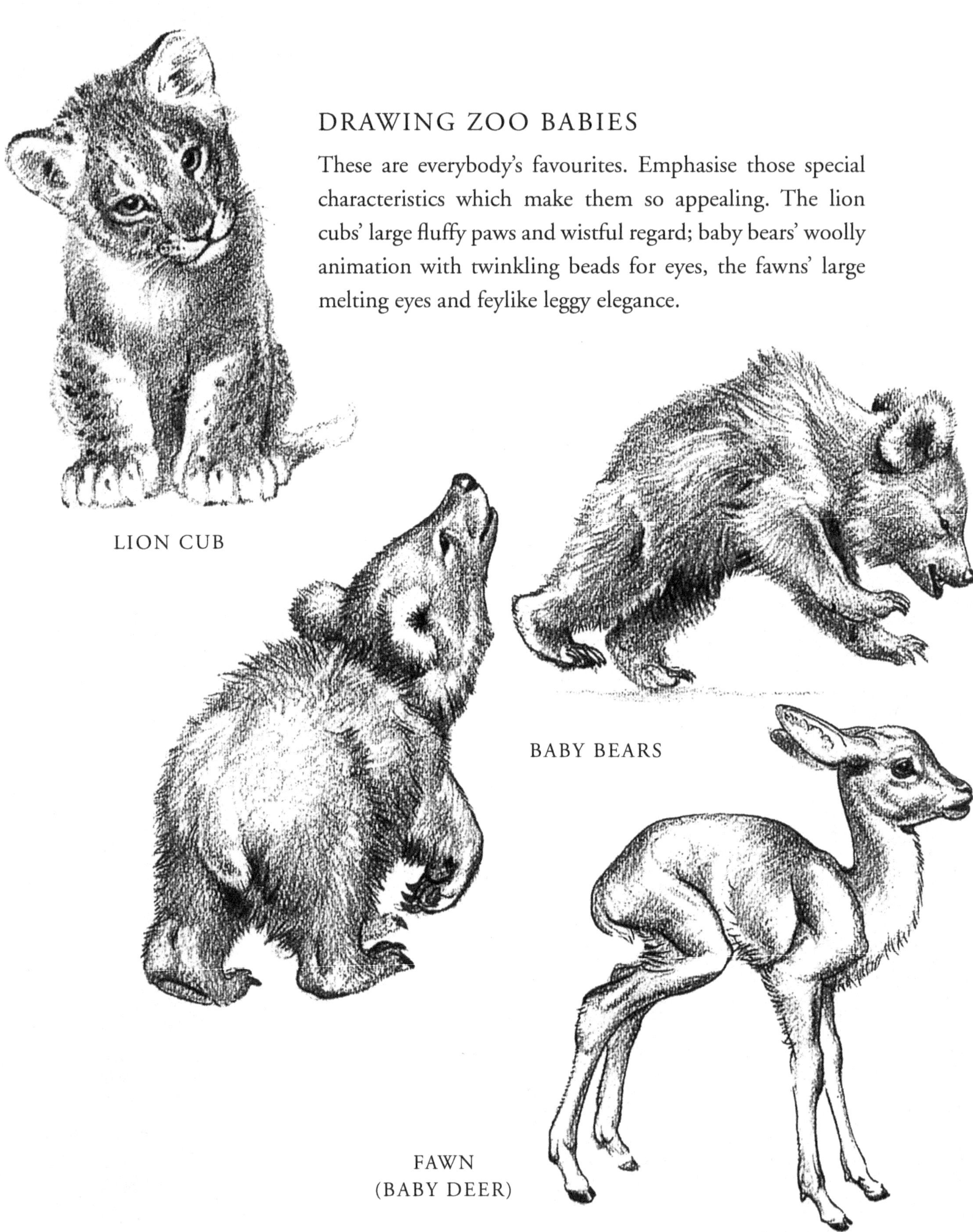

LION CUB

BABY BEARS

FAWN
(BABY DEER)

THE ANTELOPE

Here I have drawn the graceful Impala. This lovely form will stimulate you to go for all those qualities of rhythm and fluency of line I have been discussing. A nervous highly strung creature. A sympathetic approach will make your line equally nervous and sensitive as your pencil point explores the subtleties of form.

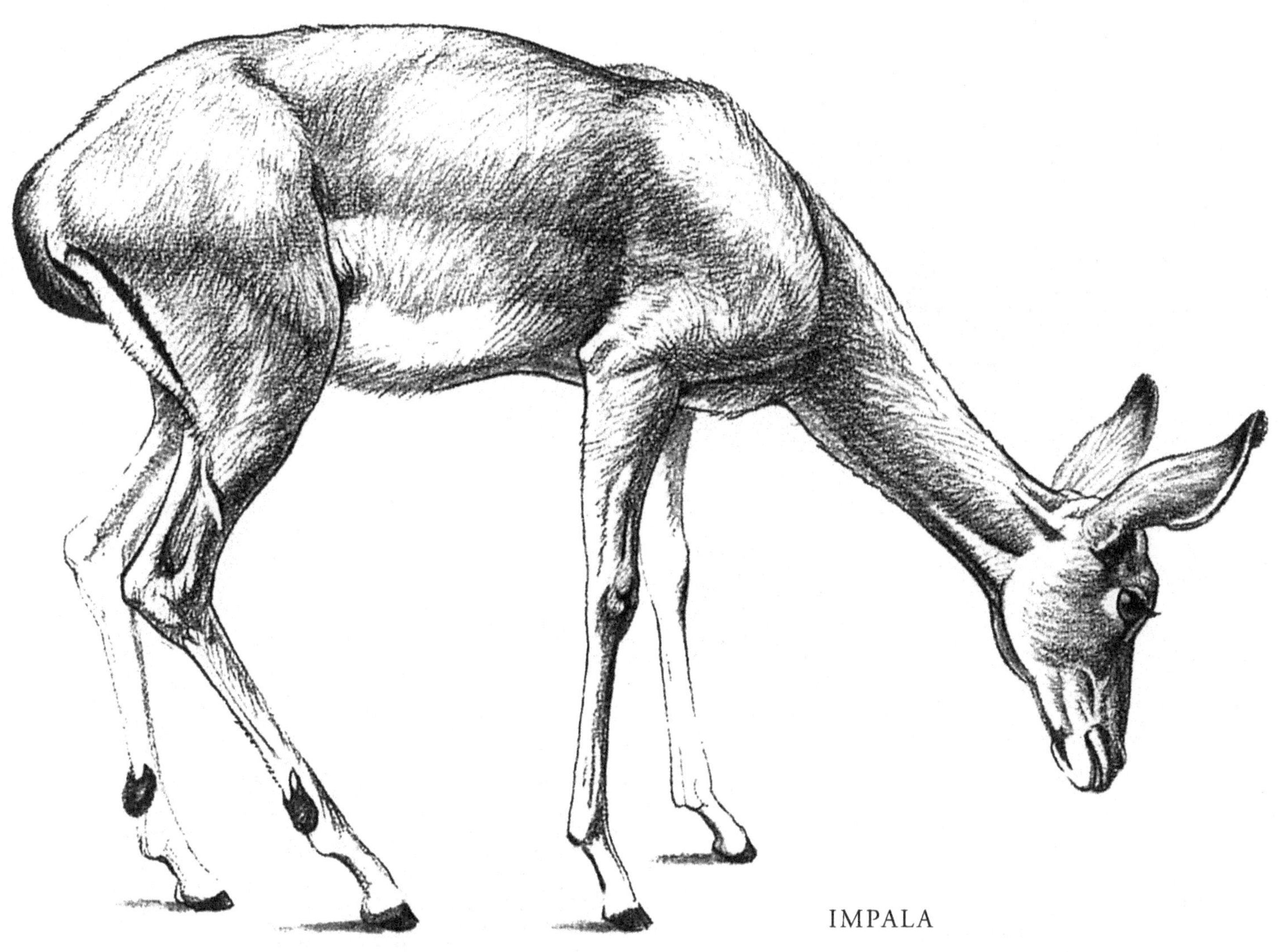

IMPALA

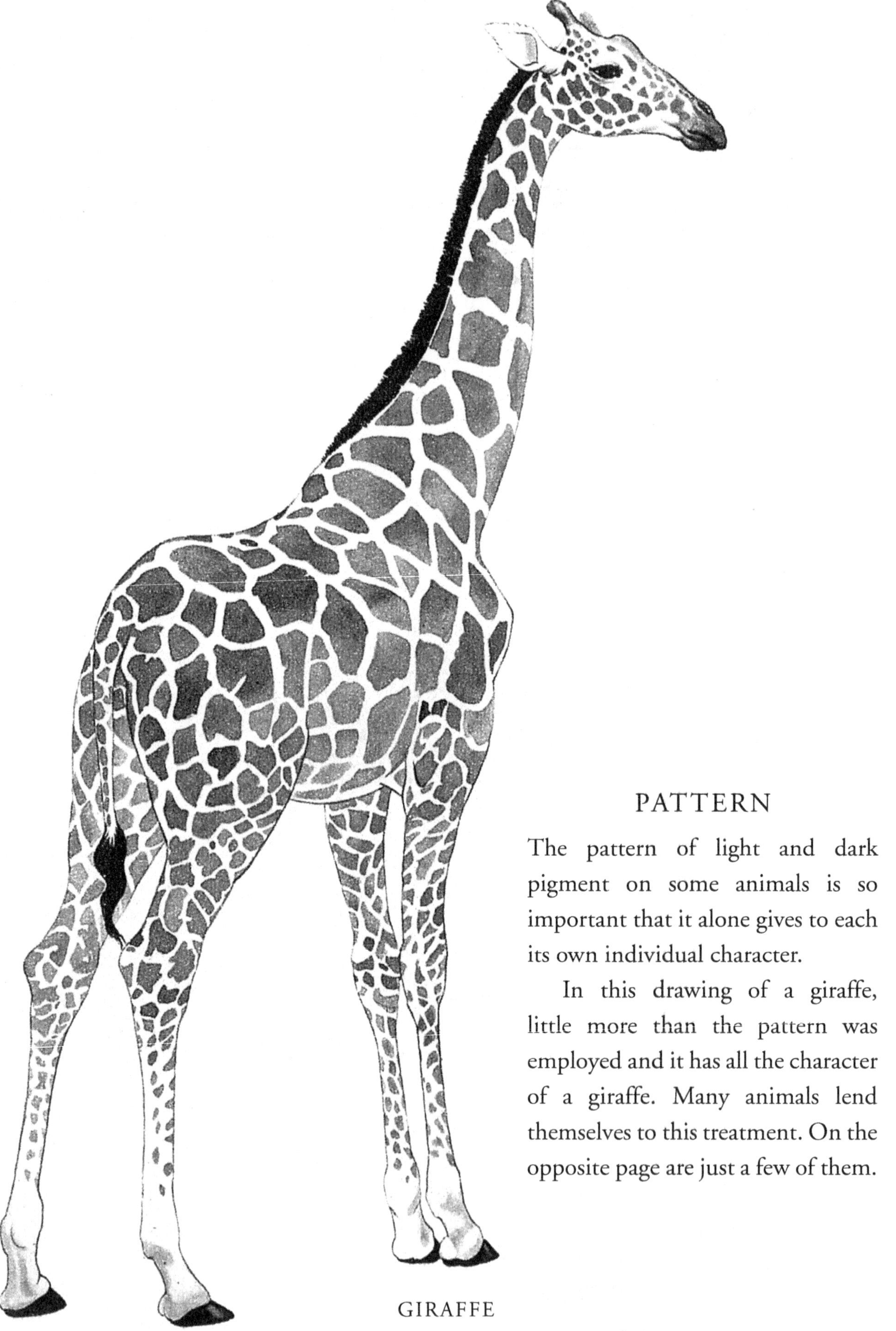

GIRAFFE

PATTERN

The pattern of light and dark pigment on some animals is so important that it alone gives to each its own individual character.

In this drawing of a giraffe, little more than the pattern was employed and it has all the character of a giraffe. Many animals lend themselves to this treatment. On the opposite page are just a few of them.

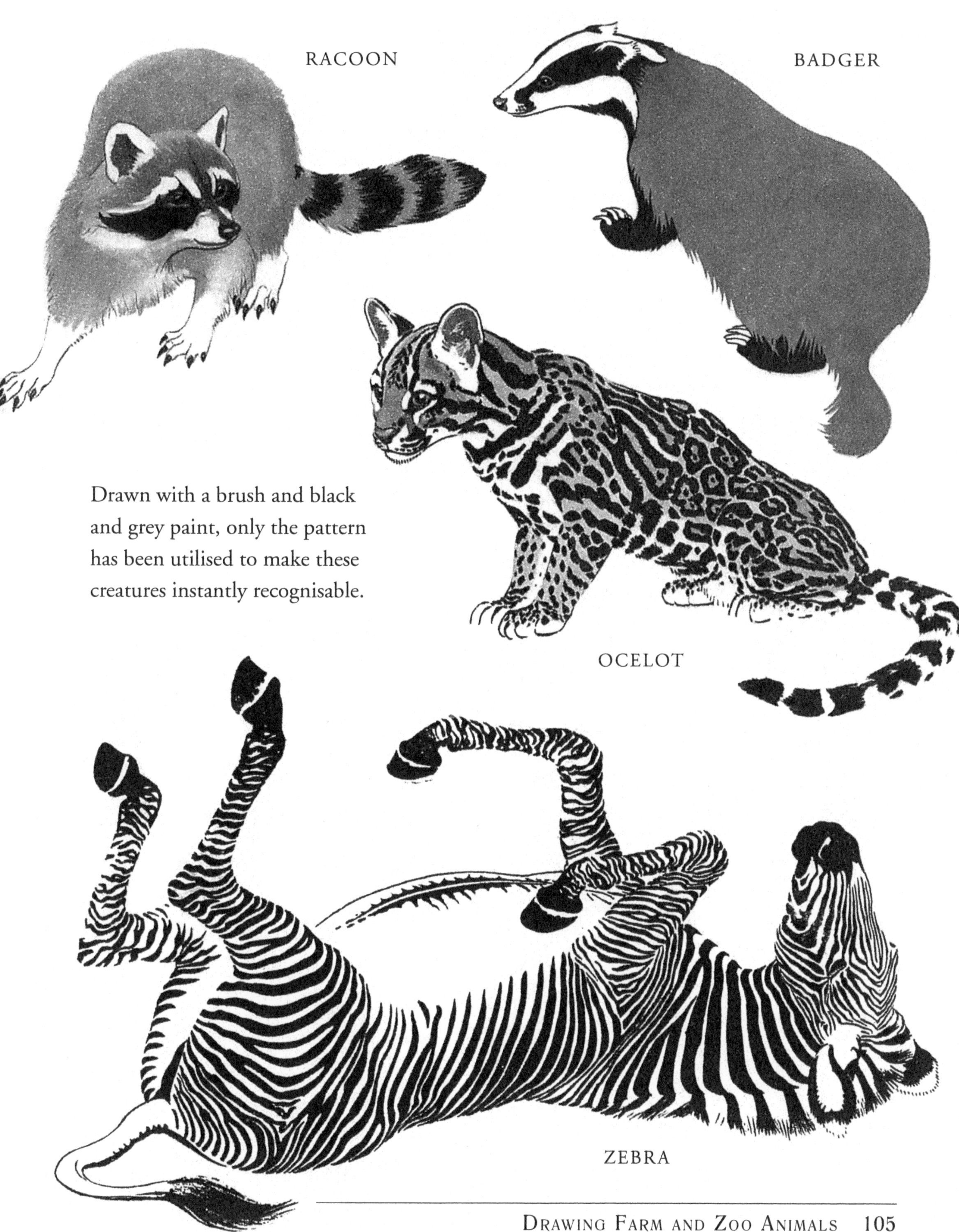

Drawn with a brush and black and grey paint, only the pattern has been utilised to make these creatures instantly recognisable.

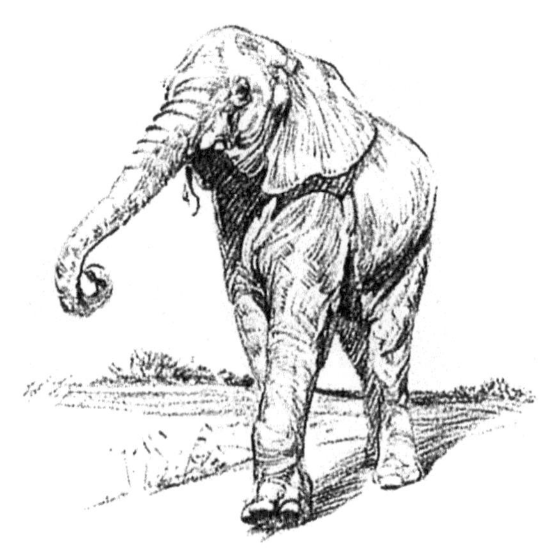

CAMELS & ELEPHANTS

One difficulty when drawing such a large animal as a camel or elephant is that, in many cases you cannot get far enough away from your subject to take in the whole animal at a glance. A large open-air zoo like Whipsnade is, of course, the ideal place in which to draw such creatures. A camel is rather quaint and I think it may help if you draw with a loose free line. Explore the forms rapidly at first in a light tentative manner and then more calligraphically. In this way you will get used to drawing a large animal on a comparatively small piece of paper.

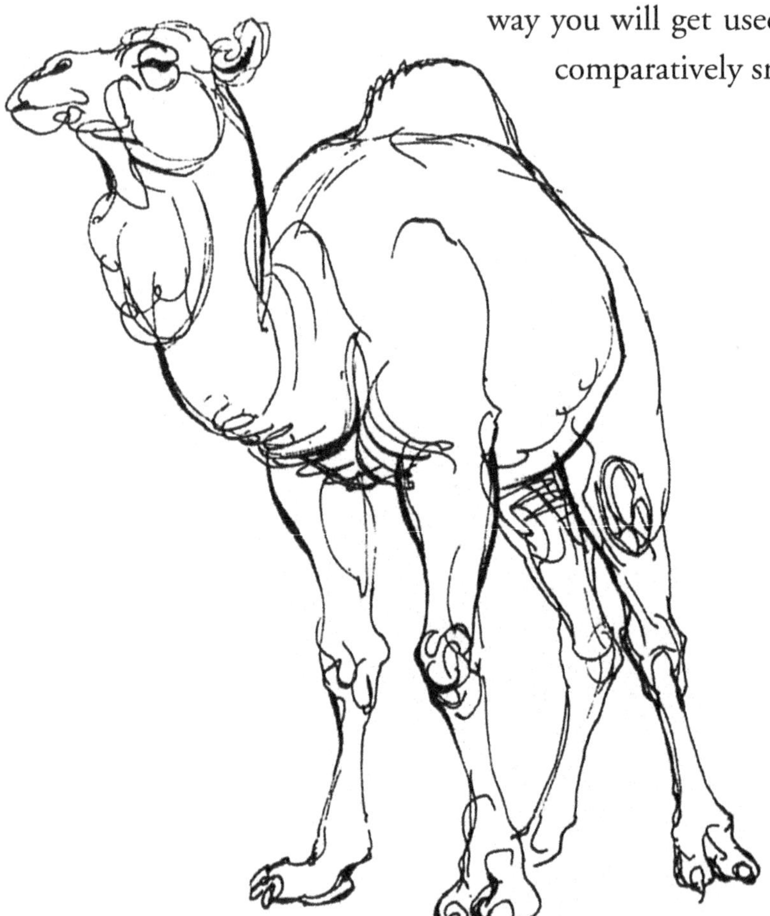

ARABIAN CAMEL
or DROMEDARY

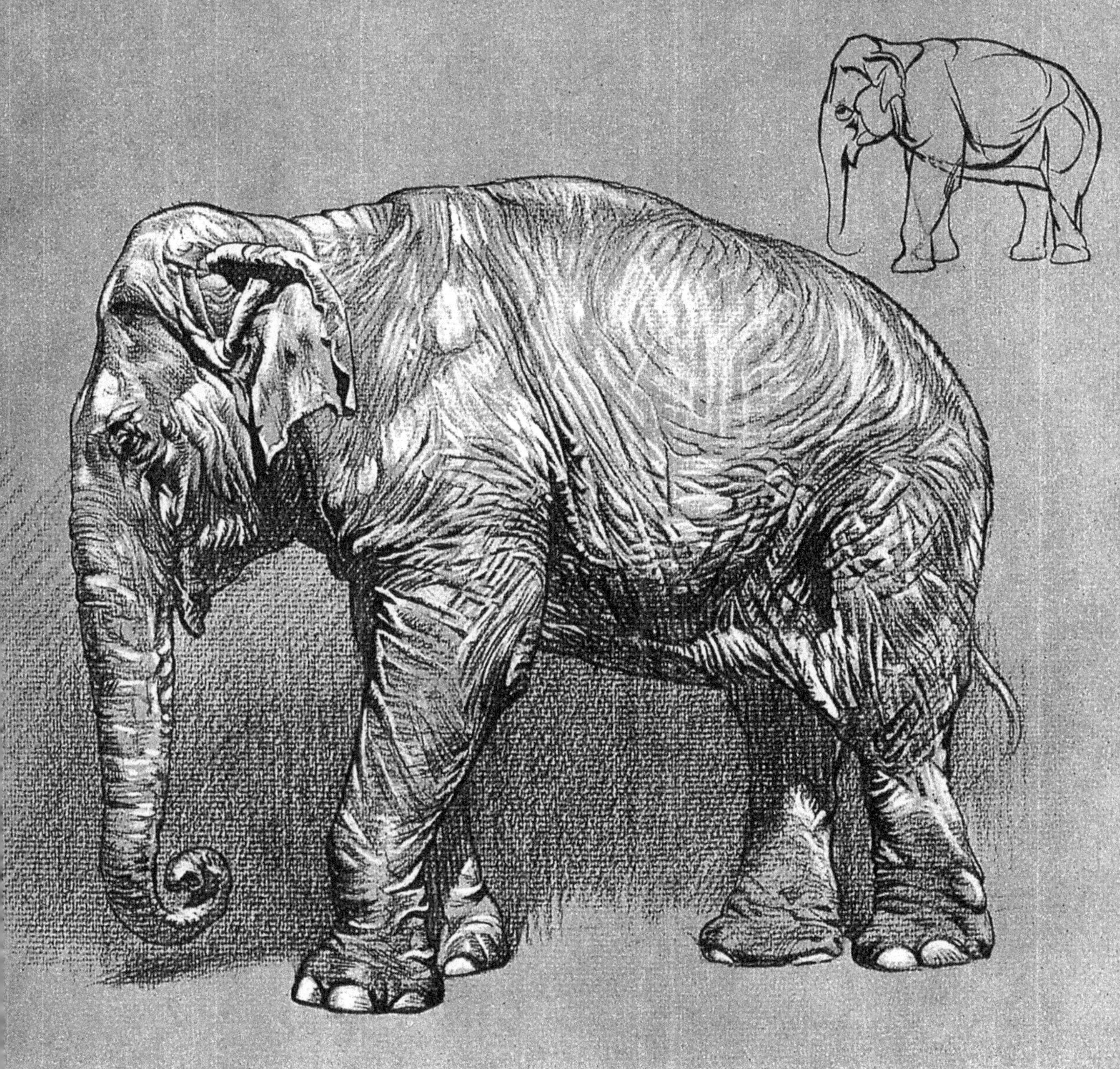

INDIAN ELEPHANT

I drew this Indian elephant on a grey paper which gave me the general middle tone of the animal. Black and white conté delineated the light and shade. The small drawing opposite is of an African elephant.

SEA-LIONS

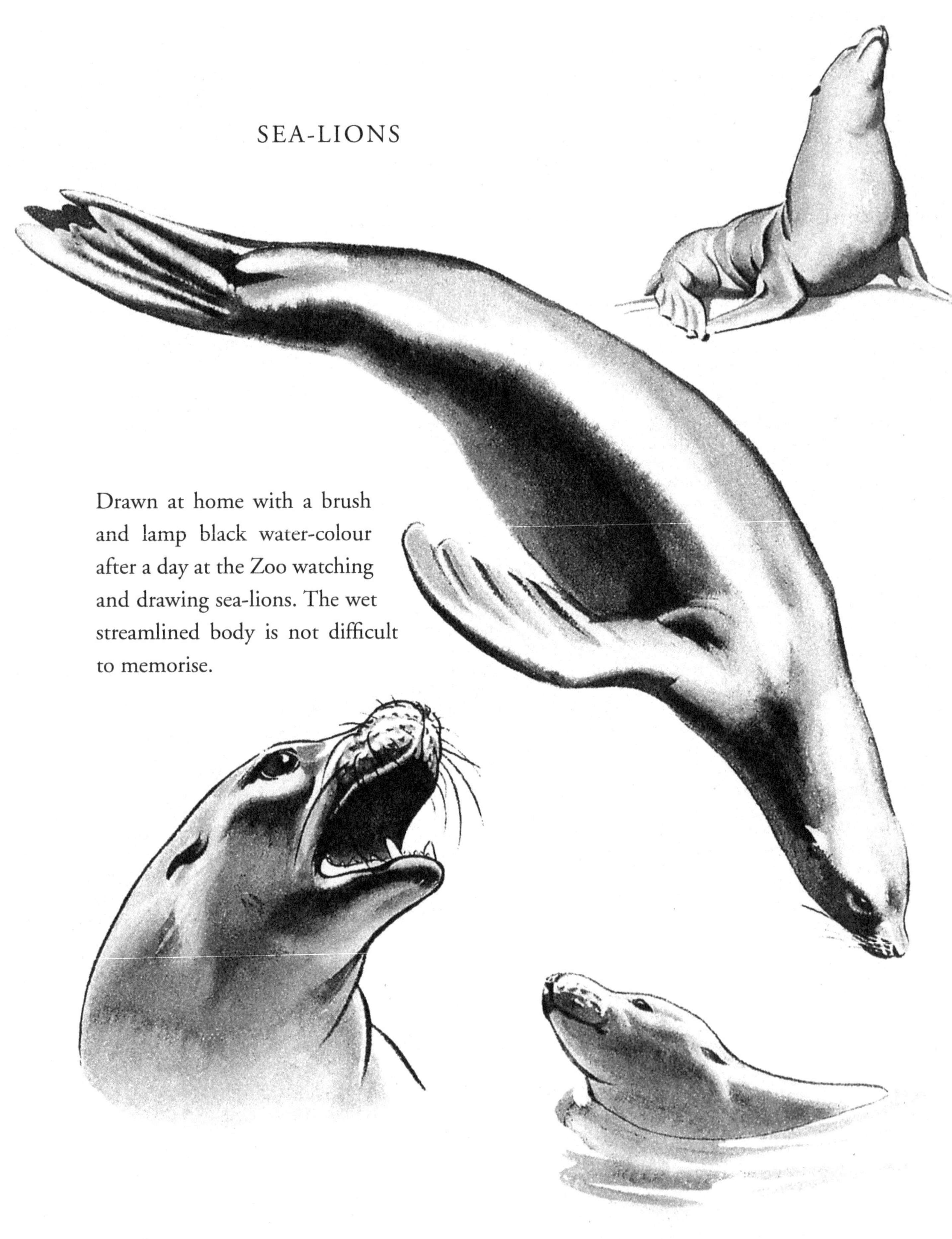

Drawn at home with a brush and lamp black water-colour after a day at the Zoo watching and drawing sea-lions. The wet streamlined body is not difficult to memorise.

ZOO BIRDS Birds require a special study on their own. If you can get R. B. Talbot Kelly's *The Way of Birds* I'm sure you will find it as stimulating and exciting as I have done. C. F. Tunnicliffe's *Bird Portraiture* explains structure well and contains many lovely drawings.

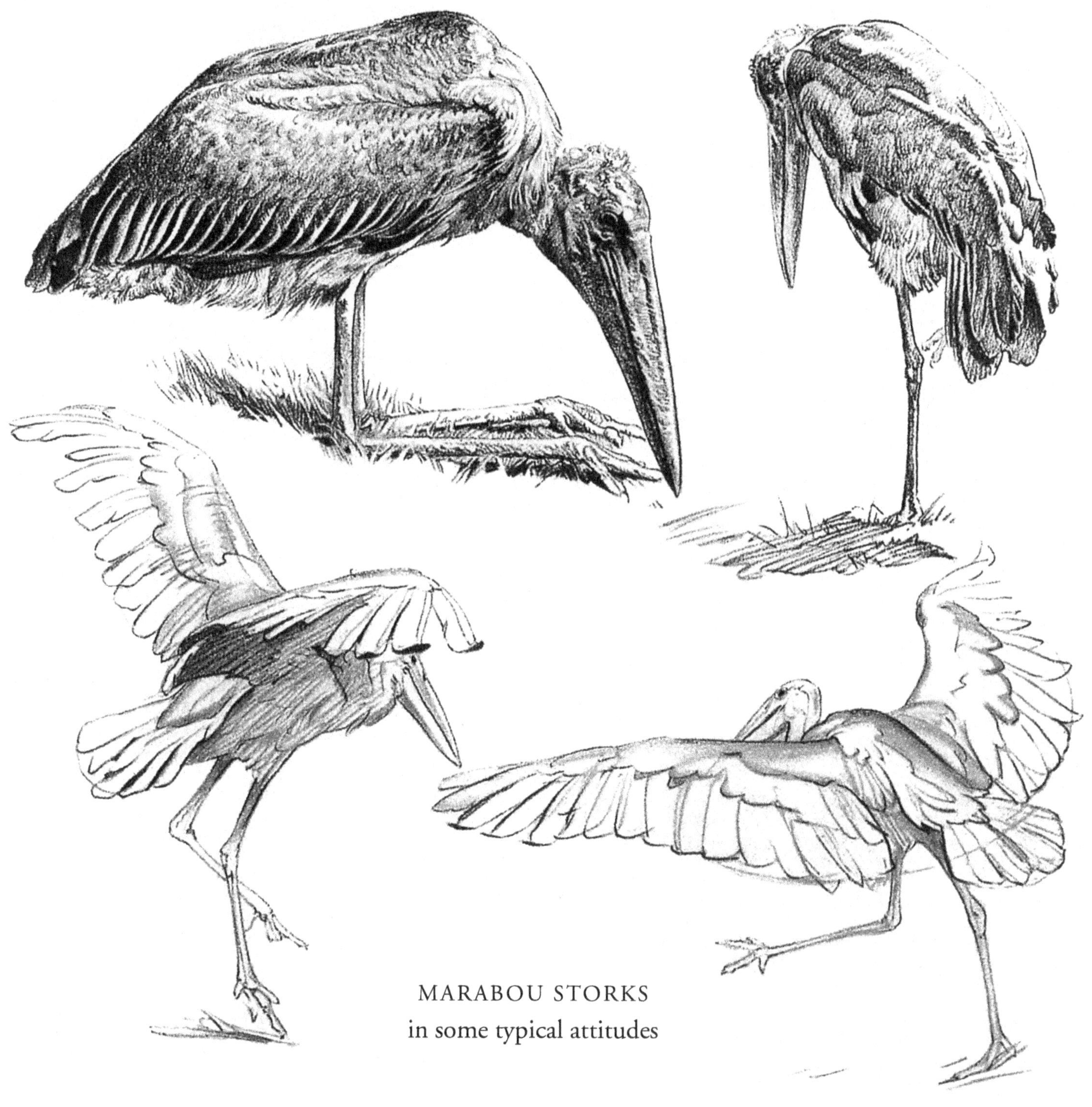

MARABOU STORKS
in some typical attitudes

FLAMINGOS

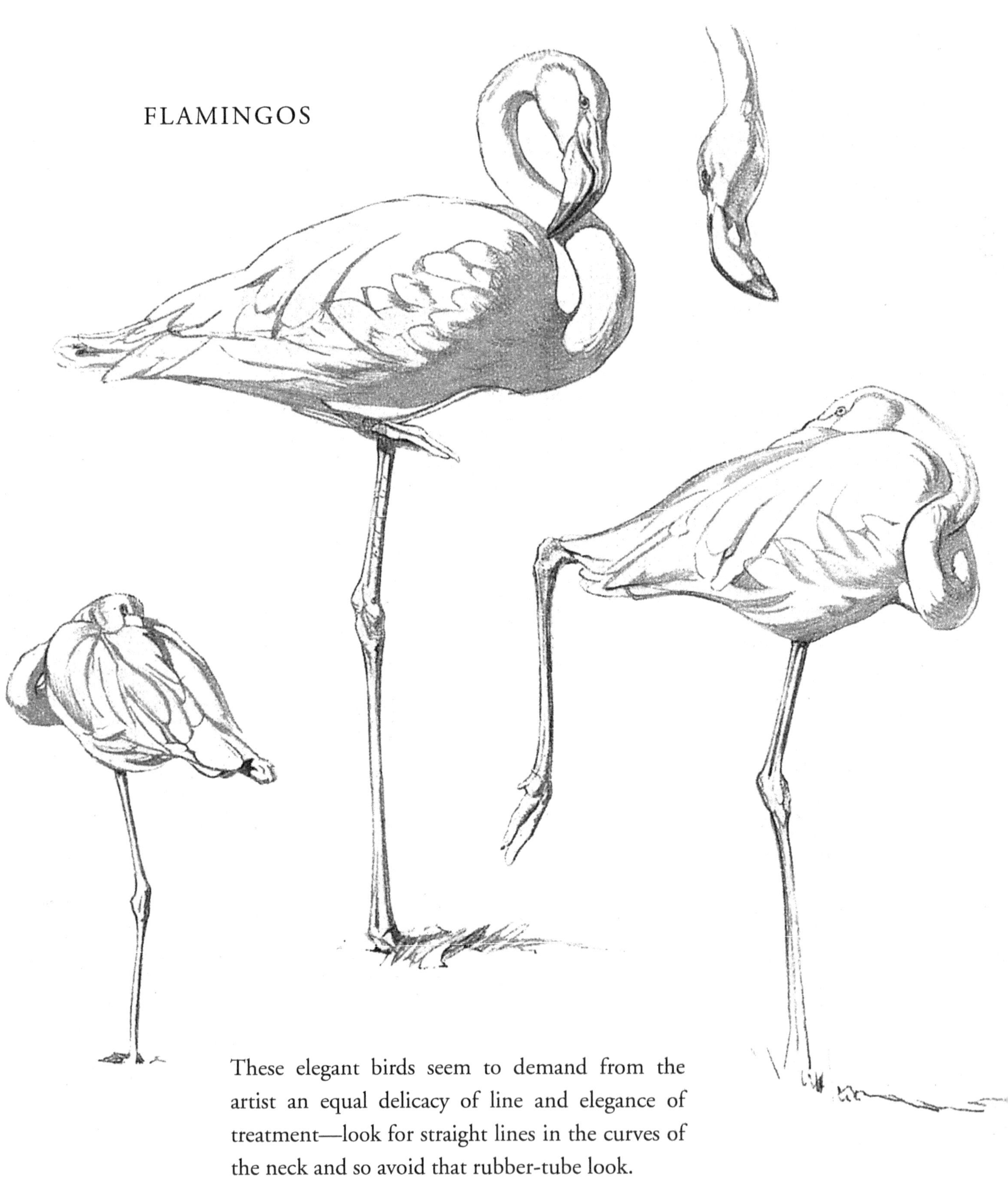

These elegant birds seem to demand from the artist an equal delicacy of line and elegance of treatment—look for straight lines in the curves of the neck and so avoid that rubber-tube look.

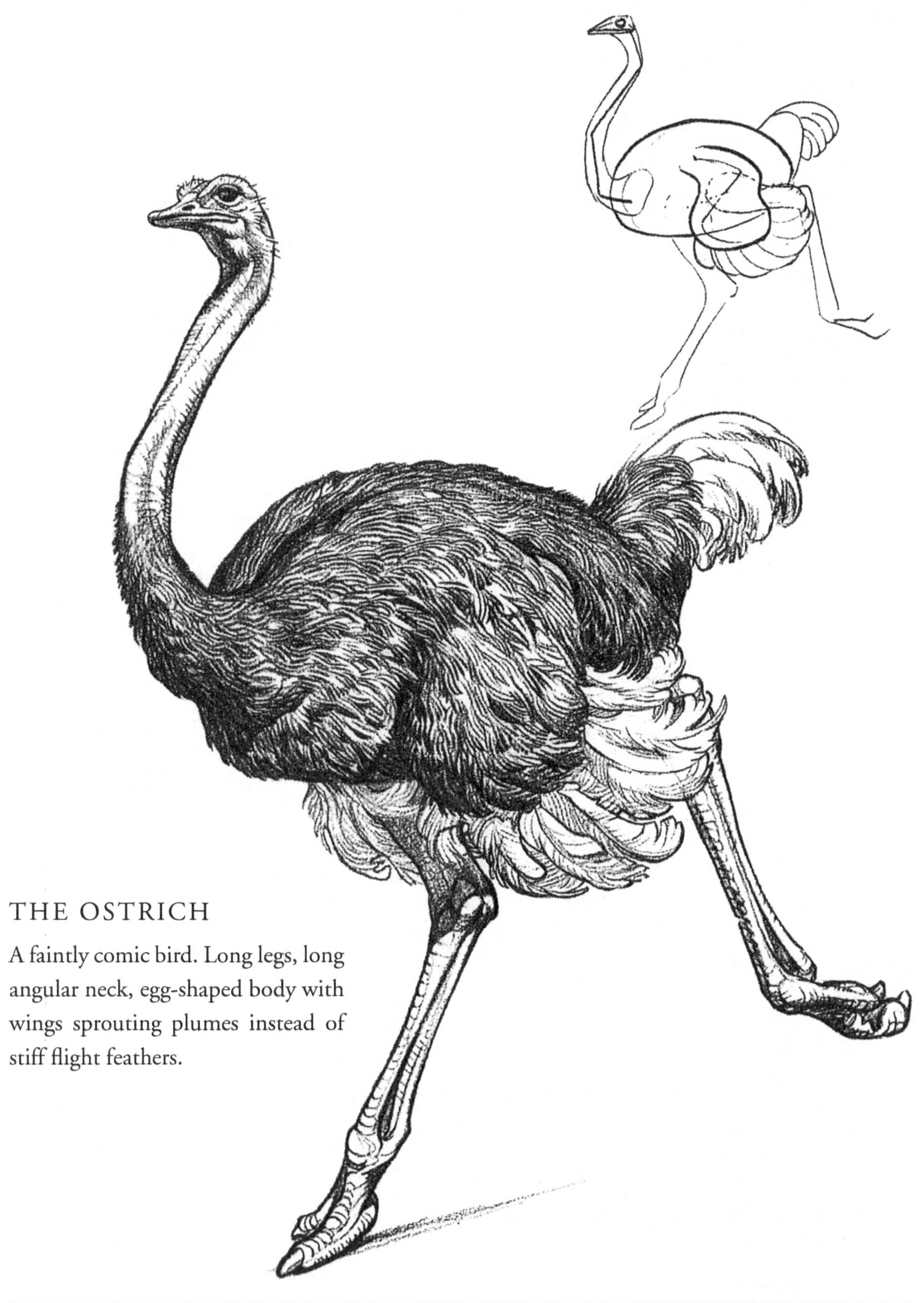

THE OSTRICH

A faintly comic bird. Long legs, long angular neck, egg-shaped body with wings sprouting plumes instead of stiff flight feathers.

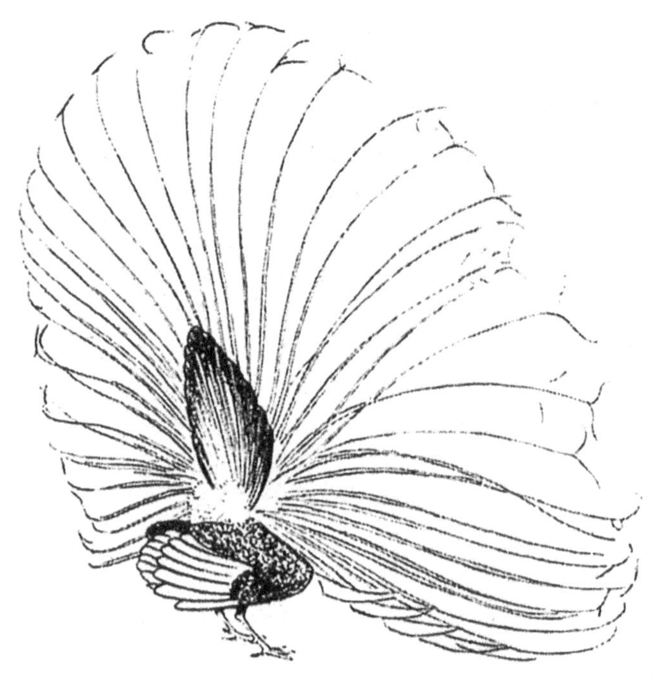

THE PEACOCK

In Edwin Noble's book of animal drawing there is a splendid drawing of a peacock in display which shows the basic geometric pattern of the so-called tail. When you understand this pattern it is fairly simple to work out a drawing of a slightly three-quarter view. The top diagram shows the stiff feathers of the real tail which support the glorious plumes which are the coverts of the tail and back.

PELICANS stand still for quite a long time, twisting their long beaks to preen their feathers. The apposition of bill to the twist of the neck makes a lively pattern.

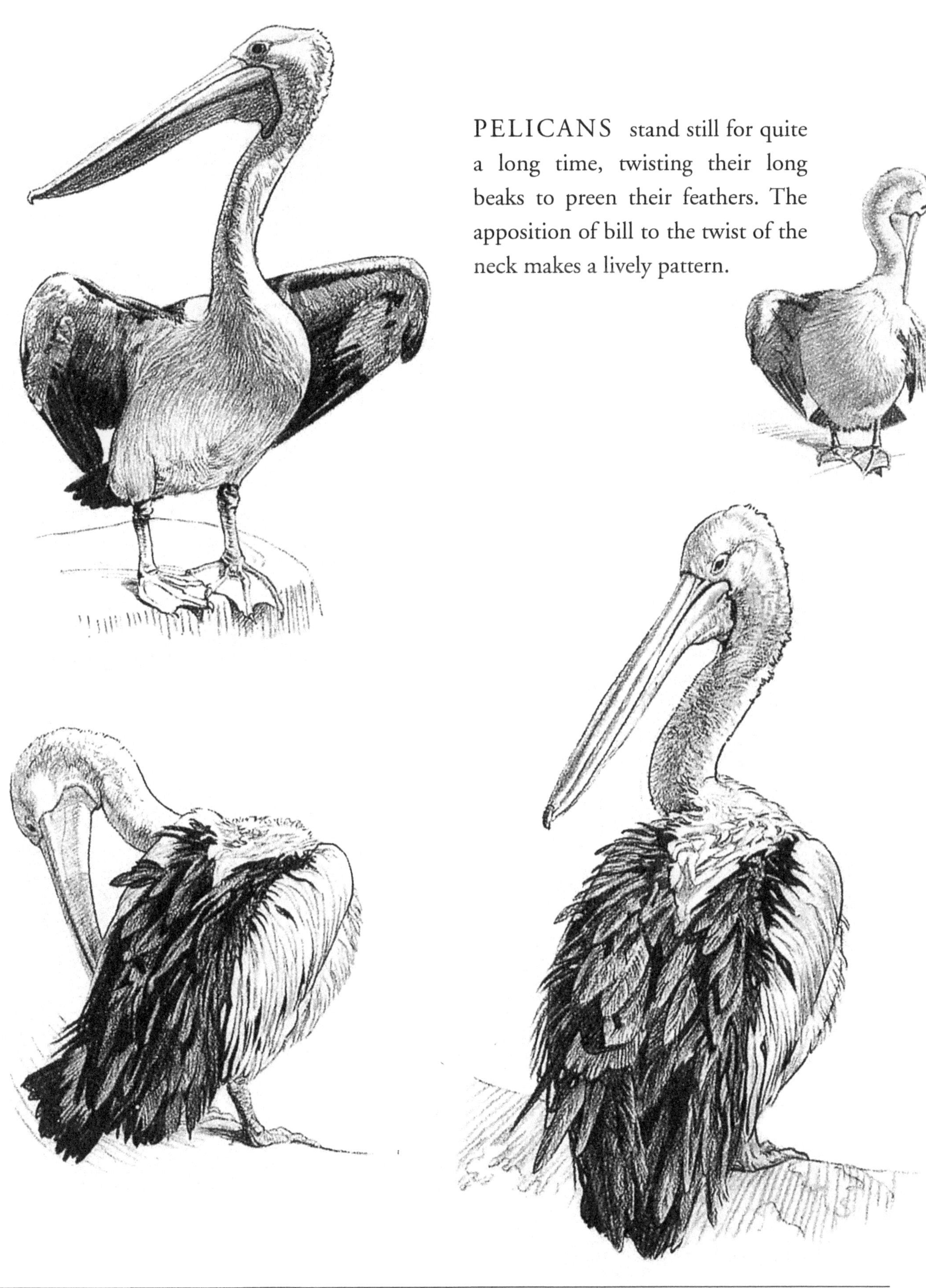

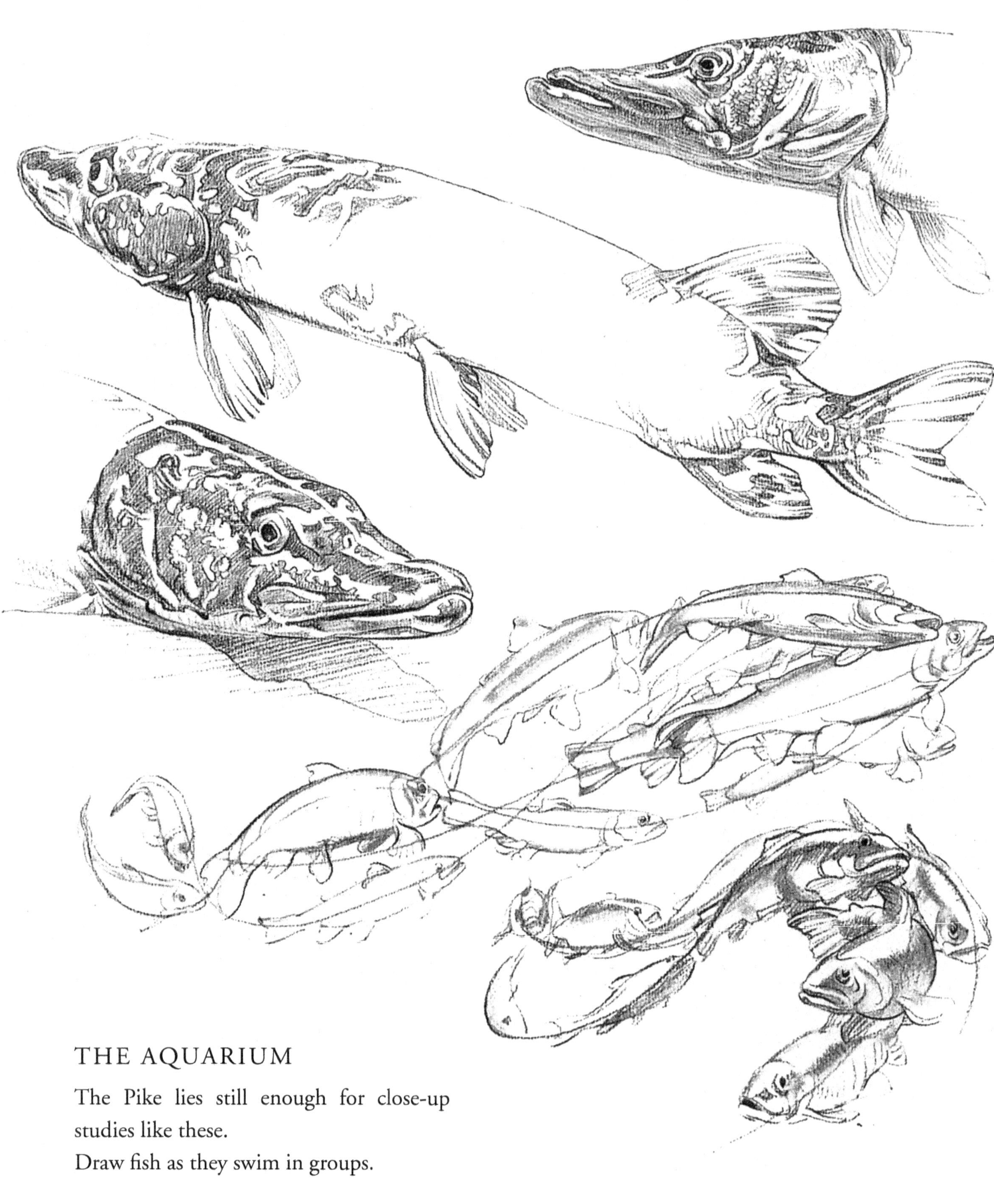

THE AQUARIUM

The Pike lies still enough for close-up studies like these.

Draw fish as they swim in groups.

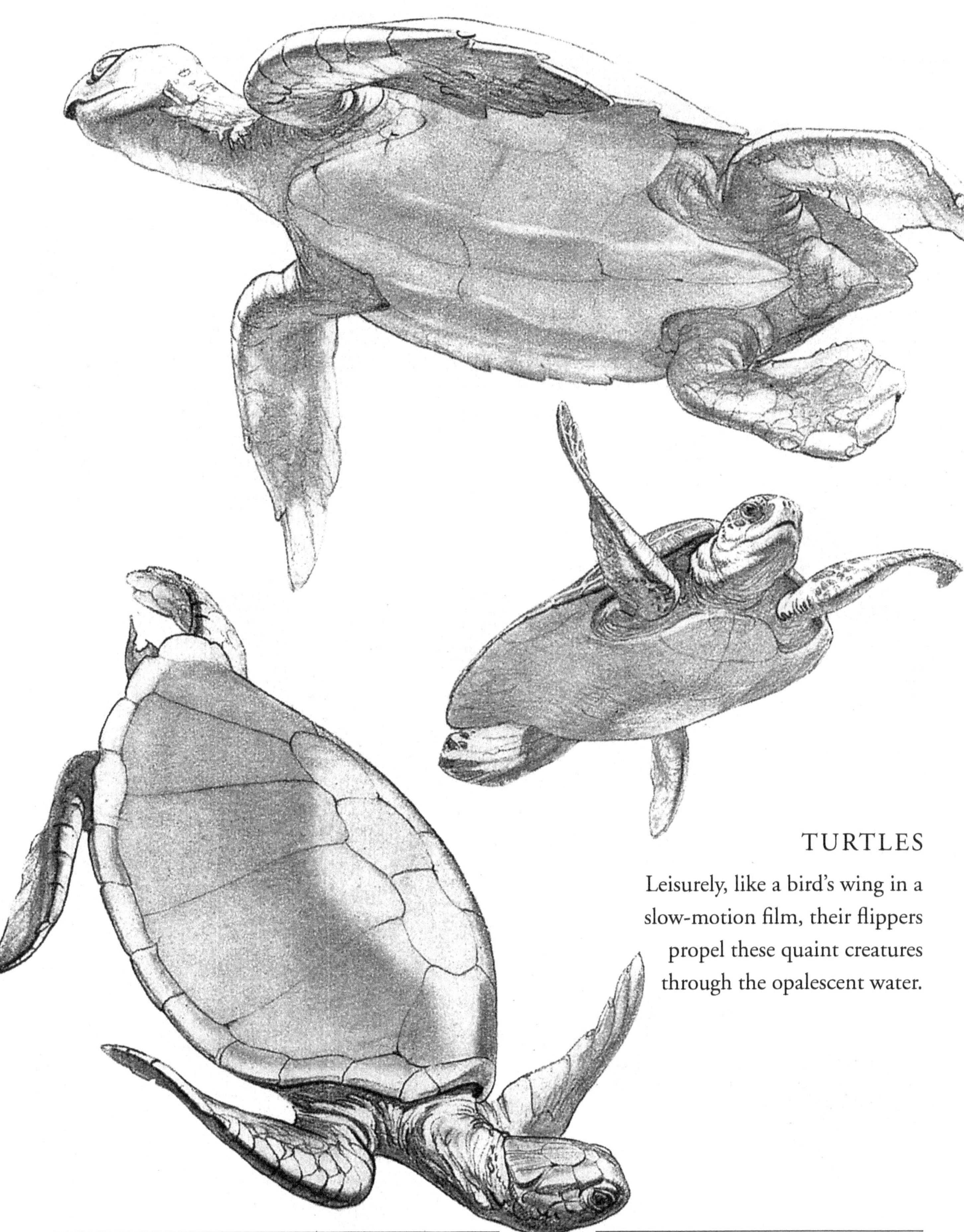

TURTLES

Leisurely, like a bird's wing in a slow-motion film, their flippers propel these quaint creatures through the opalescent water.

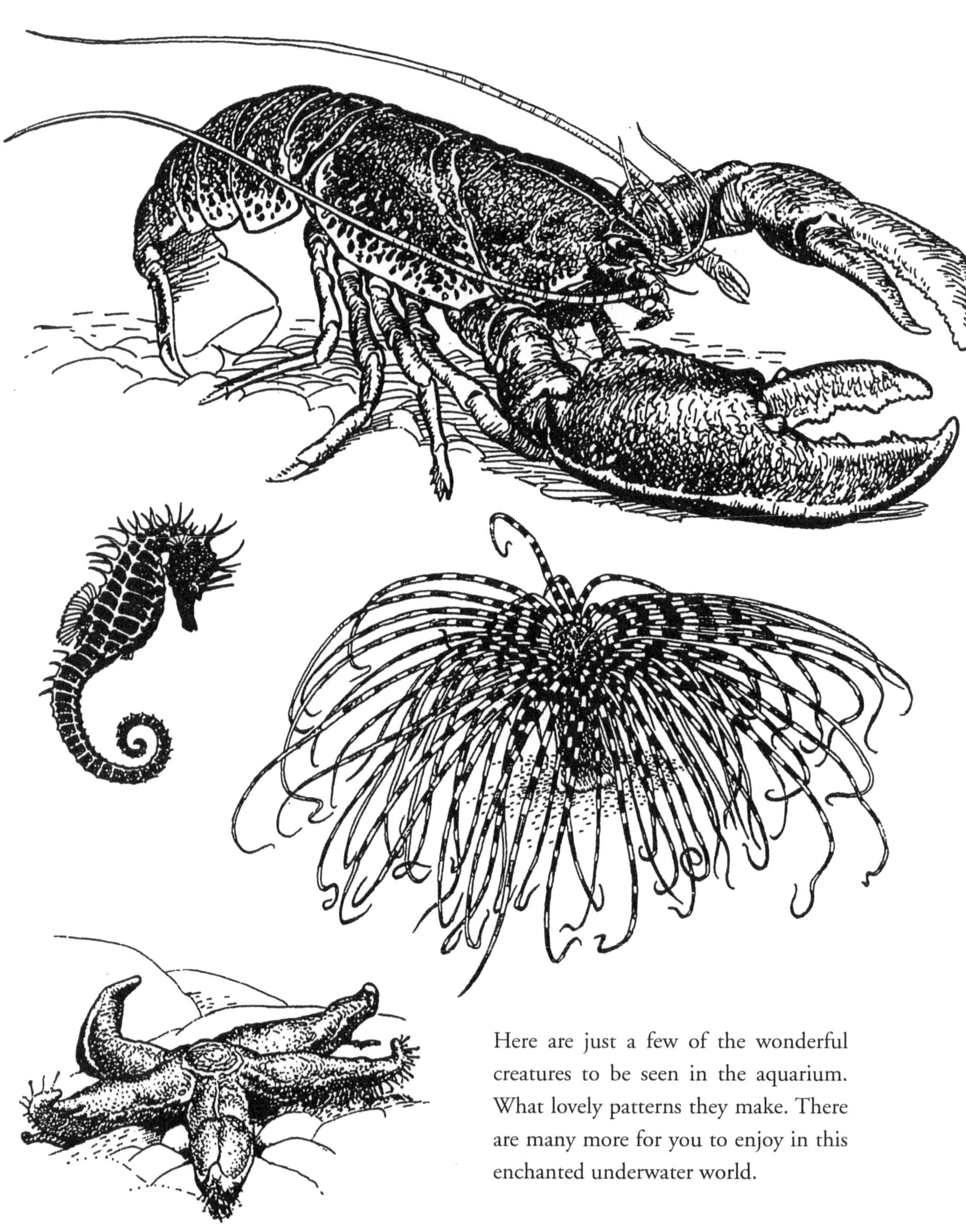

Here are just a few of the wonderful creatures to be seen in the aquarium. What lovely patterns they make. There are many more for you to enjoy in this enchanted underwater world.

USING YOUR DRAWINGS FOR PAINTING A PICTURE OR ILLUSTRATING A STORY

Many of my own zoo studies were made in order to obtain such information about a certain animal that I should ultimately be able to paint a picture or illustrate a story.

Having been at the zoo all day studying one particular animal, you may have a vague idea in your mind of doing something pictorial. Directly you get home and whilst your impressions are still vivid, make a few small scribbles (compositions really) like the one at the foot of this page. Concentrate on bold masses of light and dark and don't attempt to start a finished drawing until you have got these main elements settled, and are satisfied that you have the germ of a well-balanced picture.

When composing groups of animals or birds remember that those principles of rhythm that we found so important when drawing one animal, also apply here. Balance of mass is not enough. There must be a flow of line to knit the units together.

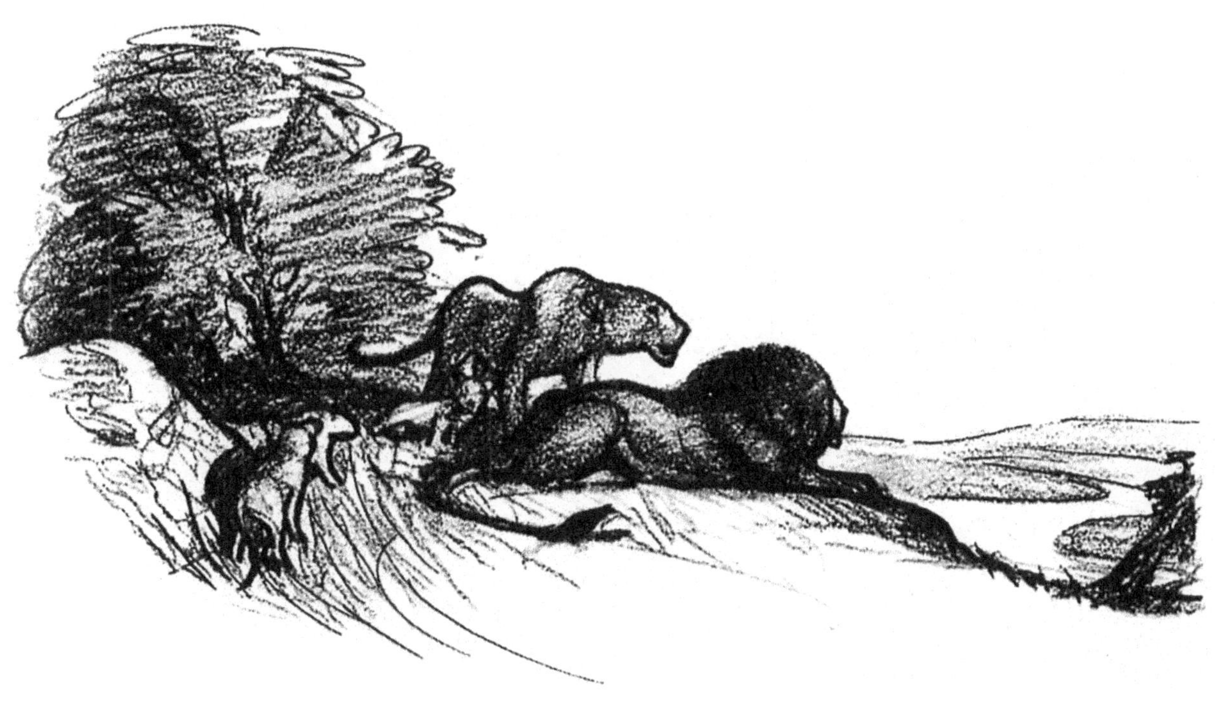

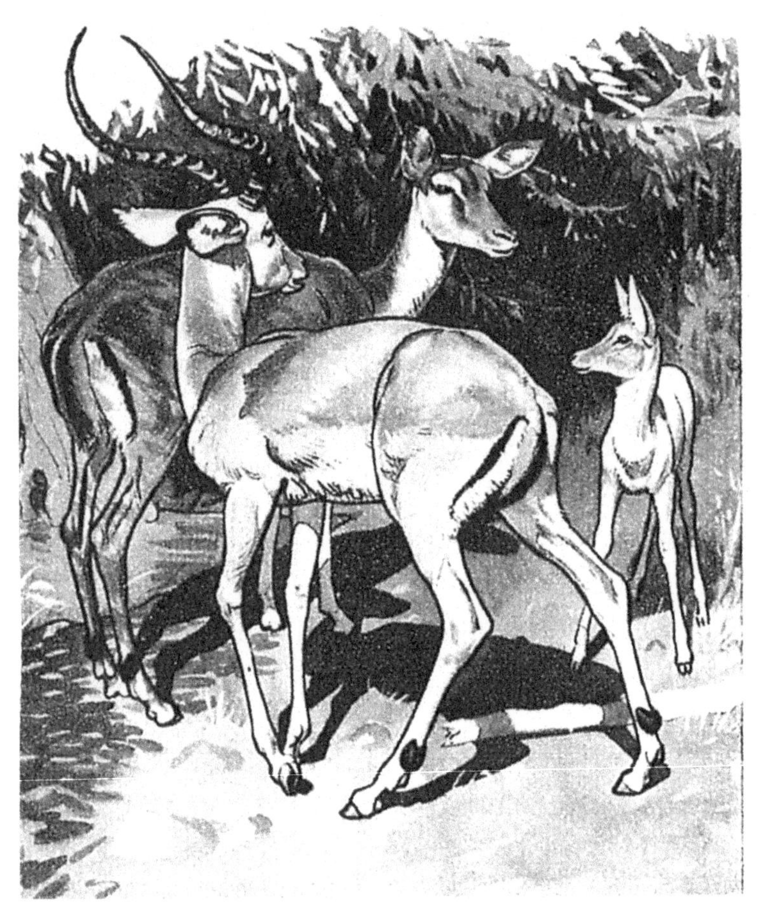

My picture of Marabou storks was considered in the first place as a collection of abstract but related shapes whose lines flowed rhythmically one into the other.

A danger to be avoided is too much subsequent over-elaboration which may tend to break up the flow of line. I had great fun making this cartoon for a painting. It shows a crowd of animals in flight from a fire. It was all done in a few hours entirely from memory. I had no studies in front of me as I wanted to give free expression to this fantasy of several species of animals all together in one painting.

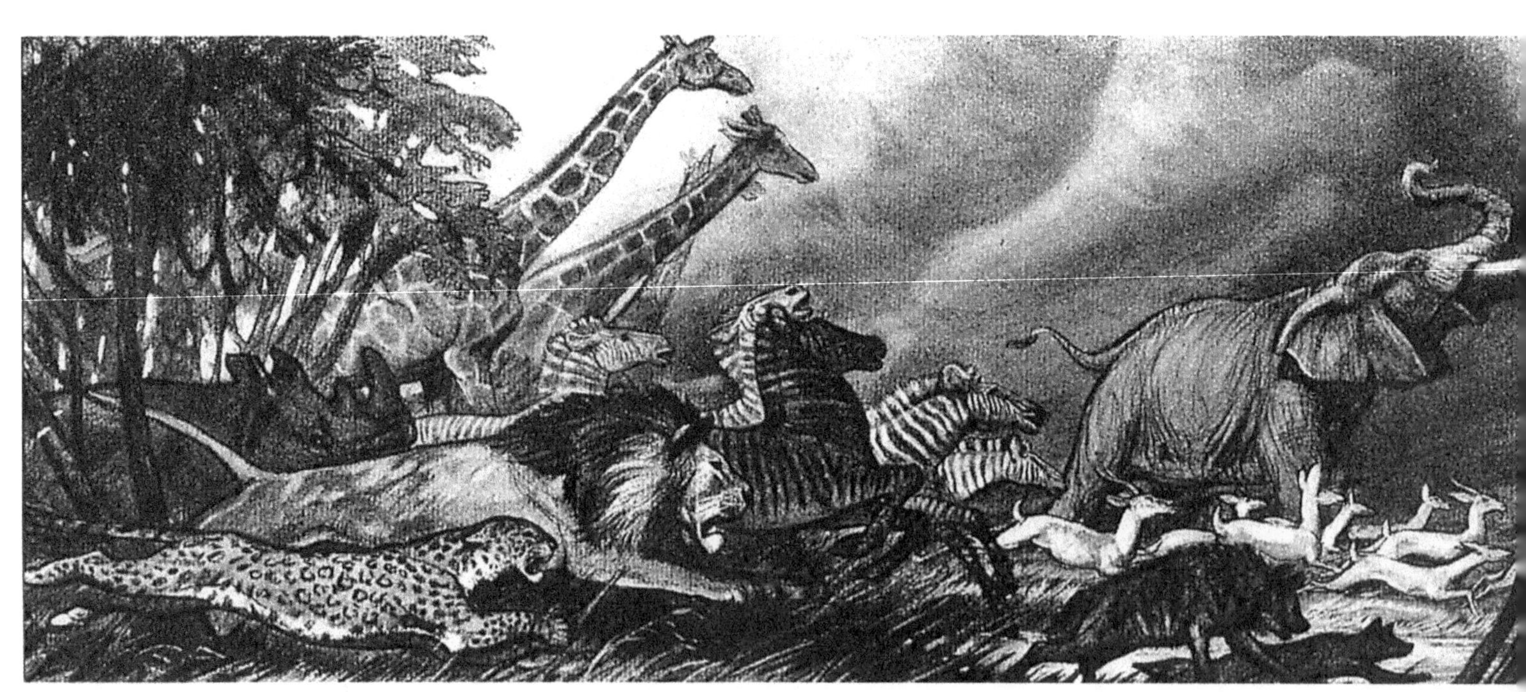

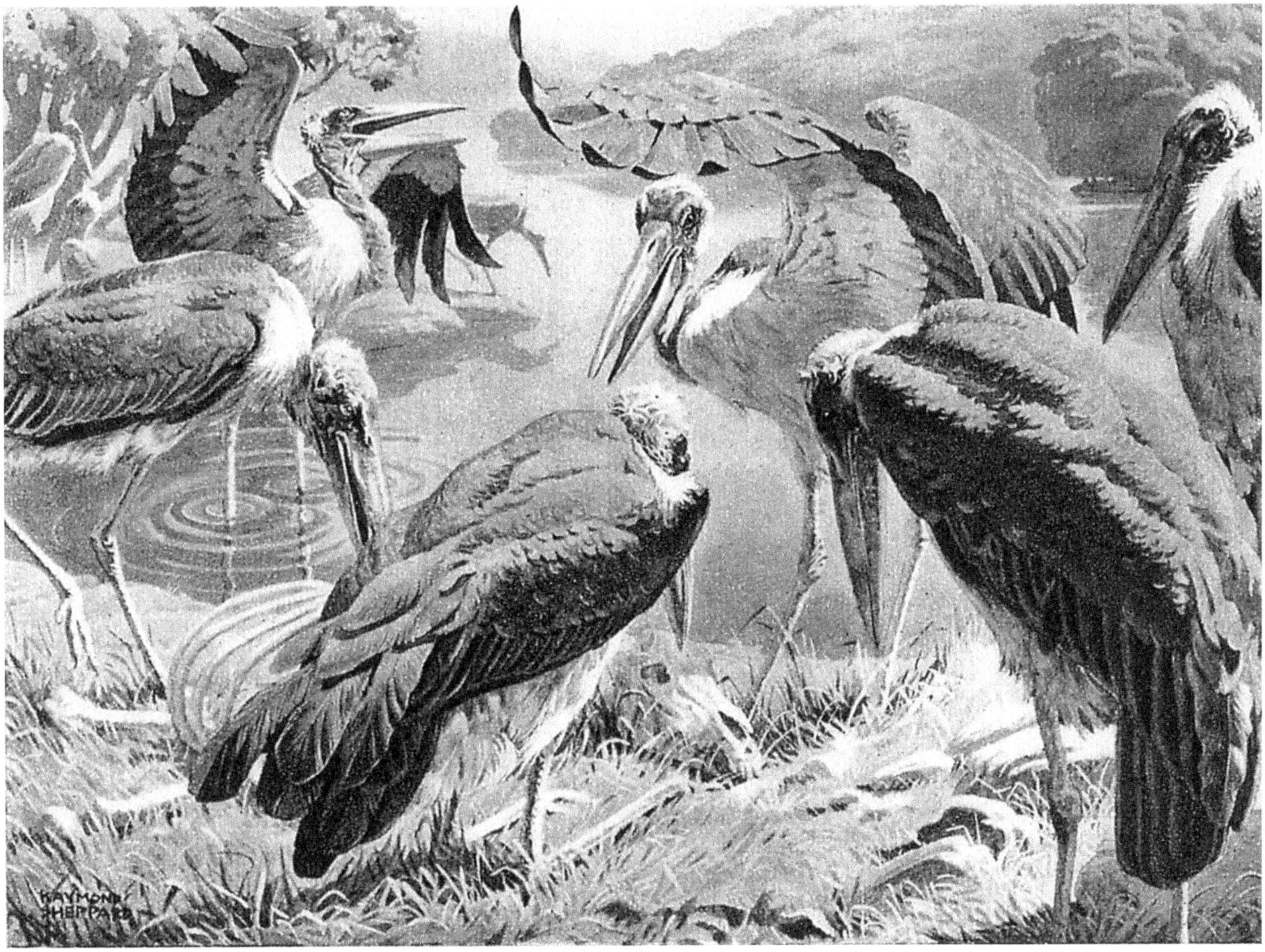

MARABOU STORKS

It is a good thing to let yourself go and experiment in this way. Go to the other extreme if you like and try abstracting pattern alone from the animals. You will enjoy yourself a lot.

To those of you who go to a zoo, not specifically to draw, but to look and enjoy, I express a hope that this book will increase both your understanding of the animal and your enjoyment in his presence.

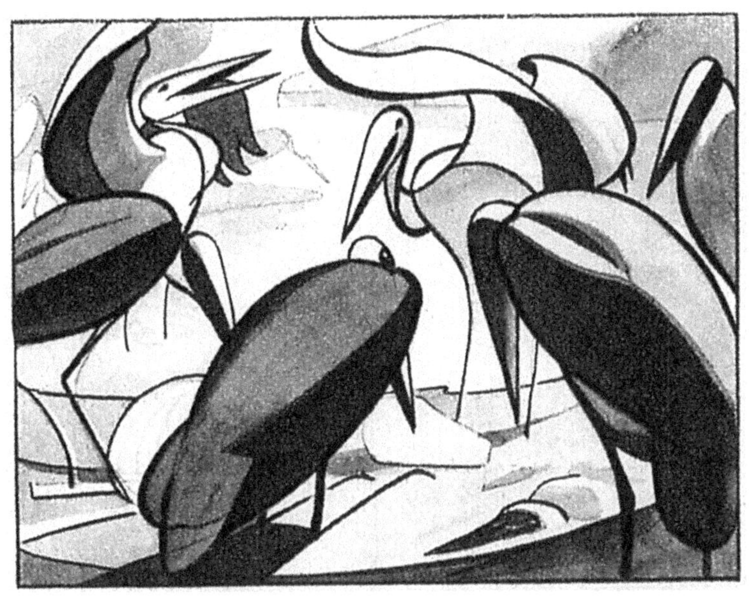

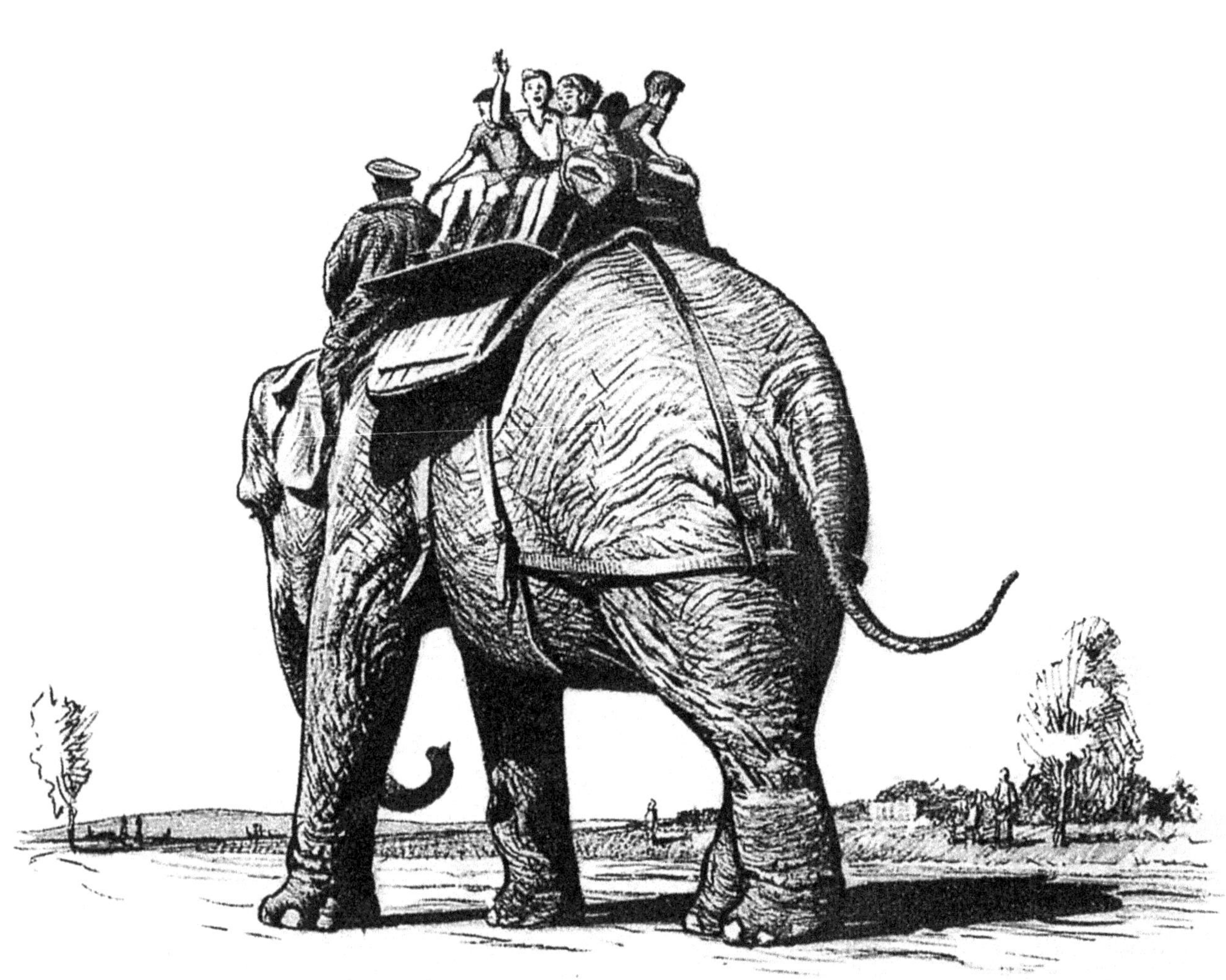